GUIDING CHILDREN'S SOCIAL AND EMOTIONAL DEVELOPMENT
A REFLECTIVE APPROACH

Janice Englander Katz

Founder and President,
The Child Care Consortium, Inc.

Boston   Columbus   Indianapolis   New York   San Francisco   Upper Saddle River
Amsterdam   Cape Town   Dubai   London   Madrid   Milan   Munich   Paris   Montréal   Toronto
Delhi   Mexico City   São Paulo   Sydney   Hong Kong   Seoul   Singapore   Taipei   Tokyo

Vice President and Editorial Director:
  Jeffery W. Johnston
Senior Acquisitions Editor: Julie Peters
Editorial Assistant: Andrea Hall
Vice President, Director of Marketing:
  Margaret Waples
Senior Marketing Manager: Christopher Barry
Senior Managing Editor: Pamela Bennett
Project Manager: Kerry Rubadue
Production Manager: Laura Messerly

Senior Art Director: Jayne Conte
Cover Designer: Suzanne Duda
Cover Image: Janice Englander Katz
Full-Service Project Management/
  Composition: Shiny Rajesh/Integra Software
  Services, Pvt. Ltd.
Printer/Binder: Courier/Westford
Cover Printer: Courier/Westford
Text Font: 10.5/12.5 ITC Garamond Std

Credits and acknowledgments for materials borrowed from other sources and reproduced, with permission, in this textbook appear on the appropriate page within the text.

Every effort has been made to provide accurate and current Internet information in this book. However, the Internet and information posted on it are constantly changing, so it is inevitable that some of the Internet addresses listed in this textbook will change.

Photo Credits: All photographs are by Janice Englander Katz.

Library of Congress Cataloging-in-Publication Data
Katz, Janice Englander.
  Guiding children's social and emotional development : a reflective approach / Janice Englander Katz.—1st ed.
    p. cm.
  Includes bibliographical references.
  ISBN-13: 978-0-13-707088-6 (alk. paper)
  ISBN-10: 0-13-707088-8 (alk. paper)
  1. Child development.   2. Early childhood education.   3. Educational psychology.
  4. Child psychology.   5. Social interaction in children.   6. Social skills in children.
  7. Emotions in children.   I. Title.
  LB1115.K38 2014
  155.4—dc23

                                                                              2012035616

10 9 8 7 6 5 4 3 2 1

ISBN 10:   0-13-707088-8
ISBN 13: 978-0-13-707088-6

BRIEF CONTENTS

CONTENTS

FOREWORD

Janice Katz's wise and practical book arrives at an important time in the field of early childhood education, child care, and early intervention. As a result of recent research findings about early brain development, we are beginning to understand with ever more certainty that social–emotional development is inextricably entwined with cognitive, language, and physical development. Infants have tremendous capacities to learn. Their brains are shaped by everyday experience, especially by social and emotional interactions in their relationships with parents and other important caregivers. Toddlers are actively exploring the world with their bodies using all their senses, their learning and growing self-confidence significantly influenced by guidance they receive from adults. Preschoolers and young school-age children, as they work and play together, continue to build cognitive power, a wide range of skills, self-regulation capacities, and a deeper understanding of themselves, others, and the physical world. All of these accomplishments in the early years hinge on whether the child is able to learn to manage emotions and behavior in ways that are acceptable within his or her family, child care settings, schools, peer groups, and community.

Katz's book reflects her unique perspective as a practicing clinical child psychologist who is also engaged daily as a provider of high-quality early care and education. The book is an extremely smart manual supporting optimal social–emotional development and mental health, written especially for professionals working with young children. Katz synthesizes and makes accessible some of the best ideas from recent child development research, practice recommendations from the mental health field, and model early childhood programs. Her emphasis throughout the book on the reader's *self-reflection* process strengthens her message and makes it more likely that teachers will be able to use the concepts and methods she offers with good effect. Within each chapter, as she introduces information that helps us to better understand children's developing emotions and behavior, she also challenges us to reflect about our own feelings, thoughts, and experiences. I believe the self-reflection process Katz suggests is truly the essential path to deeper understanding of children and one's relationship with each child. This book has the potential be transformative—for you, for the children with whom you work, and for your relationships with those children. As Jeree Pawl wisely stated, "How you are is as important as what you do."[1]

---

[1]Jeree H. Pawl & Maria St John. (1998). *How You Are Is as Important as What You Do...In Making a Positive Difference for Infants, Toddlers and Their Families*. Washington, DC: ZERO TO THREE.

For me, this book has several specific highlights:

- Accessible overviews of theories and research about social and emotional development
- Numerous clear examples of children and teachers in early childhood settings illustrating effective and not-so-effective guidance strategies
- A unique and helpful perspective and tools useful for understanding and responding effectively to what has become known as *challenging behavior* (behavior that is especially disruptive or upsetting to others in the child's environment)

Perhaps most important, Katz helps us in insightful and practical ways to sharpen our capacity to empathetically understand each child as a unique individual who is striving to have a sense of power in her own life *and* to be connected in loving and meaningful ways with others. Is there a more important goal in early care and education than helping young children find this balance of competence and connectedness?

James Elicker, PhD
Purdue University

PREFACE

Over the past few years, many books and articles have been written about the importance of social and emotional development in children. To succeed at school and function well in life, a child must be motivated to learn and able to pay attention, manage impulses, cope with emotions, and get along with people. A child needs these fundamental skills to grow and thrive, yet they do not come naturally to many children. The important adults in a child's life must intentionally and strategically guide the development of these competencies. So who should do that and how?

This increasing interest in social and emotional development comes at a time when families contend with unprecedented challenges to self-sufficiency. Although parents will always be children's first and most important teachers, greater stress on the family can hamper parents' ability to provide the time and emotional support their children need to develop in this area. Many families struggle with parental unemployment or, conversely, parents working multiple jobs. In difficult economic times, less assistance may be available from extended family and the community.

At the same time, businesses complain that young people entering the workforce lack basic "employability skills," such as communication, adaptability, problem solving, motivation, and teamwork (Cumming & Lesniak, 2000; Hansen & Hansen, 2011). All of these capacities are in the social–emotional domain and their direct guidance should be a prominent component of the educational experience.

Yet tremendous demands are placed on school systems and they often lack the resources to focus directly on building these skills. By the time students are in high school, it is assumed that they have already learned to regulate their attention, impulses, and emotions and are able to work independently and with others. When they display weaknesses in this area, their behavior is generally handled in a disciplinary, rather than a skill-building manner. This reactive approach presupposes that the skills are taught in elementary and middle school.

As early as third grade, however, elementary schools are required to engage in achievement testing in math, language, and other academic skills. The stakes are high because schools are commonly penalized for students' poor performance on these tests. As a result, the emphasis on academic skills often begins at or before kindergarten. Kindergarten teachers report that school readiness skills, the essential competencies children need to succeed in kindergarten and beyond, include more skills in the social–emotional domain than in the physical or cognitive domains (Conn-Powers, 2010). Thus in kindergarten, underdeveloped social and emotional skills are already addressed as problems needing remediation or discipline.

This set of circumstances puts the responsibility on early childhood professionals to intentionally focus on building these fundamental skills in children (Conn-Powers, Cross, & Dixon, 2011). Families rely on our support in this area, especially when their time, energy, and other resources are spread so thin. Elementary schools have increasing academic achievement demands and fewer resources available. You, the early childhood professional, are in a critically important position to promote these competencies. In fact, it may be your most important role. How are you supposed to meet this challenge?

First, recognize the need for lifelong learning in this ever-growing field. It is essential to participate in continuing education workshops and read professional publications. You may want to establish a professional learning community with colleagues focusing on social–emotional development or participate in reflective supervision.

If resources are available, your program may have access to a mental health consultant who can guide and support you as you promote these skills in children. A mental health consultant is a specially trained professional who works collaboratively with the adults in a child's life (e.g., teachers and families) to increase their competence so that those adults may, in turn, promote desired skills in the child (Perry & Kaufmann, 2009). Mental health consultants tend to think about behavior in complex ways that may seem unfamiliar to others. Their strategies emerge from a process of inquiry that incorporates self-reflection, careful observation, and analysis of many variables related to the educator, the child, and the family. Although relatively few programs currently have access to mental health consultants, in this book, you will learn some of the basic concepts and principles consultants use that can help you develop effective strategies for your children. Fortunately, you have readily available the most effective teaching resource possible: yourself.

WHAT YOU WILL LEARN IN THIS BOOK

As you read this book, you will have the opportunity to understand social and emotional competence "from the inside out" (Siegel & Hartzell, 2003). By better understanding yourself, your strengths, weaknesses, preferences, and more, you will be better equipped to guide the children in your program. By revisiting the process by which you came to be socially and emotionally competent, you will be more prepared to promote these skills in children.

Guiding Children's Social and Emotional Development: A Reflective Approach offers a unique perspective on the promotion of fundamental life skills. It is not a how-to manual with instructions for fixing challenging behavior. Nor is it a cookbook laying out recipes for creating competent young people. Rather, this book offers a process for understanding why children do the things they do and challenges us to explore what inspires us to make the choices we make as professionals. This process is called *reflection*.

THEMES AND FEATURES OF THIS BOOK

Written in an accessible style, this book includes themes and features that support an intentional, reflective approach to guiding children's social and emotional development.

Learning Outcomes. Each chapter begins with a list of learning outcomes to help you focus on the essential concepts of the chapter. As you read the material in the chapter, you are invited to apply those concepts to your daily experiences and interactions.

Pedagogical Features Encouraging Reflection. In each chapter, you will have opportunities to reflect on the material in a feature called "Looking in the Mirror…" Guiding questions reconnect you with your own journey toward social–emotional competence and can be answered only by you. Your self-reflection will help you figure out, at any given time, what course of action on your part will be effective in your work with a child or children.

In addition, throughout the book, you will have opportunities, through interactive exercises and figures posing reflective questions, to practice self-reflection and to consider how your decisions and actions might affect children and families.

Stories about Real Kids That Illustrate Key Concepts. Many of the concepts are illustrated with stories about real children from real families and real teachers in real classrooms (with changed names and details). I have come to know these individuals through my experiences along four separate but often converging paths. As a clinical psychologist specializing in the treatment of children, I have provided psychotherapy for thousands of people who would never have needed such intensive intervention had they experienced more positive care and education in their early years. Second, I am the founder and president of a NAEYC accredited child care center with 130 children from six weeks to twelve years old and 30 amazing educators. Third, I work with early childhood professionals in several capacities. As a mental health consultant for various early care and education programs, I see both the creative resourcefulness of and the challenges faced by early childhood professionals. I frequently lecture and lead workshops at professional development conferences and teach college students pursuing degrees in psychology and education. Finally, and most important, I am the mother of two sons whose energy, intellect, and curiosity have kept me on my toes for 23 years. Along these four paths, I have encountered a vast array of individuals whose stories fill the pages of this book.

Opportunities to Review and Apply Material. Each chapter includes several review questions and application opportunities, either for college courses or for professional development.

AUDIENCE

Throughout this book, the terms *educator*, *teacher*, and *professional* are used for the sake of simplicity. But others who work with children and families can easily apply the perspectives and strategies presented. If you are an early intervention therapist, a behavior consultant, a home visitor, or any early childhood professional, this book is certainly for you.

Guiding Children's Social and Emotional Development: A Reflective Approach can be used as a textbook for a college course in child development or guidance or for continuing professional education. The format, with parts that can serve as distinct modules, lends itself to ongoing learning communities, staff workshops, or professional development seminars for those already in the field.

ACKNOWLEDGMENTS

I would like to thank my husband, Jeff, and our sons, Josh and Justin, for their patience and ongoing encouragement. My wonderfully insightful sisters and supportive, loving parents were instrumental in helping me think through the various issues presented. I remain eternally grateful to the families I have seen in my clinical practice and the staff and families of Imagination Station. Thanks also to my colleague, Mary Jane Eisenhauer, whose wisdom, courage, and enthusiasm inspired the writing of this book. Moreover, I thank the reviewers of this first edition: Jennifer Aldrich, University of Central Missouri; Kimberly Austin, Kids Central, Inc.; Pamela Briggs, McLennan Community College; Stacy Burr, University of South Carolina Upstate; Johnny Castro, Brookhaven College; Susan Christian, Patrick Henry Community College; Mary Cordell, Navarro College; April Edmond, East Carolina University; Barbara Moody, Husson University; Roberta Parks, University of Arkansas Fort Smith; and Amy Strimling, Sacramento City College. And finally, I thank Julie Peters, who provided support and guidance throughout the editorial process.

ABOUT THE AUTHOR

Janice Englander Katz, PhD, is a clinical psychologist with 28 years of experience working to improve the lives of children, families, and adults. Dr. Katz is the founder and president of The Child Care Consortium that operates Imagination Station Child Development Center, a NAEYC accredited licensed educational child care center in Michigan City, Indiana. She provides mental health consulting for many early childhood programs throughout Northwest Indiana and has taught child psychology at Purdue University North Central.

Dr. Katz is an inexhaustible community organizer committed to finding systematic solutions to societal challenges. Concerned about our nation's high preschool expulsion rate and the dire ramifications of untreated early behavior problems, Dr. Katz is working to create an early childhood mental health consultation system for the state of Indiana. She is an active member of the Indiana Association for Infant and Toddler Mental Health, Infant Toddler Specialists of Indiana Steering Committee, and Indiana's Early Childhood Comprehensive Systems initiative. Dr. Katz also serves as Chair of the Public Policy Committee for Indiana Association for the Education of Young Children. She has served on many nonprofit boards, is a frequent presenter at local, state, and regional conferences, and provides workshops for physicians, educators, and parents. She earned her doctorate and master's degrees in psychology at Washington University in St. Louis and her bachelor's degree in psychology and child development at University of Minnesota. Dr. Katz and her husband have two sons, ages 23 and 19.

part 1

Reflective Guidance

chapter 1

Social–Emotional Development and the Reflective Process

"When I grow up, I'm going to be a teacher but I'm still going to have fun."

—Felicia, Age 7, First-Grader

After reading this chapter, you should be able to

- ▸ Understand the importance of promoting social and emotional skills in the early childhood setting.
- ▸ Identify your role in applying the principles and practices of the CSEFEL pyramid, developmentally appropriate practice, and the Code of Ethical Conduct.
- ▸ Explain what is meant by *reflection*.
- ▸ Distinguish between instinctive reactions and intentional responses to children's behavior.
- ▸ Understand that your own social–emotional competence is shaped by your nature and experiences and plays a role in your efforts to promote skills in children.

Four-year-old Cherese looks around before slipping the superhero into her jacket pocket. The hero belongs to the class, but she wants it to belong to her. During circle time, she repeatedly interrupts her classmates' stories, bombarding them with questions, comments, and tales of her own. Cherese enjoys the dress-up area, where she insists on playing the role of teacher, although her classmates would also like to play that role. If she can't be the one in charge, Cherese threatens to stop playing or being their friend. She insists on being first in line and pushes her peers if they are in line before her. When she is corrected, she stomps her feet and wails in distress. Cherese's teachers are fed up with her behavior.

THE IMPORTANCE OF SOCIAL AND EMOTIONAL COMPETENCE

Like all young children, Cherese must learn how to control herself and get along with others to become a successful student and an effective citizen. These and other social and emotional skills comprise a developmental domain that lays the foundation for a lifelong journey of relationships and learning. The social–emotional domain is often considered synonymous with **early childhood mental health**, the *child's ability to experience, regulate, and express emotions; form close and secure interpersonal relationships; explore the environment; and learn in the context of family and community* (Zeanah & Zeanah, 2009; ZERO TO THREE, 2002).

In an educational climate that emphasizes academic achievement, narrowly measured in terms of literacy and number skills, the promotion of social and emotional competence is often overlooked (Squires & Bricker, 2007). Yet research consistently concludes that a child's capacities to listen, pay attention, delay gratification, cooperate, and keep his hands to himself are essential ingredients for success in school and life (Conn-Powers, 2010). Hopefully, most teachers support these skills through everyday interactions with children, but we should make it a point to elevate the development of these skills to an explicit place in the curriculum. In early childhood settings, we have countless occasions to build fundamental social and emotional skills, and we should be very intentional in how we go about doing this (Eisenhauer & Katz, 2011).

There are several critical reasons for early childhood professionals to consciously create opportunities that promote these skills. Many children begin their educational career with failure resulting from underdeveloped social and emotional skills. Compiling data from nearly 4,000 preschool classrooms, a Yale University research team concluded that preschool children are expelled from early childhood programs at a rate that is more than three times the expulsion rate for all children from grades K–12 put together (Gilliam, 2005). By far, the most frequent reason for expulsion is "challenging behavior." And what is challenging behavior other than a child's solution to a personal or interpersonal problem? In the Yale study, expulsion rates decreased significantly when ongoing behavior/mental health consultation was available to help teachers help children resolve their difficulties in socially appropriate ways. Because professional consultation is not always available, however, it is imperative for early educators to have a repertoire of practical and research-based strategies for promoting social and emotional skills.

Social development and emotional health are also linked to children's academic success (Wentzel & Asher, 1995; Ladd, Kochenderfer, & Coleman, 1997; Boyd, Barnett, Bodrova, Leong, & Gomby, 2005). Children who have difficulties paying attention, following directions, getting along with others, and controlling negative emotions such as anger perform significantly less well in school (Arnold, Ortiz, Curry, Stowe, Goldstein, & Fisher, 1999; McClelland, Morrison, & Holmes, 2000).

Many undesirable long-range consequences can be prevented if we start early. Children who struggle with behavioral and emotional problems in preschool have a 50 percent chance of continuing to struggle in adolescence and adulthood (Cohen & Kaufmann, 2005). Early-onset conduct problems often predict such adolescent outcomes as drug abuse, depression, juvenile delinquency, and school dropout (Shonkoff & Phillips, 2000). Each and every day, early childhood professionals have the unique opportunity, and therefore the responsibility, to turn this undesirable trend around.

In addition, today's teacher will most certainly have children from low- or very low-income families in her classroom. At the time of this writing, over 25 million, or 46 percent of American children under age six were living in low-income or poor families (Chau, Thampi, & Wight, 2010; U.S. Census Bureau, 2011). The many stressors experienced by families struggling to meet basic needs contribute to significant vulnerability in young children. Young children living in poverty have a greater likelihood of experiencing academic difficulties throughout their school years and are at greater risk for poor health outcomes, cognitive delays, and social problems (Shonkoff & Phillips, 2000). Other risk factors include being raised by a teen and/or single parent, lack of access to health care, and unsafe neighborhoods. The more numerous are a child's risk factors, the more likely his or her developmental outcomes will be compromised (Sameroff & MacKenzie, 2003). Social and emotional competence can serve as a buffer that increases a child's resiliency in the face of stress related to poverty and other issues (Squires & Bricker, 2007). Luckily, teachers have evidence-based practices to guide them as they work with all young children.

PROFESSIONAL FRAMEWORKS TO GUIDE OUR PRACTICES

The notion of targeting the social–emotional domain and the emphasis on using a reflective approach are consistent with the principles developed by The Center on the Social and Emotional Foundations for Early Learning or CSEFEL (Center on the Social and Emotional Foundations for Early Learning, 2011). In addition, supporting social–emotional development and reflection is consistent with the frameworks presented by the National Association for the Education of Young Children (NAEYC) entitled *Developmentally Appropriate Practice in Early Childhood Programs Serving Children from Birth through Age 8*, commonly referred to as DAP, and NAEYC's Code of Ethical Conduct (NAEYC, 2009, 2011). Let's explore each of these briefly because they are a foundation for the work that you are doing. You will also learn more about them in this book.

CSEFEL's Pyramid Model

CSEFEL is a consortium of universities and organizations that focuses on promoting social and emotional competence in young children from birth to age 5. CSEFEL disseminates research and evidence-based practices to early childhood programs across the country.

CSEFEL utilizes a pyramid model to describe the relationships among prevention, promotion, and intervention strategies. The bottom, or most ubiquitous, level of the pyramid reflects the vital importance of systems and policies that support an effective early childhood workforce. The second level, nurturing and responsive relationships, and the third level, high-quality supportive environments, are critically important for all children. The fourth level, targeted social-emotional supports, refers to specific strategies and methods professionals can use to address particular emotional and behavioral skills. The second, third, and fourth levels of the CSEFEL pyramid are the focus of this book. (See Figure 1.1.)

The fifth and highest level of the pyramid, intensive intervention, involves treatment by a mental health or other professional. The need for intensive intervention can be prevented for many children if the more basic levels of the pyramid are consistently present. But some children with serious mental health issues and developmental challenges will be enrolled in typical classrooms. For example, the rate of children with autism spectrum disorders (ASD) is on the rise. ASDs are a group of developmental disabilities that can cause significant social, communication, and behavioral challenges. The Centers for Disease Control and Prevention (CDC) estimates that one out of every 110 children meets the diagnostic criteria for ASD (Centers for Disease Control and Prevention, 2011). This finding suggests that a typical teacher will have at least one child with ASD in her class every few years.

Similarly, the CDC reports that approximately one child in twenty will meet diagnostic criteria for attention deficit hyperactivity disorder. It is beyond the scope of this publication to provide detailed strategies for children with severe mental health and developmental challenges, but the reflective approach described herein will benefit all children. Consult the Autism Speaks website (www.autismspeaks.org) and the website for Children and Adults with attention deficit hyperactivity disorder (www.chadd.org) for excellent resources to help children with these prevalent conditions. Because a few children will always need a higher level of intervention, you can play an important role in getting children the services they need by making developmental screening and referral a regular part of your program.

Developmentally Appropriate Practices and Code of Ethical Conduct

In NAEYC's position statement on DAP, several principles of child development and learning are presented to inform our practices with children, regardless of our setting or specialty (e.g., teacher, therapist, administrator). Among many of the principles presented, DAP encourages us to address all developmental domains, individualize experiences to meet the unique needs of each child, and

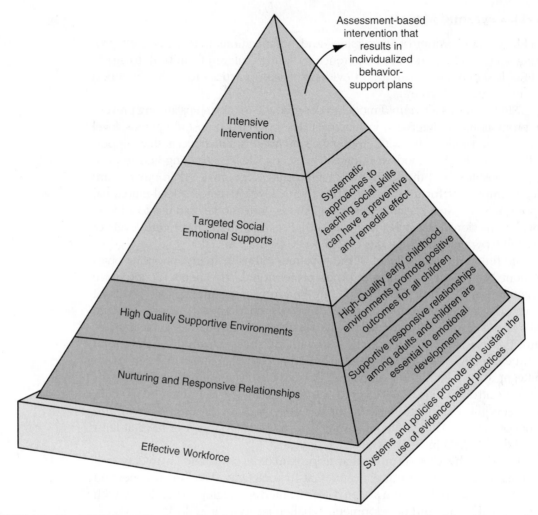

FIGURE 1.1   The CSEFEL Pyramid   *Source*: Reprinted with permission from Center on the Social and Emotional Foundations for Early Learning (2011, January). *CSEFEL: Center on the Social and Emotional Foundations for Early Learning.* Vanderbilt University. Website: csefel.vanderbilt.edu, accessed November 19, 2011.

remember that children learn best through play, all in the context of secure and responsive relationships.

In addition, the principles presented in this book are consistent with NAEYC's Code of Ethical Conduct for those who work with young children and families. The Code presents a shared framework of our professional responsibilities with children, families, colleagues, and society. It requires us to recognize the comprehensive and unique health, developmental, and educational needs of the whole child in the context of his or her family, culture, and community. Each of these ideas will be elaborated in great detail in this book, and guidance is provided for applying them in our work. For complete coverage of DAP and the Code of Ethical Conduct, please visit the NAEYC website at naeyc.org.

The children in our programs are not simple beings to be controlled with classroom-management strategies. Nor are they simple machines into which we put facts and concepts only to be recited in the future. To the contrary, our young charges are unique, complex, multidimensional, and dynamic individuals brimming with ideas, aptitudes, curiosity, and emotional needs. It is in their best interests and ours as professionals to view children in all their complexity when we guide them to become courteous and effective human beings.

REFLECTIVE PROCESS

> *"When I look in the mirror, I see a happy girl*
> *who hates lima beans and loves jelly beans."*
>
> —MOLLIE, AGE 6

Why do we like what we like? Why do we do the things we do? Our preferences and our actions, the ways in which we choose to behave, come from somewhere. They don't just emerge randomly. But what underlies our behavior choices and patterns? What underlies the behavior choices and patterns of the children with whom we work? These are the questions of reflection.

DEFINING REFLECTION

Reflection has several meanings. At one level, reflection refers to the ability to see ourselves as others see us. Self-reflection, or reflecting on oneself, is like looking into a magical magnifying mirror. Through this mirror, we have access to the hidden world of our thoughts and emotions in the context of our life history, current circumstances, and aspirations for our future. Reflection also refers to a thinking process that allows us to consider the many variables that result in the behavior of others. If we angled that magical mirror to see inside another person, we would be able to put his behavior into the context of his thoughts, emotions, and other unique attributes. Daniel Siegel, founder of the Mindsight Institute, refers to "me-maps" and "you-maps" to describe the brain's process for insight into ourselves and others (Siegel, 2011). For our purposes, **reflection** includes *both the ability to look within ourselves and to look in depth at children so that we may use our enhanced understanding to determine the most effective ways to promote their social and emotional competence.*

The field of education and the field of mental health have somewhat different definitions of the word *reflection*. The education literature emphasizes teaching practices. **Reflective practice** in education is *a cycle that involves stopping to consider [teaching] practices and the reasons for them, thinking critically about alternative perspectives and changing practices based on new understandings"* (O'Connor & Diggins, 2002). As summarized by McFarland and her colleagues, self-reflection allows educators to distance themselves from their thoughts and actions, make sense of how and why particular practices worked or didn't work, and use new understanding of these processes to adapt practices to be more effective in the future (McFarland, Saunders, & Allen, 2009; Arthur, Beecher, Death, Dockett, & Farmer, 2005).

In contrast, early childhood mental health practitioners believe that the purpose of reflection is not to distance oneself from her thoughts and actions, but precisely to examine those thoughts, emotions, intentions, and actions in the context of her history of being in relationships. Rather than setting them aside, the reflective practitioner uses her self-awareness in the very work of promoting positive development in others (Heffron, Ivins, & Weston, 2005). **Reflective functioning** in mental health refers to *the essential human capacity to understand behavior in light of underlying mental states and intentions* (Slade, 2005). It involves a cluster of related skills that includes the adult's awareness of her own mental states and those of the child, as well as the ability to understand how these mental states affect the child's behavior and her own caregiving behavior (Tomlin, Sturm, & Koch, 2009). In the following example, Ms. Keisha demonstrates reflective functioning when helping five-year-old Charlie manage more effectively in the classroom:

> Charlie is new to Ms. Keisha's kindergarten class. His constant motion, disruptive outbursts, and aggressive behavior bring chaos to the otherwise peaceful, organized classroom.
>
> Keisha steps back and realizes that she is feeling particularly frustrated by Charlie's behavior. Keisha's own parents and teachers would never have tolerated such behavior and would have imposed severe consequences. She believes that children this age should know how to control their anger and impulses better than Charlie does. Sometimes she feels like his behavior is intentional.
>
> Keisha then remembers that Charlie and his mother, a victim of domestic violence, have moved in and out of homes of relatives and shelters for the past five years. His hair-trigger tendency to fight most likely is an adaptive response to experiences in his past. Charlie has never been in a group setting for longer than a week and probably has no idea how to behave in a classroom.
>
> At first, Keisha considers using a firm, assertive voice with Charlie, looking him in the eye and imposing time-out. But then Keisha remembers that children who have been traumatized often feel threatened by a firm voice and direct eye contact. She remembers that

she hasn't taken the time to establish a supportive relationship with Charlie, so she decides to focus on building Charlie's trust and sense of security. She knows that his cooperation will improve when he feels safe and respected.

By examining her own reactions, putting the child's behavior in context, and intentionally deciding on the most effective response, Keisha's reflective process has positive results for Charlie.

Keisha recognizes that her role as an early educator goes beyond teaching Charlie and his classmates how to read and write. She knows that she is also responsible for promoting their social skills and emotional health during the many hours that they are together. Keisha acknowledges the importance of looking within herself and also reflecting on the unique attributes of each child in fulfilling this tremendous responsibility.

What Reflection Looks Like

Psychologist and researcher Carl Rogers introduced "client-centered therapy," a therapeutic technique that emphasized a communication technique called **reflective listening** (Rogers, 1951). As the name suggests, *the reflective listener serves as a mirror to the speaker. Rather than answering the client's question, challenging his idea, asking questions, or offering advice, the reflective listener confirms the idea the speaker expresses.* This reflection includes reference to the words, emotional tone, and nonverbal messages that are expressed. In therapy, reflective listening might sound like the following example:

CLIENT (holding head in hands and looking at the floor): "I just can't get my husband to listen to me! I've been trying for years!"

THERAPIST: "It sounds like you've tried and tried for a long time and you can't seem to get your husband to listen to your concerns."

Virginia Axline adapted Rogers's then "person-centered" approach to her work as a psychologist with young children (Axline, 1947, 1989). Axline's "play therapy" is an approach to helping children between ages 3 and 11 work through anxiety and other emotional issues through play in the context of a supportive, responsive relationship (Swenson, 2010). Reflective listening with young children recognizes that children express themselves differently from adults and requires that we observe the way they play and interact with others to understand their thoughts, feelings, and needs. A therapy session with a five-year-old might look like this example:

CHILD (bouncing the plastic tiger up and down and hiding the boy doll behind the playhouse): "Grr! I'm going to get that little stinker."

THERAPIST: "That tiger is very angry!"

CHILD: "She won't find him back here."

THERAPIST: "It looks like the boy feels safe behind the house."

Early childhood educators are not expected to be therapists and should not attempt to practice therapy without proper qualifications. But you can learn a great deal about the children in your care by reflective listening. To be more precise, when working with young children, the term *reflective listening* tells only part of the story. Young children often express themselves through nonverbal means, such as make-believe play, art, movement, and emotional displays (e.g., tantrums, pouting, whining, hiding); thus, the term *reflective observation* is more accurate. The purpose of reflective observation is to learn about children's perceptions, thoughts, and feelings through their play, stories, and other behavior. Reflective observation in the classroom may look like the following scenario:

Ms. Marsha asked her students to draw a picture of their family and to narrate the stories while she wrote them down. Four-year-old Lawrence, a playful, sometimes aggressive and defiant child, is the youngest of seven brothers. He drew three big people and about 15 small people standing and sleeping in every corner of a small house, including the roof and the front lawn. Lawrence asked Ms. Marsha to write these words, "I don't know all these people but they live at my house. This one is Bruce and he's mean so he sleeps in the doghouse. That's what the aunties say."

MS. MARSHA: "There are lots of people and you don't know some of them. Your aunties say that Bruce is mean so he sleeps in the doghouse?"

LAWRENCE: "He's mean to Mommy and me and Lenny and Jack."

MS. MARSHA: "Sometimes he's mean to you and the people you love like your brothers and your mom?"

LAWRENCE (tugging on his hair, sucking on his collar):   "I hope he doesn't hurt the dog."

MS. MARSHA: "You are worried about the dog and the people you love."

Marsha's comments reflect Lawrence's concerns expressed through his art and descriptions. Marsha might feel helpless to do anything to relieve Lawrence's anxiety, but her reflective responses have made a contribution to his mental health and well-being by conveying to him that his feelings are valid and he has been heard and understood. She has helped Lawrence "feel felt," an essential emotional connection that will buffer the impact of difficult experiences and enable Lawrence to work through troubling emotions and situations (Siegel & Hartzell, 2003).

The next time Lawrence behaves in a manner that is aggressive, Marsha interprets his behavior against the backdrop of a child who has witnessed aggressive behavior modeled by an adult who is important to his family. The next time he is defiant, she considers the likelihood that Lawrence has very few ways in which he can safely assert his autonomy at home. She recognizes that sometimes he needs to feel that he is in charge because at home, many other people control his circumstances and he feels powerless to control how things turn out.

It takes time and practice to be able to tune in accurately to what children are communicating in these indirect ways. One should consider this time and effort as an investment in becoming an effective interpreter of children's behavior.

Reflection also involves looking within oneself to unearth the deeper mental states that shape our actions. Throughout this book, the reader is invited to explore those **mental states (or inner states)**, *thoughts, feelings, preferences, intentions, and biases,* in the context of a variety of subjects. Behavior does not occur in a vacuum, but rather works in a three-way partnership with the emotional domain and the cognitive domain, as Ms. Marsha contemplates:

> Ms. Marsha takes a moment to consider her experience with Lawrence. Her feelings and Lawrence's situation remind her of how she used to feel with her childhood friend, Carla. Carla lived with her extended family of ten in a two-bedroom apartment. The crowded environment resulted in frequent irritable outbursts by adults who in turn scolded the children. Although Carla had little influence on the activities and relationships at her home, Marsha remembers her to be very bossy with their group of friends. With the support of Marsha and a cadre of compassionate teachers, Carla grew up to be a strong leader and the owner of a successful company. As a teacher, Marsha recognizes the importance of her responses to Lawrence so that she can support him and positively influence his development.

WHY REFLECTION IS IMPORTANT

Innumerable strategies can be used to teach a skill or solve a problem. Some approaches are very effective, others are less effective, and some actually work against our desired outcome. For example, when a child is having a temper tantrum, giving him some tools to calm down is usually effective, scolding him is less effective, and spanking him will increase the intensity of the emotional outburst. Reflection enables the adult to articulate the goals he is trying to accomplish, explore the many variables he must consider, and determine the most effective strategy for accomplishing his goals.

INSTINCTUAL REACTIONS AND INTENTIONAL RESPONSES

Reflection is a key element of the distinction between a reaction and a response. A **reaction** is *an emotion or behavior that immediately follows a triggering event with no time taken for consideration of outcomes or other factors. It is a rather impulsive action that follows an event.* In contrast, a **response** is *an emotion or* *behavior that follows a triggering event and is the result of thoughtful examination of personal and contextual variables, determination of desired outcomes, exploration of all possible actions, and an intentional selection of the most effective course of action.* A split-second reaction is a good thing when someone is in immediate danger. When the goal is to foster skills in young children, however, it is more effective to take the time to develop a thoughtful, intentional response.

This is not always easy. We do many things on instinct. An **instinct** is *an inherent inclination toward a certain behavior that occurs below a conscious level.* Sometimes our instincts are right on target and other times they are off base. Our instincts are based on a combination of built-in survival reflexes, life experiences, and our immediate interpretations of our perceptions, which may or may not be accurate. When we pay conscious attention to the ways in which we interpret our circumstances, we can turn otherwise instinctual reactions into intentional responses. By going through this reflective process over and over, the accuracy of our instincts improves. Like any new skill, however, honing our instincts takes mindful practice (Gladwell, 2005). According to scientists who study the development of expertise in the business world, "through an ongoing process of honest and continuous self-assessment, we can develop expertise in anything. It requires struggle, sacrifice, and honest, often painful self-assessment. There are no shortcuts" (Ericsson, Prietula, & Cokely, 2007).

We do many things out of habit, too. Actions that took some time to learn at first have become so automatic you don't have to think about them at all, such as brushing your teeth, driving a car, or proceeding through the grocery store. We behave in habitual ways in our classrooms, too. The steps you go through to serve snacks, organize the children for circle time, and gather your things to go home are examples of activities that once required thought but over time have become habitual. Sometimes, the ways we relate to certain people or react to particular behaviors become habitual, too. For example, when a child whines, your hands may go instantly to your ears to muffle the sound. It may take conscious effort on your part to stop and consider the personal origins of your behavior and the need the child is expressing.

LOOKING IN THE MIRROR...

Consider the ways you typically respond to challenging behaviors:

- What do you do when a child grabs an object from another child?
- What do you do when children fight?
- What do you do when a child whines?
- How do you handle tattling?

These problems are not easy to solve, and yet you may find yourself in the habit of addressing them in very predictable ways.

FIGURE 1.2

The Child's Behavior: Its Meaning and Your Goals

In responding to a child's need or outward behavior, we should first consider our desired outcomes, think through the various response choices, and then act accordingly. You can start by asking yourself these questions:

- What is this child's behavior telling me about his or her needs?
- What do I wish to accomplish right now with this child?
- What factors do I have to consider to accomplish that goal?
- What are the possible ways in which I can accomplish that goal?
- What would be the positive and negative consequences of those various approaches?
- What is the best course of action to accomplish my goal?

We behave in habitual ways because we always have, or we haven't taken the time to really think about it. We are on autopilot. In fact, automaticity is an essential brain function because it allows us to focus on learning new material. But just because an action is automatic, it is not necessarily the best way to accomplish our goal. Especially when it comes to addressing challenging behavior, it is important to stop and think about what we are trying to accomplish. We should consider if our action will help us accomplish our goal or if it is simply a habitual reaction to a trigger. Keisha, whose classroom was described at the beginning of this chapter, was in the habit of using a firm, assertive voice to correct children's behavior. It took conscious reflection for her to stop and consider the individual needs of the child and the various approaches that would be more effective in accomplishing her goal of improving Charlie's coping skills. Please see Figure 1.2 for questions to guide our thinking about child behavior.

A REFLECTIVE APPROACH TO PROMOTING ESSENTIAL SOCIAL AND EMOTIONAL SKILLS

What social and emotional skills does a child need to be successful in school and in life? Researchers and authors have clustered social and emotional skills into various groupings to communicate their findings. For example, *Mind in the Making* is a highly recommended summary of the research to date on the importance of skills in this domain, and it organizes them into "seven essential life skills every child needs" (Galinsky, 2010). Pam Schiller also describes seven essential skills for school success, though they differ slightly from Galinsky's seven skills (Schiller, 2009). Ann Epstein explores eleven skills in her coverage of social–emotional learning in preschool (Epstein, 2009). As a clinical psychologist and behavior consultant, I have found that the competencies children need to thrive can be summarized by two sets of emotional skills and two sets of social skills. This discussion is consistent with the other texts on the subject, but our emphasis on the reflective process lends itself to this organizing structure. The essential skills discussed in this book include the following:

Emotional Skills	Social Skills
Self-regulation	Empathy/sense of community
Autonomy	Communication

Reflection and Self-Regulation

Research suggests that a caregiver's ability to reflect on her own personal life story predicts the quality of the attachment relationships she will have with children in her care (Siegel & Hartzell, 2003). The caregiver's self-reflection enables her to hold and manage the child's emotions when those emotions overwhelm the child's ability to cope. Over time, such a pattern of responsive caregiving enables the child to regulate his own emotions.

Early childhood professionals also promote self-regulation in children by modeling self-reflection. If you have ever tried to break a habit or respond differently to circumstances, you know that before you can change your patterns of behavior, you must heighten your awareness of yourself in those circumstances where the behavior has become automatic. For example, to use relaxation strategies to calm down when you are angry, you must first identify that you feel emotionally aroused, ascertain the nature of that feeling (anger? frustration? impatience?), consider alternative ways of coping, and consciously replace the automatic angry outburst with practiced strategies. So it is with children. When we model self-reflection, it allows children to see the underlying basis of our decisions and actions, as can be seen with Ms. Keisha in the following vignette:

> It has been a week of cold rain and slush. Getting the children outside for recess has been impossible and everyone is cranky. Ms. Keisha has worked tirelessly to keep the children engaged and active, but today is Friday and the children are bouncing off the walls! Poking and pestering each other, the children are producing a continuous stream of tattling and whining.
>
> Keisha invites the children to the circle-time area for a chat. She begins the conversation with self-reflection:
>
> "Children, I feel frustrated and irritable. We have had to stay inside all week, and I wish we could get out and run around, but the weather is awful. Sometimes when I can't get outside, everything seems to bother me. I get angry about little things. It is hard to remember to calm myself down so I don't hurt other people with my words or actions. I wonder if some of you feel the same way?"

Keisha is thinking aloud about her feelings and concerns so that the children can observe self-reflection in action. Through repeated exposure to adult self-reflection, children become increasingly able to develop these skills themselves.

Reflection and Autonomy

Three ingredients are necessary for children to develop **autonomy**, *the sense that one is able to do things for himself or herself.* These ingredients are wonder, confidence, and motivation. Children are born wondering about the world in which they live, and it is our job to support their natural inclination toward

discovery. With our society's emphasis on educational outputs such as test scores, we often lose sight of the importance of the process of wonder and discovery in children's learning. It can be tempting for educators to use worksheets and flashcards to ensure that children are learning the facts necessary for success at their next stage of development. When we reflect on our own learning, however, we realize that our richest educational experiences have come from our self-directed exploration of the environment, seasoned with conversations and fortified by time for contemplation. Upon reflection, we realize that confidence and motivation emerge over time as a function of our successful interactions with the world. To promote the confidence and motivation necessary for the development of autonomy, we must provide children with opportunities to explore and interact with a healthy array of materials, people, and circumstances.

Reflection, Empathy, and Sense of Community

"How would you like it if he did that to you?" This question is common in early childhood settings. The question has two parts and both parts require self-reflection. "*If he did that to you*" is a hypothetical premise that requires a child to step into the shoes of another person and imagine that person's experience. "*How would you like it…?*" is a question that requires a child to look within and reflect on how she would feel in a similar situation. It is by imagining oneself as having the experiences of another person that we are able to understand the way others feel.

During a typical day with young children, we have countless opportunities to model the use of self-reflection to promote empathy. We model self-reflection when we say, "That would make me feel sad (or angry or scared), too." We model the capacity to reflect on the feelings of others when we say, "Look how sad Tina feels when you hit her." When young children observe reflective

processes offered by role models, they are more inclined to practice these processes themselves in their own interpersonal relationships.

Self-reflection is also useful in building a sense of community. When we stop
to consider the qualities of a group experience that make us feel connected to
that group, we can more effectively create such an atmosphere in our classrooms.
For example, by creating opportunities for small and large group goal-oriented
activities, children are able to see their important role as part of the community.
A classroom garden is one such experience wherein all students can have roles
and responsibilities that are important to the success of the project as a whole. By
discussing each child's contribution, they all can recognize their important place
in the classroom community.

Reflection in Communication

Scientists use the term **meta-cognition** to describe *the process of thinking about
thinking*. We use reflective words every day to describe our inner states and
the thoughts and feelings of others. Self-reflective words that describe our inner
states include "I think," "I feel," "I remember," "I wonder," "I wish," "I suppose,"
and "I imagine." Similarly, "You seem," "You appear," and "It sounds like you
feel" are phrases we use when we reflect on the verbal and nonverbal expressions of others, essentially putting words to other people's inner experiences.
That we use all of these words with such regularity is a testament to the central-
ity of reflection in everyday communication.

Expressive communication refers to the *process involved in the transmission of oral, nonverbal, or symbolic communication to another person*.
Self-reflection increases the effectiveness of our communication and includes
filtering, considering the desired outcome, selecting the best communication
approach from among alternatives, and delivering the message effectively.
Sometimes we must **filter** what we say, or *inhibit the expression of words or
gestures that might offend other people, get us in trouble, or interfere with accomplishing our goals*. Imagine, for a moment, that a parent in your program spent
all day cooking stew for you. It looks awful, smells putrid, and tastes even
worse. Think of how hard you have to work to resist making a face of disgust
or saying, "Ugh!" If you are like most people, as a young child, you did not
have the capacity to reflect on the impact of your communication on another
person's feelings. The ability to stop, filter, and judge the best response after
a reflective analysis of choices only *begins* to emerge in early childhood and
develops throughout the lifespan. But when you model self-reflection by thinking through communication issues aloud, you provide children with a strategy
that they can use for the rest of their lives.

Reflection is also important in **receptive communication**, *the process
of perceiving and interpreting the communication of others*. Because young
children are relatively inexperienced in communicating their inner states, we
must observe closely and recognize that they are communicating through their
behavior, play activities, and creative art. We must tune in to the nuances of the

child's behavior, in the context of the child's developmental level and family and cultural influences, to fully understand his underlying messages. When we then put words to the child's behavior, his emotional vocabulary will grow and he will increasingly be able to communicate more directly in the future.

Summary

Working with young children is complicated, and many variables must be considered when determining the most effective ways to support their social and emotional growth. As an early childhood professional, you may have dozens of children to get to know. Busy as a typical classroom day can be, we must make time to reflect on the unique attributes of each child and our own inner states as we attempt to meet their needs. Each child enters our classroom with his own unique array of interests, sensory needs, skills, strengths, and weaknesses in the physical, cognitive, social, and emotional domains of development. Each comes from a family with its own structure, cultural values, educational status, and socioeconomic background.

Just as each child is complicated and unique, you the professional also bring a unique profile into the classroom. You have your strengths, weaknesses, biases, and preferences. You are influenced by your own history of having been cared for and taught. You are guided by the values of your culture and family as well as by the principles you have developed over the years as a result of your training and experience.

Because of the complex and often intensely emotional nature of early childhood work, it is important that early educators have regular, built-in opportunities for self-reflection and supportive conversations with coworkers or supervisors. These conversations should provide a safe, secure space for the professional to think aloud about his thoughts, feelings, ideas, and concerns regarding the children in his care. Many early childhood programs have designated time periods for staff to participate in individual, group, or peer reflective supervision (Weigand, 2007). Reflective supervision is highly recommended because it enables us to work through the complexity and emotional intensity we experience in our work so that we can better promote children's development.

Review and Apply

1. Explain why reflection is important in promoting social skills and emotional competence.
2. Five-year-olds Tonja and Bonita are arguing loudly about who will play the mom and who will play the child in their story.

   a. Describe how you would react to their argument out of instinct or habit.
   b. After reflecting on yourself and on the needs of the children, what strategies could you use to help them resolve their conflict?

chapter 2

Teacher Self-Reflection

> *"There is no job in the world that is more important than mine. I plant the seeds of wisdom, water them with love, nurture them with mindfulness, and watch them grow and thrive."*
>
> —Ms. Rachael, Age 38, Teacher of Three-Year-Olds

After reading this chapter, you should be able to

▸ Define emotional intelligence and multiple intelligences.

▸ Describe how the dimensions of your temperament influence the ways in which you approach your work.

▸ Recognize the ways in which your early relationships influence your relationships and interactions today.

▸ Assess your level of comfort with, and competence in, the cognitive, social, and emotional skills you are trying to promote in children.

▸ Describe the strategies you use to manage stress and minimize its impact on your work with children.

EMOTIONAL INTELLIGENCE AND MULTIPLE INTELLIGENCES

The groundbreaking works of Howard Gardner, father of the theory of multiple intelligences, and Daniel Goleman, creator of the concept of emotional intelligence, have reframed the way we understand intelligence. Their efforts expand intelligence beyond the purely cognitive domain to include physical and social–emotional components. According to Gardner's theory, each of us has strengths and weakness in several types of intelligence. The seven most studied intelligences are logical-mathematical, spatial, linguistic, bodily-kinesthetic, musical, interpersonal, and intrapersonal. Gardner initially proposed these seven intelligences, and subsequent research suggests that there may be even more, including naturalistic and existential. Debate continues about whether Gardner's intelligences are merely patterns of strengths and weaknesses within one global concept of intelligence or are, indeed, distinct intelligences. This debate is beyond the scope of this book, but Gardner's theory is useful as we explore how we make sense of our experiences.

In *Emotional Intelligence*, Daniel Goleman proposes that emotional skills like "self-control, zeal, persistence, and the ability to motivate oneself" are perhaps more important for life success than the cognitive capacities typically associated with intelligence. He explains that the abilities to recognize one's own emotional life, regulate one's feelings, understand the emotions of others, work with others, and have empathy are critically important skills for effective living (Goleman, 1995).

Gardner and Goleman emphasize the importance of developing "interpersonal" and "intrapersonal" capacities to function successfully (Gardner, 1999; Goleman, 1995). **Interpersonal intelligence** refers to *a person's capacity to understand the intentions, motivations, and desires of other people and, consequently, work effectively with others.* Interpersonal intelligence is vital for teachers, clinicians, and leaders (Gardner, 1999).

Among his proposed intelligences, Gardner states that perhaps the most important for success in any person's career is **intrapersonal intelligence,** *the capacity to understand oneself, to have an effective working model of oneself—including one's own desires, fears, and capacities—and to use such information effectively in regulating one's own life.* This is the stuff of self-reflection. *Intra*personal intelligence is especially important in working with young children because the work elicits such strong emotions.

The capacity for self-reflection as a component of emotional intelligence varies a great deal between people and develops over time. We use words such as *insightful* and *introspective*, both of which mean *able to look within*, when we describe people who seem naturally self-reflective. Even some young children demonstrate an amazing capacity to look within themselves and describe their perceptions, thoughts, and feelings. Perhaps you are someone who can *look within* with ease. In contrast, you may find self-reflection to be difficult, perhaps uncomfortable, and you may have to consciously work at it. Self-reflection, introspection, intrapersonal intelligence, or whatever we may call it, is an aptitude that can be improved with concerted effort.

An intern once told me, "I'm an after-thinker." She was explaining that she cannot always grasp what she is feeling and thinking at the moment an event occurs; only later can she look back and describe what she had been experiencing. This retrospective analysis is very common and, in fact, describes

LOOKING IN THE MIRROR...

Developing a habit of reflective practice takes time and commitment, but will help you become more effective in your work. It is helpful to write about your experiences in a journal for later review. Try journaling for a few weeks, and then ask yourself the following questions:

- What themes do you notice in your thoughts and feelings about your work?
- Do situations or specific children appear repeatedly in your writing?
- Do you tend to respond to those situations or children in predictable ways, or do you vary in your responses?
- When you look back at your journal over time, what patterns or trends do you notice in your thoughts, feelings, and responses?

This reflective experience can be enhanced when you have the opportunity to review recordings of classroom interactions with a supervisor. When the technology is not available, you may invite a trusted colleague to observe difficult situations in your classroom or review your journal:

- What individuals can you call on to observe your interactions when you encounter difficult situations with a child?
- With whom would you feel comfortable sharing parts of your journal?

how we develop skills in many areas. Think for a moment about how athletes learn to improve their performance. Many athletes use video clips to look back at their event or game to determine how to perform more effectively in the future. Therapists develop the capacity for self-reflection by sitting with supervisors and poring over audio or visual recordings of interactions with clients for the purpose of understanding the perceptions, thoughts, and intentions behind the therapist's responses. Humbling as this experience can be, it greatly increases the self-reflection skills of the therapist. As an early childhood professional, you can improve the effectiveness of your work by taking a few minutes after your interactions with children to think about your underlying perceptions, thoughts, and intentions as well as how you might improve such interactions in the future.

In the following scenario, Dianna invites Patti, another teacher, to observe a challenging classroom experience to help her gain insight to the problem:

Dianna has been struggling to get Jayson to settle down for activities and finds herself increasingly frustrated. Patti agreed to spend a few minutes observing Dianna's classroom during certain problematic transition times. After lunch, Patti and Dianna took a few minutes to talk.

DIANNA: "See what I mean about Jayson? He's so hyper. I've never seen anybody move around so much. He's just wild!"

PATTI: "He *does* move around a lot! When he knocked over his paint, what was your first thought?"

DIANNA: "I was ready to scream at him! If he'd just settle down, things like that wouldn't happen!"

PATTI: "You are really frustrated with him. You don't know how to help him settle down, which makes you want to scream. It sounds like you feel helpless."

DIANNA: "I mean...he's a sweet little boy. He's always wanting to help, but he's always bumping into things because he moves too fast and too much. I feel like I need to be in overdrive to keep up with him. I just don't move that fast!"

PATTI: "So you can see nice qualities in Jayson, but he's more active than you are and moves faster. You're kind of a mellow person...and he's *not*! I noticed that when you stopped to take a deep breath, he did the same thing. Did you notice that after a few deep breaths, he became a little calmer? I wonder if you can use that as a strategy?"

Dianna was fortunate to have a reflective observer in Patti. Patti could see some events that Dianna missed, and those observations proved very useful in changing Dianna's way of thinking and interacting with Jayson. Trusted colleagues can provide different perspectives for us. With practice using our magical magnifying mirror to look within ourselves and look deeply into the unique qualities of the child, we can begin to develop multiple perspectives for ourselves as well.

In any given situation with a child, there are limitless ways you can respond and limitless reasons for why you respond the way that you do. A fast-moving child like Jayson can lead one teacher to feel frustrated, helpless, or angry, while another feels energized. Our responses differ from one another because we differ in our temperaments, relationship histories, strengths, weaknesses, and expectations. We also vary from one day to the next because of the inevitable realities and stresses in our own lives. It is important to reflect on and understand these unique and interacting aspects of ourselves so that we can be intentional in our responses.

Understanding Your Temperament and Personality

In the field of child development, we talk quite a bit about child temperament, but we adults came into this world with our own temperament as well. **Temperament** refers to *individual differences in emotional reactivity and regulation that appear early in life, are relatively stable, and are at least partly biologically based* (Rothbart & Bates, 2006). Developmental scientists Buss and

Plomin (1984) proposed that to be considered a temperament dimension, a trait has to be evident in the first two years of life, at least somewhat hereditary, and continuous into later personality. Your temperament is every bit as important as the temperament of the child in understanding your interactions.

Extensive research has been conducted on the subject of temperament and the various behavior qualities that make up temperament. Scientists have looked at ways certain characteristics cluster together, how stable they are, how they correlate with brain processes, whether they predict mental health problems, and the roles they play in relationships (Thomas & Chess, 1977; Zentner & Bates, 2008; Dougherty, et al., 2011; Goldsmith, Lemery, Aksan, & Buss, 2000; Kagan & Snidman, 2004). In an excellent review of the temperament literature, Zentner and Bates (2008) report that the most evidenced-based temperament traits cluster into five general categories: (1) behavior inhibition, (2) irritability/frustration, (3) positive emotionality, (4) activity level, and (5) attention/persistence. This vast body of research gives us information about why we do the things we do and why we are the way we are as adults. Because the original nine dimensions described by Alexander Thomas and Stella Chess are well known and straightforward, discussions of temperament in this book utilize their classification system.

The concept of temperament became the subject of study in the 1950s when Thomas, Chess, and their colleagues noted that environmental differences alone could not account for all the variability between children and that children bring their own unique attributes into their environments. This observation inspired the New York Longitudinal Study (NYLS), where researchers followed 133 individuals from 84 families from the age of three months to adulthood.

The results of NYLS suggested that there are nine basic dimensions of temperament, each of which is characterized by specific patterns of behavior and that these dimensions can differentiate between individuals. The nine temperament dimensions on which people were found to differ are summarized in Table 2.1. These include sensory threshold, intensity of reaction, activity level, initial response (approach/withdrawal), rhythmicity (regularity), adaptability, quality of mood, distractibility, and persistence. According to Thomas and Chess, "Temperament can be equated with the term *behavioral style*. Each temperament dimension refers to the 'how' rather than the 'what' (abilities) or the 'why' (motivation) of behavior" (Thomas & Chess, 1977; p. 9).

Everyone, you the professional as well as the children with whom you work, entered the world with a distinctive temperament. Your personality as an adult is the result of your inborn temperament and the experiences you have had over the years. On each of the temperament dimensions, our behavior tendencies fall somewhere on a continuum. You may rate yourself high on the adaptability dimension and high on activity level but low on intensity and low on persistence. If that profile describes you, you are someone who enjoys new things but would not go out of your way to look for them. Or, you may rate yourself low on sensitivity, low on activity level, high on adaptability, and high on mood. If that profile describes you, you might be someone who cheerfully goes with the flow, but you have trouble keeping up if things move too quickly.

TABLE 2.1 • Dimensions of Temperament

Dimension	Description
Sensitivity threshold	How easily aroused or disturbed is the individual by sensory stimulation?
Intensity	How intense is the individual's response to stimulation?
Activity level	How much movement and activity does the individual typically display?
Adaptability	How does the individual respond to changes in routine or expectations?
Approach/withdrawal	What is the individual's first response to a new situation?
Persistence	Does the individual continue an activity until it is finished?
Rhythmicity	What is the regularity of the individual's rhythm of activity, bodily functions, sleep, arousal, and so forth? Is the rhythm predictable?
Quality of mood	Is the individual generally pleasant and friendly or fussy and unpleasant?
Distractibility	How easily is the individual drawn away from an activity?

Based on Thomas and Chess (1977)

LOOKING IN THE MIRROR...

Using the nine dimensions of Thomas and Chess, we can explore our own unique temperament patterns. Look at Table 2.2. Rate yourself on the dimensions listed in the first column by circling 1 if you are low in this dimension, 2 if you are at a medium level, and 3 if you are at a high level on this dimension. (When completed, put Table 2.2 aside. We will use it again in Chapter 3.)

You might find that on one dimension or another, the answer will be, "Well, it depends the situation." That is true. Sometimes we are more or less positive in our mood, more or less active, and so forth. For the sake of identifying your temperament profile for further exploration, please think about your most typical behavior style when you complete the chart. Your results will reflect your behavior style in many situations. This exploration will help you understand yourself in relation to the children in your program.

- When you identified your levels on the temperament dimensions, were you surprised by anything?
- Do these observations about yourself help you understand why some situations, interactions, or people are enjoyable and easy for you, while others are more difficult?

TABLE 2.2 • Your Temperament

Dimension	Compared to Your Peers:	Example	Low Medium High		
Sensitivity	How easily are you bothered or aroused by sensory stimulation? (Easily bothered or aroused = 3)	Penny doesn't like loud music, wool shirts, roller coasters, or bright lights. She is very sensitive.	1	2	3
Intensity of reaction	How intense is your reaction? (Most intense = 3)	Maggie screams when upset and laughs with her whole body when amused.	1	2	3
Activity level	How active are you? (Most active = 3)	Jazzi is in constant motion.	1	2	3
Adaptability	How well do you respond to changes in routine/expectations? (Very comfortable with change = 3)	Polly can easily go with the flow.	1	2	3
Approach/withdrawal	How comfortable are you when approaching new situations? (Most comfortable = 3)	Rebecca actively seeks new experiences.	1	2	3
Persistence	How well do you continue an activity until it is finished? (Can stay with it well = 3)	Jeff won't stop working on the huge jigsaw puzzle until every piece is in place.	1	2	3
Rhythmicity	How regular is your rhythm of activity, sleep, arousal, and so forth? (Very regular = 3)	Regardless of circumstances, Anna wakes up, needs a midday snack, and falls asleep at the same times each day.	1	2	3
Quality of mood	How positive is your mood? (Most positive = 3)	Caryn is upbeat and cheerful most of the time.	1	2	3
Distractibility	How easily are you drawn away from an activity? (Easily distracted = 3)	Zach has trouble finishing what he starts because his attention is drawn to everything around him.	1	2	3

Relationship between Temperament and Environment

The temperament with which you came into the world is only part of the story. Your temperament interacts with the environment every minute of the day. It is the culmination of those interactions that determines how you behave, the friends you pick, and the activities you choose. Thomas and Chess emphasized that there is no good or bad temperament, but it is the goodness-of-fit between a person's temperament and the environment that provides the basic dynamic influence for the process of development (Thomas & Chess, 1977). **Goodness-of-fit** refers to *the degree to which an individual's temperament is compatible with the demands and expectations of his environment.*

One aspect of that environment is the other people in it. When a person's temperament is incompatible with that of another, tensions may arise. Think about the goodness-of-fit between your temperament and the temperaments of the teachers and other caregiving adults with whom you have interacted in the past. The memories of the two professionals described next were discussed at a recent workshop:

Mildred said, "My first grade teacher was *scary*. As you can see, I'm a wiggler, and what you see today is calm compared to how I was in first grade! Mrs. Smith liked peace and quiet. I've always been a social butterfly. Mrs. Smith liked order and routine, and if something was out of place, even coloring outside the lines, she scolded us in front of the whole class. I could not concentrate if I wasn't moving, and I was always dropping pencils or whatever else I was fidgeting with. If we got out of our chair, she put our name on the board. You would have thought the blackboard was named after me because it always said *Mildred* in big letters! First grade was awful!"

Patrice said, "As a child, I was terrified to try new things. Now I'm not scared. I just get nervous. Routines make me feel comfortable because I know what to expect. I hate surprises! I'll never forget my first day of preschool. My dad dropped me off and there was so much commotion. The kids were loud, the lights were bright, and Ms. Saylor was super-hyper! She would break into song unexpectedly. She moved very fast from one thing to the next. The whole thing was overwhelming. Our aide, Mr. Brian, was very mellow, and I think that if it weren't for him, I never would have made it through that unbearable year!"

Mildred and Patrice were so profoundly affected by the mismatch in temperaments between themselves and their early educators that those classroom experiences are still vividly remembered with shadows of the discomfort they felt as children.

LOOKING IN THE MIRROR...

Think about a teacher from your childhood whose temperament was similar to yours:

- What emotions do you feel when you think about your relationship with that teacher?

  Now think about a teacher whose temperament dimensions were different from yours:

- What emotions do you feel when you think about your relationship with that teacher and the memories of that classroom?
- What might have made those experiences more positive?

UNDERSTANDING YOUR EARLY RELATIONSHIPS: ATTACHMENT, GHOSTS, AND ANGELS

Early childhood educators assume many different roles with young children, including **caregiving**, *being the provider of physical and emotional care and support.* **Attachment** is an important aspect of caregiving and refers to *a child's sense of security and support from a particular adult—the attachment figure— especially in situations that arouse anxiety or distress.* Trust develops from the caregiver being psychologically and physically available to provide comfort, protection, and safety when the child is upset or needs help managing stress. The caregiver is the child's "safe haven." The attachment figure also serves as a "secure base" from which the child can confidently explore and engage with the environment (Powell, Cooper, Hoffman, & Marvin, 2009). Secure attachment fosters feelings of **self-efficacy**, *the sense that an individual can have an effect on the world* (Shonkoff & Phillips, 2000). From early attachment relationships, the child develops **internal working models**, *or cognitive-emotional expectations for relationships that influence*

how he experiences and reacts to the caregiver and, over time, to other people (Boris, Aoki, & Zeanah, 1999).

You, like all adults, grew up with your own internal working models of caregiving relationships. **Ghosts in the nursery** is a term borrowed from the field of infant mental health that suggests that *the ways in which our primary caregivers (parents and guardians) related to us, for better or for worse, profoundly influence our present relationships with children in our care* (Fraiberg, Adelson, & Shapiro, 1975). Fraiberg's group was the first to articulate how our past experiences exert ongoing influences on our values, expectations, and interactions with others. More recently, the term **angels in the nursery** was coined to describe *the influence of positive early relationships on ongoing caregiving relationships* (Lieberman, Padron, Van Horn, & Harris, 2005). Lieberman and colleagues explain that angels in the nursery are those early relationships that have given messages of unconditional love and provide the child with an ongoing sense of worth and security.

Each of us has our own ghosts or angels from our past. The stories of Linda and Marla illustrate the continued influence of early relationships on current caregiving styles:

> Linda and her mother lived in a one-bedroom apartment above a liquor store on a busy city street. Although they did not own any books and Linda had few toys, Linda's mother made sure that their regular bus rides to the library were filled with stories, conversations, and games like "I spy." Linda remembers that her mother often worried about paying bills but always told her that they were "a clever family that could handle anything." As a teacher now, Linda has particular sympathy for children whose families struggle with poverty, and she instinctively engages them in activities that promote their creativity and self-efficacy.
>
> In contrast, Marla and her brother, as children, were careful to stay quiet during meals and at bedtime. Even when their parents were not fighting, the ever-present, ominous tension in the air warned of an impending temper explosion by one parent or the other. Disobedience was severely punished and complaints were not tolerated. Marla was prohibited from playing with neighbors because, according to her mother, "They are ignorant." Her father insisted that the world was unsafe and people were out to hurt her. As a teacher, Marla is appalled by students who do not obey immediately. She also feels intimidated by her students' parents who are assertive. She finds herself avoiding conflict and controversy.

Linda and Marla relate to their young students in ways that mirror their relationships with their primary caregivers. Although Linda lacked material possessions, her mother was sure to attend to Linda's needs and inner states, as evidenced by her reassurance about their ability to make ends meet. Marla's parents were preoccupied with their own emotional states and demonstrated little regard for Marla's needs. Marla's ghosts in the nursery strongly influence her relationships in the present and make it difficult for her to tolerate the challenges of working with young children and their families.

We might conclude that Marla's attachment to her parents was insecure, largely due to their unpredictable moods and lack of regard for her inner states. Nonetheless, there is hope for Marla as a professional. Research suggests that a person's ability to reflect on her own early relationships and to recognize their impact on present interactions is a strong predictor of her capacity for healthy attachment with children in her care. In fact, those abilities may matter more than whether those early relationships were positive or negative (Siegel, 2001). To improve her effectiveness in guiding the children, Marla's task is to explore in depth her childhood experiences within the context of a supportive relationship in the present, such as in therapy or reflective supervision. Through the process of developing her own narrative of her life story, she is likely to learn to trust herself and the world around her. As she improves in her ability to reflect on her own life history and inner states, she will increase her ability to attend to the needs and inner states of the children in her care (Siegel & Hartzell, 2003).

Understanding Your Competence and Preferences in the Domains of Development

In the various domains of development—cognitive, physical, and social–emotional—we vary in our levels of competence and pleasure. Naturally, we tend to select activities that complement those areas in which we feel most comfortable and competent. The teacher who loves to create art but is physically uncoordinated might offer children more artistic opportunities than physical ones. Although this is understandable, we should always remember that all the domains of development are important for all children. In fact, early learning standards require that we actively and directly address all the domains of development and content areas in our everyday work with children. Your awareness of your own strengths, weaknesses, and preferences can remind you to make a variety of activities available for the children in your program. This is why a reflective examination of your lesson plans is a good step toward becoming a reflective practitioner.

Physical and Cognitive Domains

Some of us are extraordinary athletes or dancers with wonderful coordination, endurance, and grace. Many of us are not. We vary a great deal in our gross-motor development. We also vary in our fine-motor skills, such as writing, drawing, sewing, and tinkering with appliances. It is important to recognize how we subtly encourage or discourage children's activities on the basis of our own preferences. Again, we must remember that children need many assorted opportunities to develop their gross- and fine-motor skills and be sure to provide them—whether we enjoy them or not.

The cognitive domain has many components, including language, literacy, number skills, problem-solving, abstract reasoning, creative thinking, and the integration of all of those. We differ from each other in our patterns of strengths and weaknesses among the various cognitive areas, as is evident in the following classroom description:

> The two-year-olds are lucky to have Katrina and Leila as their co-teachers. Katrina is a by-the-book, follow-the-rules, detail-oriented person. If Katrina is in charge, there are no worries that a licensing regulation or curriculum standard could be overlooked. She struggles, however, with handling unexpected events, thinking creatively to solve a unique problem, or acting spontaneously when novel opportunities arise.
>
> Leila, in contrast, is a big-picture, go-with-the-flow, think-outside-the-box kind of person. No problem is too difficult to solve with a little creative ingenuity. She has to work very hard, however, to remember such details as documenting important events, bringing emergency contact information on field trips, and putting on a hairnet to serve snacks. Leila's creativity and spontaneity are matched only by her lack of attention to details. Together, Katrina and Leila are an effective team whose skills complement each other.

Like in the other skill areas, we must be sure to utilize our strengths, work on improving our weaknesses, and offer our students the opportunities they need for their optimal development.

Social–Emotional Domain

Just like in the physical and cognitive domains, we also have strengths and weaknesses in the social–emotional realm. As early childhood professionals, we play a critical role in fostering the skills that let children experience, regulate,

---

LOOKING IN THE MIRROR...

- Do you enjoy physical activities with children, for example, chasing them, shooting baskets, or kicking around a soccer ball?
- Do you feel confident and competent about creating art?
- Do you enjoy puzzles, word games, or number games?
- Do certain activities that children invite you to participate in make you feel incompetent, clumsy, or bored?
- Do you like some activities that you organize for the children more than the children do?

While it is important to enjoy our work, we must always remember that our role is to build children's competence in *all* the domains of development.

and appropriately express their emotions so they may confidently explore the world. We are also responsible for supporting their development of empathy, sense of community, and the ability to communicate effectively (Goleman, 1995). With such an important task, we must first reflect on our own competencies in those emotional and social areas.

SELF-REGULATION

As our students get older, we expect better and better impulse control from them. We expect them to delay gratification for increasingly longer periods of time. For example, it doesn't surprise Leila when the two-year-olds grab for snacks as soon as the serving platter is placed on the table. But when Leila visits the kindergarten classroom, she is shocked to see a child grab rather than wait for everyone to be served.

We also assume that children will be able to regulate their emotions more and more effectively as they get older. Again, Leila expects some aggressive behavior or temper tantrums from her two-year-olds but is surprised when she sees those reactions in the kindergarteners.

Like any skill, you have strengths and weaknesses in these important skill areas. It is useful to think about times in our own lives when we have done impulsive things only later to regret them and wish for a do-over. Step by step, we tried, made mistakes, and eventually became competent enough with our skills to become early childhood professionals. In fact, we will continue to work to master these competencies throughout our lives. We know that these skills don't develop in children without support from the adults in their world and that we *are* those adults. But how well do *we* control our own impulses, delay gratification, or regulate emotions?

LOOKING IN THE MIRROR...

- Can you resist the impulse to eat the chocolate cake, yell at a bad driver, or bite your fingernails?
- How difficult—or easy—is it for you to pass up fun activities in the moment and instead work toward a long-range goal?
- What experiences helped you learn to regulate your impulses and delay gratification?
- When you are angry, how well do you stop to calm down, consider your options, and select the most appropriate response?

Think about a time when you had an emotional outburst. For example, maybe you were extremely angry and blew up at someone. Or, maybe you were unable to control your laughter at a time when laughing was inappropriate:

- What were the consequences?
- What did you learn about emotional regulation from that experience?
- What factors helped you learn to manage those emotions more effectively?

When helping children develop self-regulation, we can use experiences from our past to guide us in what to do (or *not* to do) for them.

AUTONOMY

We can also use experiences from our past to help us support children's emerging sense of autonomy. As with other competencies, we have strengths and weaknesses in the components of autonomy. Autonomy requires a sense of wonder, confidence, and motivation. It can be enlightening to think about experiences in your past that encouraged or discouraged these components of autonomy.

LOOKING IN THE MIRROR...

- As a child, were you encouraged to explore, try new things, and even get messy?
- As an adult, are you still driven by curiosity and a desire to learn about the world?
- If not, did specific experiences inhibit your exploration?
- What did your caregiving adults do to encourage or discourage your autonomy?

EMPATHY AND SENSE OF COMMUNITY

If you ever walked into a room with multiple infants, it probably didn't take long to notice that babies cry or laugh in sympathy with one another. We come into the world with a certain level of empathy for the emotions of others around us. Over the years, some of us become jaded and we no longer feel the pain and suffering of others as much as we did when we were young. Others

LOOKING IN THE MIRROR...

You received messages from your family, school, and community about how to treat others. Perhaps you were encouraged to "turn the other cheek" or to reach out and help the less fortunate. Sometimes adults advise children not to put up with mistreatment from other people and, indeed, it can be unsafe to back down from a threat in some circumstances. It may even have been the case that you received all these messages about empathy, and many more, over the years:

- What messages did your family or community give you about how to treat others?
- Were you encouraged to overlook negative behaviors of others?
- Were you encouraged to stand up for yourself or to back down?
- Were you ever encouraged to intimidate others?

become more in synch with the distress of other people. How is that we are so different from one another in the dimension of empathy? Perhaps we are born with variable predispositions for empathy, but it is also likely that our level of empathy was more or less influenced by our experiences.

You can use the lessons you learned from your past to create environments and deliver messages for children that promote empathy and foster their sense that they belong to a community that cares about them.

COMMUNICATION

Recall that communication involves both expressing your needs, thoughts, and feelings in such a way that others can understand you as well as comprehending the messages expressed by others. For example, Linda, described earlier, enjoyed a warm and open relationship with her mother, who made it a point to ask her about her thoughts, ideas, and feelings. In contrast, Linda's colleague Marla was strongly discouraged from expressing her inner states for fear of negative consequences. Messages like these can diminish a child's willingness to practice the complicated skill of communicating.

People vary a great deal in their communication styles. Some people are dramatic with their gestures or can turn a simple event into an epic tale. Some people like to expound on every imaginable detail, going off on tangents and focusing on minutia until the listener backs away looking at his watch. Others communicate in short sentences, giving only minimal answers to questions and volunteering very little information. Some can express a thousand words simply with their facial expressions, shrugging their shoulders, or rolling their eyes. These communication styles and everything in between result from a combination of your temperament, your experiences, and your comfort level with your audience.

Listening with your ears and eyes takes practice and is important in your work with young children, especially as you guide them to express their needs, thoughts, and feelings.

LOOKING IN THE MIRROR...

Think about how well you express yourself.
- Is it easy or difficult for you to share your experiences and opinions?
- Is it easy or difficult for you to find the words that accurately describe your thoughts and feelings?
- Do you prefer to use words or to express yourself through art, poetry, dance, or music?

Communication also involves listening and observing, focusing on both the verbal and the nonverbal aspects of communication:

- How well do you listen?
- How well are you able to read the emotional messages conveyed by another person's tone of voice, selection of words, body language, and facial expression?

Understanding Your Beliefs about Teaching and Learning

It is important to be aware of the beliefs and expectations with which you entered the profession of early childhood educator. At a recent workshop, teachers were asked the following question: "Why did you become a teacher of young children?" Some of the participants were new to the field and some were "quite seasoned," as one experienced teacher described herself. A partial list of their answers includes the following:

XAVIER: "So, I can be a strong role model for them."

CLARISSA (with a chuckle): "Because I have a lot to say! Isn't that obvious?"

MAUREEN: "Children inspire me with their innocence and curiosity. My role is to observe and guide, not unduly influence them."

NORVILLE: "If I can get them to read before they start kindergarten, I'll have set them on the right course forever."

LAVERNE: "The little ones just need so much loving. Sometimes they don't get what they need at home, and I can show them they are special and teach them right from wrong at the same time. That's my job and I love it!"

Your beliefs about your role as a professional strongly influence how you structure your program and your approach to teaching. In later chapters, we

LOOKING IN THE MIRROR...

- Why did you decide to be an early childhood professional?
- What is your motivation to pursue this challenging work?
- What comes to your mind when you hear the word "teacher?"
- Do you see yourself doing the following?
  - Playing with children
  - Telling them what to do and how to do it
  - Standing back and supporting their natural curiosity
- Is classroom management a high priority for you?
- Do you consider challenging behaviors to be teachable moments or inconveniences?

will explore how these beliefs and expectations shape your relationships and interactions with children and families.

Understanding Stress and Your Coping Strategies

Stress is an inevitable and important part of life. It keeps us alert and growing. Sometimes, we knowingly seek out stressful experiences, like when we enroll in college, take on a new sport, or begin dating after a relationship ends. Sometimes, stress finds *us* and brings along fear, anxiety, and frustration. Unwelcome stress may come in the form of financial, employment, or transportation difficulties. Sometimes relationships with coworkers or family members are stressful. Problems with our health or the health of our loved ones are stressors that can seem to take over our every thought.

We need healthy outlets for our stress because holding it in can lead to the soda-can effect. A little stress is like shaking a closed can of soda a little, which builds up pressure in the can. A little more stress shakes it up a little more, creating more pressure. Without letting off some of the pressure created by the stress in our lives, we do what the soda can does with the last fateful shake: we explode!

If we do not have healthy outlets, our stress can result in health problems, irritable interactions with coworkers and children, or worse, aggressive behavior. The first principle in NAEYC's Code of Ethical Conduct, indeed in all codes of ethics, is that we "do no harm" (NAEYC, 2011). When our responses to children are driven by unmanaged stress in our lives, we can do devastating and lasting harm. As one gauge for measuring the impact of stress on your interactions, listen to the sound of your voice when asking a child to do something. If the voice you hear is a voice with which you would like to be addressed, then you probably have found healthy outlets for your stress. If the voice you hear is overly harsh (like the bark of a dog), you might need to develop some more effective outlets.

Countless positive and healthy behaviors can help handle stress. Some people relieve stress physically, like with deep breathing, physical activity, or relaxation exercises. Others prefer verbal strategies, such as talking with a close friend or writing in a journal. Some feel better through artistic activities, like drawing, molding clay, creating and listening to music, or acting out scenarios with a friend. Regardless of what stress-management technique you use, remember that the result does much more than just make *you* feel better: it influences every interaction you have with children, parents, and coworkers. It can change the atmosphere in the room from one of impenetrable tension to one of safety and security for all.

Summary

To provide optimal learning experiences for children, it is helpful for you to look within yourself and understand the factors that underlie your choices and responses. Your temperament is as important as a child's temperament in your interactions with him. Your self-awareness and the goodness-of-fit between temperaments and the learning environment can make learning experiences productive. The attachment relationships you had with your parents or guardians, that is, your ghosts or angels in the nursery, continue to influence your relationships today, so it is important to reflect on the nature of your early relationships.

In addition, understanding your pattern of strengths and weaknesses in all domains of development will facilitate your efforts to promote skills in young children, especially in the social and emotional domain. It is also useful to keep in mind your expectations and beliefs about your role as a teacher. And finally, day-to-day experiences, such as stress and how well you manage it, can impact the quality of your relationships with children and the effectiveness of your guidance strategies.

Review and Apply

1. Describe how your emotional intelligence, temperament, relationship history, expectations, and stress management influence your approach to your work.

2. You have been assigned to teach a class of four-year-olds. Your co-teacher differs from you in temperament, classroom expectations, and coping strategies.

   a. What do you need to consider in order to work effectively with your co-teacher?

   b. What steps can you take to work through those differences?

part 2

· ·

Guiding Principles for Promoting Social– Emotional Skills

It's Margie's first day as lead teacher of the three-year-olds. She aced most of her classes while working toward her bachelor's degree in early education. She knows what should be expected of a typical three-year-old across the domains of development. She has written a well-balanced lesson plan consistent with the curriculum guide recommended by her favorite professor. Margie has all sorts of creative ideas about teaching children. She is ready to dive in.

Margie connects immediately with Donnie and his grandma, who warmly shares an amusing story about the family's summer vacation. This family reminds Margie of her own childhood. Donnie is outgoing and looks adoringly at Margie with his twinkling hazel eyes.

In contrast, Rochelle's hurried mother dropped her off at the front door. When Margie attempts to engage with the little girl, she stands at the outskirts of the classroom activities and looks at the floor. Margie feels anxious and uncertain about working with Rochelle.

Naptime allows Margie a few minutes to wonder aloud with her co-teacher: What's up with Rochelle's reluctance to connect? Doesn't her mother realize the importance of the departure experience? Why isn't this mother warm and attentive like Donnie's grandmother? And, by the way, why does Donnie live with his grandparents?

Margie learned on her first day that simply applying a curriculum or a lesson plan is not sufficient for working with young children. While she was well versed in theories of child development and knowledgeable about best practices, she felt surprisingly unprepared for the range of experiences that characterize real children—children who are each influenced in different ways by their unique temperaments and families—in real dynamic care and education settings.

One of the most important responsibilities for an educator is to support the intricate process of social and emotional development in each of her young learners. This process is not simple but rather requires thoughtful consideration of several factors, each influencing the others. Five guiding principles should underlie our efforts in this domain:

1. The process should be *relationship-based*, emphasizing self-awareness in the educator and mutual respect with the child.
2. The process must be *individualized* to meet the unique needs of each child because children differ from one another in so many ways.
3. The process must take into account the *developmental* differences between children as well as developmental variability within a given child.
4. The process should occur with the recognition that *contextual* variables play a role in children's functioning and development.
5. The process must be *culturally appropriate* for each child.

chapter 3

Relationship-Based Guidance

"I don't remember what my preschool teacher taught me, but I know she liked me and cared about my family and me."

—MARA, AGE 6, KINDERGARTENER

After reading this chapter, you should be able to

▶ Explain how your expectations of your role, internalized messages from your past, and your personality influence your relationships with children in your program.
▶ Describe strategies you can use to improve the goodness-of-fit between you, the children, and the environment.
▶ Apply strategies for getting to know the needs, preferences, and inner states of children.
▶ Apply the principles of parallel process in your interactions with children.

The people who have had the greatest impact on our own learning are generally remembered for the ways in which they interacted with us rather than what they were trying to teach us. In a similar vein, it is through our relationships with young children that they will learn life's important lessons.

Relationship-based guidance is *an approach to teaching and guidance that emphasizes the emotional connection between two individuals, the adult and the child.* Children learn best when these connections are characterized by attunement and emotional responsiveness. **Attunement** occurs when the adult *aligns her own internal state with that of the child, accomplished by attending to the nonverbal, often subtle communication of the child* (Siegel & Hartzell, 2003). For example, infants who feel overwhelmed tend to turn their heads away from the stimulus, even when the stimulus is a playful, actively engaged adult. When the adult responds to the infant's signal by pulling back and quietly waiting for the child to reconnect, the pair is in attunement. **Responsiveness** occurs *when one person responds intentionally and specifically to the emotional states and needs of another.* For example, when the first-grader spills her milk in a crowded lunchroom, her teacher recognizes the child's embarrassment and responds with quiet reassurance. By placing a priority on establishing and maintaining respectful, warm, attuned, and responsive relationships with children, the children feel more secure and free to explore, learn, and connect with others (Elicker & Fortner-Wood, 1995; Pianta, 1997).

WHAT YOU BRING TO RELATIONSHIPS WITH CHILDREN

To be able to relate to young children with the level of attunement and responsiveness necessary for relationship-based guidance, you first must be attuned to yourself. The days of an early childhood professional are hectic, filled with planning, reading, singing, documenting, managing mini-crises, and wiping tables and noses. It is often difficult to find time to reflect on your own internal states, such as your perceptions and feelings at the moment, or to ponder the basis for those states. When you are mindful of your inner states and open to understanding and respecting a child's state of mind, however, your relationships will become stronger (Siegel & Hartzell, 2003). It is also important to be aware of your expectations, your personality traits, and the messages you have internalized from your past.

Your Expectations of Your Role

Of the many career paths you might have chosen, you decided to be an early childhood professional. Your reasons for this decision influence the nature of your day-to-day interactions, which over time will shape the quality of your relationships with the children. The quality of those relationships determines how well they learn (Hyson, 2008).

Perhaps you decided to work with young children because you believe you have important wisdom to share about right and wrong and how the world works. You have interesting things to tell children, like a sage on the stage. A sage on the stage is an educator who sees his role as a holder of information who imparts knowledge on a more or less passive learning recipient (McKenzie, 1998). The sage might be frustrated because children learn life's lessons best through experience, play, and active engagement, rather than through listening to information told to them.

On the other hand, you might expect to be more of a guide on the side who encourages exploration and self-discovery on the part of the learner. If you are a guide on the side, you probably envision yourself sitting on the floor beside a child as he constructs a block tower and letting his curiosity lead the way. You allow children to knock over block structures and observe their reactions. You listen to their language and try to understand what motivates and interests them as they build their creations. You participate when they invite you. The guide on the side stands by ready to support and assist children as needed (McKenzie, 1998).

Maybe you decided to teach because you love to read and you want to instill literacy skills and a love for reading in children. Many young children greatly enjoy hearing stories. You may be surprised to discover, however, that many other children are not inclined to sit quietly and listen to a story. If this were your expectation, you might find yourself uneasy with children who get restless during story time or who find reading instruction tedious.

Perhaps something else entirely sparked your interest in working with young children. Where did that interest originate? In what ways has your understanding of your role evolved over time?

Your expectations influence your approach to teaching and your level of satisfaction each day. Sometimes your experiences will be right in line with your expectations and sometimes they will be at odds. Regardless of *what* you expect your role as a teacher to be, your *awareness* of those expectations is essential.

LOOKING IN THE MIRROR...

- What do you see as your major role in the classroom?
- What are your most important values as an educator?
- Did some of the responsibilities involved in teaching young children surprise you?
- What situations or duties do you find to be challenging?
- What strategies can you use to make those situations successful for you and for the child?

Your Personality

It is also important to be mindful of the unique components of your **personality—**
the stable set of traits or patterns of affect, behavior, and cognition that define you, as
well as your characteristic adaptations to situations and self-defining life narratives
(DeYoung & Gray, 2009). Aspects of your personality include your temperament,
preferences, values, strengths, and weaknesses. (See Table 3.1 for definitions.) It
takes intentional examination of those personality aspects to recognize how they
impact your interactions with children. One way to gain this self-awareness is to
listen carefully to the words you use spontaneously to describe a child's behavior.
Consider this typical classroom scenario:

> Terri has asked you five times in five different ways to share her book
> with the class. When story time finally arrives, Terri announces three
> times that it is *her* book. Is Terri annoying or persistent?
>
> Carlie can't seem to listen to Terri's story without enthusiasti-
> cally acting out the emotions of the characters. Is Carlie disruptive
> and impulsive or entertaining and spontaneous?
>
> Mateo tells Terri that he doesn't like her book and would rather
> hear a different story. Is Mateo rude or assertive?
>
> Later, Danica runs into the classroom, springs from her cubby to
> greet Oli at the puzzle table, and bounces to the block corner where
> she bumps into Jack's tower and plops down to play with him. Is
> Danica hyperactive or exuberant?
>
> Jack storms with fury like it's the end of the world when Danica
> destroys the mile-high tower he meticulously constructed. Is Jack
> overly dramatic or passionate?

TABLE 3.1 • Definition of Terms for Self-Awareness

Term	Definition	Example
Temperament	A constitutional predisposition to react in a particular way to stimuli; an inborn pattern of behavior that tends to remain constant throughout life.	Josh's temperament is characterized by a high activity level, positive mood, and comfort in new situations.
Strength	A skill or activity at which one excels.	Working with impulsive children is one of Meg's strengths.
Weakness	A flaw or a weak point; a skill or activity with which one struggles.	Rick's weakness is working with children who whine.
Preference	A person, quality, or activity with which one likes to engage rather than a different person, quality, or activity.	Kenisha has a preference for child-directed activities rather than teacher-led activities.
Value	A quality or outcome that one feels is most important to achieve.	Justin places a high value on creativity.

Your interpretation of and emotional reaction to children's behaviors will influence your responses as well as your relationships with them. When a child's style or behavior elicits strong positive or negative feelings in you, look within yourself to determine the underpinnings of your feelings. Your feelings can result from internal factors like your temperament or from experiential factors, such messages from caregiving adults in your past.

Goodness-of-Fit

Temperament is one internal factor that contributes to how we feel about and handle situations. Earlier, you used Table 2.2 to describe yourself on the dimensions of temperament. You bring those aspects of your temperament into all of your interactions and experiences, as do the children with whom you work.

The goodness-of-fit between you and the child shapes the quality of your interactions and developing relationship. If you are uncomfortable with disruption to your routine, for example, and you have an active, highly distractible child in your program, the two of you may have a temperamental mismatch that can lead to conflict. That same child would be likely to have positive, enriching days with a teacher who has a high level of activity and is comfortable with unpredictability. And yet, that highly active teacher might be overstimulating to a child who is sensitive and uncomfortable with change.

As an early childhood professional, you do not have to change your temperament or personality to be effective. You also don't have to excuse yourself from working with a child whose temperament differs from your own. To the contrary, reflective and relationship-based practice requires that you first recognize the different, incongruous behavior styles that exist between you and a given child. The difference in temperament profiles between the two of you is

LOOKING IN THE MIRROR...

Look at your temperament ratings from Table 2.2. Plot those ratings on Figure 3.1 and connect the dots that represent your level on each dimension. This is your temperament profile.

Now, think about a child with whom you interact, preferably a child whose behavior puzzles or challenges you. Use Table 3.2 to rate the child's temperament. Plot the child's temperament ratings and connect the dots on Figure 3.1 like you did with your own. Compare your temperament profile to the profile of the child:

- On what dimensions is your temperament similar to that of the child?
- On what dimensions does your temperament differ?
- How can you use your understanding of goodness-of-fit to improve your interactions with a child whose temperament differs from yours?

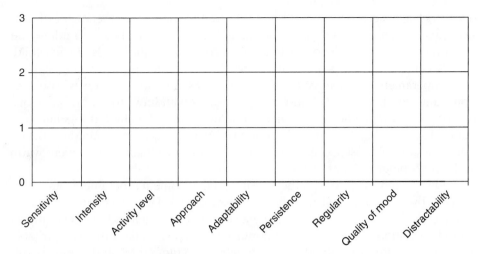

FIGURE 3.1 **Temperament Profile**

TABLE 3.2 • The Child's Temperament

Dimension	Compared to other children:	Low	Medium	High
Sensitivity	How easily is the child bothered or aroused by sensory stimulation? (Easily bothered or aroused = 3)	1	2	3
Intensity of reaction	How intense is the child's reaction? (Most intense = 3)	1	2	3
Activity level	How active is the child? (Most active = 3)	1	2	3
Adaptability	How well does the child respond to changes in routine/expectations? (Very comfortable with change = 3)	1	2	3
Approach/withdrawal	How comfortably does the child approach new situations? (Most comfortable = 3)	1	2	3
Persistence	How well does the child continue an activity until it is finished? (Can stay with it well = 3)	1	2	3
Rhythmicity	How regular is the child's rhythm of activity, sleep, arousal, etc? (Very regular = 3)	1	2	3
Quality of mood	How positive is the child's mood? (Most positive = 3)	1	2	3
Distractibility	How easily is the child drawn away from an activity? (Easily distracted = 3)	1	2	3

one important piece of a complicated puzzle. By bringing temperament dimensions and differences into your conscious focus, you can begin to adjust the environment and your responses to better accommodate the needs of each child.

Recent research has given us some clues to matching caregiving style to the temperament characteristics of a child. For example, children whose predominant mood was fearful and who tended to withdraw from new situations developed self-regulation best when the adult guided the child in a gentle way rather than in a harsh manner. In contrast, active and fearless children developed self-control most successfully when they were with adults who were warm and fun (Zentner & Bates, 2008).

One pattern observed in the research is that some temperaments are more affected by environmental modification than others. Differences in the quality of the child-rearing environment have a strong detrimental or beneficial impact on only a minority of children. Children whose predominant mood is irritable and negative are considered "temperamentally vulnerable" and seem to suffer disproportionately from negative caregiving environments. These same children are more likely than their peers to benefit from supportive environments (Belsky, Bakermans-Kranenburg, & van Ijzendoorn, 2007). In other words, the whiny, irritable child benefits greatly from warm, gentle support and is psychologically injured more significantly by harsh, negative caregiving than other, less vulnerable children.

When there is a temperamental mismatch, your challenge is to decide how to improve the goodness-of-fit. Three components of the situation should be considered: you, the child, and the environment. As an example, think about how to improve goodness-of-fit between an exceedingly active, emotionally reactive child and a highly sensitive, slow-moving teacher in a program that requires lots of seatwork. The teacher might work to increase her energy level, physical stamina, and stress-management skills. She might exercise, meditate, or modify her diet. The child may benefit from learning strategies to adapt his responses so he can function in environments he finds challenging. The teacher's role is to support him as he attempts to navigate situations that challenge his natural behavior style or temperament. This highly active and reactive child could be coached in deep breathing and other self-calming techniques, sometimes called *down-regulating* (Williamson & Anzalone, 2001). The environment can also be modified to include calm background music, more outside time, and a greater number of gross-motor activities. It is important to examine goodness-of-fit to determine, with a given child in a given situation, in what ways you, the child, or the environment need to adapt or be adapted. In many cases, the answer would be all three, as illustrated in this scenario:

Peggy was a theater major and performed in musicals before she became an early childhood educator. Known for her emotional expressiveness and high energy level, she won many awards for her theatrical roles. She loves singing and dramatic storytelling with her three-year-olds. Peggy often turns tasks like cleaning up into dramatic play activities.

Nolan moves slowly and cautiously. He is highly sensitive to noises and becomes very anxious with change. As a toddler, he used to bite children when they were too close or too loud. At three, he puts his hands over his ears and covers his eyes when there is too much stimulation. When Peggy breaks into song and exaggerated movements, the other children giggle, join in, or ignore her. Nolan cowers in the corner.

Three things can be modified to improve goodness-of-fit in this situation. Peggy needs to tune into the emotional states of each child and, in this case, recognize that Nolan and perhaps other sensitive children are easily overwhelmed. These children become agitated with her high volume and energy level, so Peggy can try to move more slowly and sing more quietly. Nolan needs help learning to up-regulate, starting with the level of stimulation with which he is comfortable and gradually, with support, increasing the amount of energy and stimulation (Williamson & Anzalone, 2001). Third, the environment should have places where Nolan and the other children can go when they feel anxious or overwhelmed, such as a quiet corner or a book nook.

Messages You Have Internalized

We are profoundly influenced by the messages we received from our early relationships, although much of this influence occurs at an unconscious level. Take, for example, the messages your family gave you as a child regarding

LOOKING IN THE MIRROR...

Consider the messages you received as a child:

- How was conflict handled in your family?
- How did the adults handle your expressions of physical states like pain or illness?
- How did they respond if you were sad or frightened?
- How did they respond if you were angry?
- Did they ask you about your ideas and opinions?
- What sorts of discipline practices did your parents use when you misbehaved?

The adults' level of regard for your inner states has likely influenced and will continue to influence the ways you respond to the thoughts and feelings

(continued)

of the children in your care. Sometimes we repeat the patterns of our elders and sometimes we behave very differently:

- In what ways do you respond to children's inner states or outward behavior like your caregivers responded to you?
- In what ways do you respond that are different from the adults in your past?
- Are there any children or other individuals with whom you would like to improve your responses to their inner states?

how to handle conflict. In some families, conflict was avoided at all costs. Family members might have developed such conflict-avoidance maneuvers as turning everything into a joke, being sarcastic, changing the subject, eating, lying, or retreating into fantasy. In other families, conflict was encouraged, and dinnertime debates were exciting and dynamic. In still other families, conflict turned into personal attacks or violence. Those messages about conflict are deeply ingrained in who we are. We have also internalized messages about emotional expression, roles, behavior, values, priorities, and countless other life occurrences.

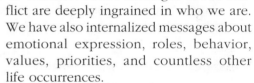

All of these considerations about yourself come into play in your everyday interactions. They interact with the unique attributes of each child in ways that define your relationships with them.

Reflecting on the Child

All behavior has meaning. It comes from some motivation. The better we know a child, the more easily and accurately we will be able to gather the meaning behind the behavior he exhibits. So, what do we mean by knowing the child? In later chapters, we will explore ways to understand a child's unique developmental, temperamental, familial, and cultural characteristics. Here, we will discuss ways to tune into the child's internal states, needs, and motivations.

Conversation

One of the best ways to get to know children is through conversation. When we engage with children in rich back-and-forth conversations, we are providing them with mechanisms for thinking and tools for understanding the world (Bodrova & Leong, 2007; Vygotsky, 1987). Research that links teacher-child conversations to literacy and language development sheds light on the characteristics of those exchanges that are typical in early education settings. Studies examining teacher-child interactions in Head Start classrooms revealed that the majority of teacher utterances were very brief and did not promote extended conversation nor deal with the kind of content that promotes language development or relationships (Dickinson, 2003). In some settings, over half of teacher verbalizations centered on helping children obtain items, managing behavior, directing peer interactions, and providing instruction. These verbalizations offer limited opportunities for children to elaborate on their ideas or share their experiences (Massey, 2004). Yet only through their elaborations will you be able to get to know the children in all their complexity.

Children thrive when they participate in conversations that use **extended discourse**, *reciprocal (back-and-forth) interactions with opportunities to hear and produce explanations and personal narratives* (McCabe & Peterson, 1991). They benefit tremendously when they engage in pretending with adults where they can experiment with a variety of roles and ideas. As they elaborate on their ideas through dramatic play and extended discourse with you, there is a cascade of benefits to their development. They come to see themselves and their ideas as valid and important. They see you as someone who likes and appreciates them, thereby increasing their sense of trust and security in the relationship. Their language skills become more and more fine-tuned and sophisticated. They come to understand the social and material world with increasing complexity. All of these gains support the emotional intelligence they need to succeed in school and in life.

The relaxed back-and-forth nature of conversation with young children yields abundant information about their values, beliefs, and misconceptions about the world. It was through one such conversation that my kindergarten teacher learned why I was terrified about our impending field trip to neighboring Chicago. The horrific "trolls in the troll booth" brought fear and trepidation. The teacher gently explained that there were no "trolls" in the "*toll* booth," that the "*toll* booth was for money and not operated by trolls." Through extended discourse we, like my kindergarten teacher, can learn a great deal about how children make sense of their experiences.

Many children love to tell stories about their loved ones and their adventures. They casually pepper their recounting of real experiences with fantasy. It is not unusual for children to bring dinosaurs, tigers, and monsters into their stories of home and family. When we engage in such child-driven conversations, we enrich their language and literacy skills and, what is quite important, our mutual relationships.

Close Observation

How do we know what is in the mind of a child? When people can communicate through words, their thoughts and feelings are often clear. But the youngest children do not have this capacity. It can take many years of guidance for children to develop the skills to communicate in the affective, or emotional domain. In later chapters, we will explore ways to help children with the important skills of emotional expression. Here, we will focus on observing the ways young children naturally communicate their internal states and how we can read the cues they provide.

When we tune into the nonverbal aspects of a child's communication, we get important clues about what underlies his behavior. **Nonverbal communication** refers to *the process of sending and receiving information through wordless messages and includes gestures, facial expressions, eye contact, and body language.* Young children also communicate their inner states nonverbally through *play, art, dance, and behavior.*

From the first moments of life, infants communicate what they are feeling through nonverbal cues. They gaze to tell us they are ready to explore the world. They flail their arms and legs when they are startled or excited. They cry to tell us they need something, and this is where the detective work begins. By the time a child is a few months old, her attuned caregivers can usually distinguish the tonal quality of her cries and know what need she is expressing. Her repertoire of communication tools increases every day. When she is overstimulated, she turns her head. When she is awake and ready to play, she kicks her feet or shakes a rattle. During the first year, she coos and babbles to invite conversation and reaches for objects to convey her curiosity. As a toddler, she points and grunts, pouts and bites, and eventually tells you *"No!"*

The emergence of verbal communication does not end the important task of tuning in to nonverbal communication. In fact, nonverbal communication is often more telling of a person's underlying inner state than the words they use. In the following examples, you can see that nonverbal communication is at least as important as the words the child uses to communicate the intended message:

> Usually bubbly and cheerful, five-year-old Danielle clung to her father's leg and buried her face in his jacket one morning. When Dad finally extricated her from his leg and left, Danielle sat down at the table and looked blankly at the floor. In her hands, she fondled a tattered scrap of cloth. Ms. Margie knelt down to talk with her, but the child abruptly turned her body away.
>
> Danielle was telling Ms. Margie loud and clear that something was bothering her. Although Ms. Margie was very curious and eager for Danielle to voice what she was experiencing, Ms. Margie

respected what Danielle was communicating through her body language. She had turned away from Ms. Margie, which meant that she was not ready, willing, or able to express directly what was bothering her.

Sometimes the most respectful way to listen is to step away and give a person some space. Waiting can be difficult for those whose tendency is to fix things or take away the pain.

Ms. Margie used a different strategy to understand Javen:

Javen's aggressive behavior was throwing the class into chaos. Ms. Margie paid close attention to his facial expression that looked like a cross between pride and authority. His look suggested that he felt justified in pushing and grabbing his classmates. On several occasions, Ms. Margie had taken Javen aside to talk about his behavior, but he was unable to explain it and the aggression continued.

Later that day, Ms. Margie asked the children to draw a picture of and narrate a story about what they wanted to be when they grew up. Javen drew a picture of a masked man holding a gun and sporting an arsenal of weapons under his cape. He told Margie he wants to grow up to be a vigilante who destroys everything that gets in his way, just like the character in his brother's video game.

By giving Javen a different way of expressing himself, Ms. Margie was able to reveal the underlying motivation for his behavior. Armed with this information, she could be more intentional and effective in her efforts to prevent aggressive behavior in the future.

Contrary to what we were told as children, mothers do not have eyes in the back of their heads. What they do have, when they are attuned to the needs and communication cues of their children, is the ability to detect deception and mischief as well as the capacity to know the emotions that underlie their child's behavior. In a healthy attachment relationship, the parent can read the facial expression and body language of the child and know with a high degree of certainty what inner states the child is experiencing. This skill also comes naturally to some early childhood professionals, although others have to develop it through close observation and ongoing practice.

Demonstrating Respect for the Child

While teaching styles vary widely, promotion of social–emotional development in young children requires relationships firmly grounded in reciprocity and respect. As an added benefit, compliance and cooperation improve dramatically within the context of positive teacher-child relationships, as can be seen in the following story of one child in two very dissimilar relationships:

> Five-year-old Dorie attends Mrs. Johnson's kindergarten class in the mornings and goes to Tasha's Tots Child Care in the afternoons. Mrs. Johnson, who highly values classroom management and orderly schedules, often scolds Dorie for getting messy and not following the rules. In contrast, Ms. Tasha asks Dorie every day about her puppy, her morning at school, her preferred activities, and her feelings when upset.
>
> Dorie's mother received a note from Mrs. Johnson expressing concern about Dorie's restless and disobedient behavior. The note was puzzling because Dorie is cooperative at home. She asked Tasha if Dorie was also restless and disobedient at child care. Tasha was very surprised. At Tasha's Tots, Dorie is delightful, engaged, warm, and cooperative.

Like most of us, Dorie is inclined to cooperate with people who seem to care about her. If you ever find that a child is unwilling to comply with your rules or requests, ask yourself if you have taken the time to establish a warm, mutually respectful relationship with that child. By consistently asking Dorie about her experiences, Tasha let Dorie know that she is important to her. In contrast, Mrs. Johnson did not take the time to get to know Dorie or to convey a sense of respect for the child. As a result, Dorie tended to be disrespectful to Mrs. Johnson.

So how do we come to know a child when the child is new to our class? How do we know the child's preferences and needs? Although we all differ in many ways, there are some universal truths about how people like to be treated. In a nutshell, we like to be treated with dignity and respect. At a very minimum, we can expect that children like to be treated with dignity and respect, too. Thus we can use the golden rule as our guide: *do unto* others *as you would have them do unto* you. Treat children the way you like to be treated.

Think about how you like to be treated when you are sharing news. Many children love to tell their stories about new toys, *owies*, and adventures. In the flurry of our busy days as teachers, we need to pause and consider how *we* like to be heard when we have something to share. The words, "Stop talking, George," feel very different from the words, "George, your story is important and I'd like to hear it, but it's quiet reading time now. Let's try to remember to talk about this at lunch, OK?" If you don't like to be told to "stop talking," you can assume that George doesn't like it either.

Similarly, think about how you like to be guided or corrected. If you have ever been called out and criticized in front of your peers, you may have found the experience to be an affront to your dignity. When correcting the behavior of a child, then, we can assume the child would also benefit from private consultation instead of public reprimand. Moving physically close to the child, getting down to his level, and speaking quietly about his behavior is more effective than correcting him from across the room. It is also safe to assume that a child would rather hear a tone of voice that emits support instead of one that implies irritation or disgust. In the throes of our busy days, it is easy to forget to keep correction private and supportive.

PARALLEL PROCESS IN THE CLASSROOM

Parallel process is a term borrowed from the literature on reflective supervision in the field of infant mental health. It refers to *the process by which the nature of one relationship is replicated in another relationship.* Underlying the concept of parallel process is an extension of the golden rule. Jeree Pawl, past president of ZERO TO THREE: National Center for Infants, Toddlers and Families, states the following:

> *...it is not possible to work on behalf of human beings...without having powerful feelings aroused in yourself...I have coined a short-hand* **platinum rule** *to supplement the golden rule in order to convey a sense of this parallel process "Do unto others as you would have oth-ers do unto others.* (Pawl & St. John, 1998; Parlakian, 2001).

By this, Dr. Pawl means that we need to treat other people, including the children in our care, the way we would like them to treat others. To illustrate how parallel process works, imagine this scenario from a day at the child care center where you teach:

> On his way to the center for his unannounced site visit, the licensing agent had a flat tire that disrupted his whole schedule. In his irrita-tion, he was loud and critical as he presented his findings to Donita, the director. Unfortunately, at the same time, a prospective parent happened to be waiting outside Donita's door for a tour. Donita was embarrassed and anxious as a result of the agent's tirade and had to apologize to the parent who was waiting.

LOOKING IN THE MIRROR...

- How do your beliefs about your role as a teacher influence your expecta-tions for your young learners?
- How do those beliefs influence your teaching style and communication with children?
- What strategies can you use to learn the beliefs, preferences, and inner states of children?
- What strategies can you use to create an atmosphere of dignity and respect in the classroom so that children can benefit from the plati-num rule?

A short while later, during snack time, Donita stormed into your classroom demanding that you take care of your paperwork because the agent just cited the program for having incomplete records. You felt inadequate and humiliated by Donita's angry tone of voice. Your heart was pounding. The very moment Donita left your room, three-year-olds Jonas and Leo began to play wrestle. An elbow hit a cup and milk went flying.

You had a choice to make. If you reacted on the basis of what you were feeling at that moment, you would probably transfer your feelings of inadequacy and humiliation onto Jonas and Leo. You might have criticized them harshly and scolded them. Because children learn how to treat other people by observing adult models (Bandura, Ross, & Ross, 1961; Bandura, 1989), the boys would likely display this harsh, critical behavior in their subsequent interactions with others. If, instead, you chose to slow down, calm yourself, and think about the impact of your response on the boys, you would be able to break the chain of negative energy that began with the licensing agent's flat tire. You can respond intentionally and maintain the warmth and respect that is characteristic of your classroom.

The ways we treat the children in our classroom influence the ways they treat one another. Our demeanor and our actions set the tone of the classroom. Bobbi Fisher, a widely published author with 25 years of experience teaching young children, states, "Children look to us to set the tone for caring and learning, and they copy what we do. If we listen to them, they listen to each other. If we value them and support, encourage, and celebrate what they do, they will do the same for each other" (Fisher, 1995). Children learn through observing the behavior modeled by others, especially adults. They watch how we treat each other and they imitate our words and the level of respect we show. More important, they feel how we treat them and replicate that affective tone in their relationships with others (Pawl & St. John, 1998).

Summary

A relationship-based approach to guiding social–emotional development rests on a foundation of self-awareness on the part of the teacher as well as knowledge of and respect for the unique qualities of the child. By keeping in mind your own temperament, personality, and inner states, you can more effectively interact with children. The ability to tell your own story of having been nurtured, regardless of whether that story involves ghosts or angels in the nursery, enables you to form richer relationships with the children. Your relationships become even more powerful vehicles of social and emotional growth when you have an intimate knowledge of the child, his thoughts, feelings, beliefs, and misconceptions. This knowledge enhances your ability to respond intentionally and with respect. Not only should we treat children the way we like to be treated, but we should also treat them the way we want them to treat other people.

Review and Apply

1. Explain what is meant by "relationship-based guidance" and include in your answer the concepts and terms described in this chapter.
2. Rodrigo's constant motion and impulsive touching are disrupting your calm program and the activities you have organized for the children.

a. What do you need to consider to help Rodrigo function effectively in the program, and how can you get that information?
b. What strategies can you think of to improve the goodness-of-fit between Rodrigo, you, and the program?

chapter 4

Individualized and Developmentally Appropriate Guidance

"I try to listen, but sometimes my brain takes a nap and my body keeps doing stuff."

—ALEJANDRO, AGE 4

After reading this chapter, you should be able to

▸ Explain the link between children's sensory preferences and their behavior.
▸ Describe the ways a child's history and family dynamics can influence behavior.
▸ Discuss ways you can find common ground with parents whose expectations differ from your own.
▸ Determine if a child's challenging behavior results from a lack of knowledge, underdeveloped skills, or unwillingness to cooperate.
▸ Apply strategies to detect any underdeveloped skills so that you may target them for additional support.
▸ Implement a strategy for analyzing the function of a child's negative behavior.

An important principle to guide your early childhood work is that your approaches and strategies should be individualized based on a variety of factors. Information about a child's nature, history, and development should serve as the springboard from which you understand the child and teach him new skills. This information is especially crucial when working with children who have challenging behaviors.

INDIVIDUALIZED GUIDANCE

No two children are alike, of course. Just like in the cognitive domain, learning plans in the social and emotional domain should be individualized to meet the unique characteristics and needs of each child. But in what ways do children differ from one another socially and emotionally, and how can we use our knowledge of each child to individualize our strategies and approaches? Some differences in social and emotional development can be explained by biologically based characteristics, such as sensory preferences and temperament profiles. Other differences result from events in the child's history or his family dynamics. Each of these aspects influences children's emerging skills and behaviors. When we consider children with these attributes in mind, we can tailor our approach to meet each child's unique developmental needs.

SENSORY PREFERENCES

We learn about the world around us by what we see, hear, touch, smell, and taste. We then process the information from all our senses and turn it into knowledge and meaningful action. Sensory processing is an important component of temperament and plays a role in the behavior we see in children. Each child has his own sensory preferences—the pattern of sensations that make him feel comfortable or uncomfortable. For example, one child may be fascinated with the flashing of a strobe light, while another finds strobe lights disturbing. Some children are troubled by coarse fabrics, while others prefer the tactile stimulation of corduroy or wool. **Sensory integration**, a concept well known to occupational therapists, is *the process of organizing sensations from the body and the environment for adaptive use* (Ayres, 1979). We can learn a great deal about children's sensory preferences and integration by observing them closely.

Occupational therapists have given us additional information about sensory processing that can help us understand certain child behaviors, such as fidgeting, squirming, and constant motion. They describe two *inner* senses that play an important role in children's ability to function in the environment: vestibular processing and proprioception. Early childhood professionals might not use these terms on a regular basis, but they are included here because they explain some of the challenging behavior we see in young children. **Vestibular processing** refers to *a person's sense of balance and perception of his or her body in space. The vestibular sense is processed in the inner ear.* Information from the vestibular system contributes to coordination, balance, equilibrium, eye movement control (to maintain a stable visual field when moving), state of arousal, and level of attention (Williamson & Anzalone, 2001). Consider the infant who can be calmed only when held upright, the toddler who is soothed by swinging, or the six-year-old who stumbles and falls whenever he runs. These characteristics are a function of vestibular processing.

Proprioception refers to *the communication system between the muscles and the nervous system that provides the child with information about movement or the position of his body parts* (Williamson & Anzalone, 2001). Some children crave movement, while others prefer to take in the world by sitting and watching. The child who is compelled to climb on and jump off furniture or who spins until he falls down may be seeking stimulation in the vestibular and proprioceptive sensory modalities. When you see these behaviors and recognize that they are sensory based and not intentional or defiant, you can help the child find ways to meet his need for more stimulation in these areas. For example, the bouncy, squirmy child could sit on an inflatable dome that allows for contained wiggling, push a shopping cart with a little extra weight, or carry a backpack with a few blocks from one room to another.

Very young children often lack the self-awareness and verbal ability to communicate a mismatch between their sensory preferences and their environment. A child who feels overwhelmed by the noisy demands of a large group activity may instead act out her feelings by crying, running away, or hitting. Kiki's story illustrates how behavior might represent a child's coping response to sensory overload:

> Eighteen-month-old Kiki was a frequent biter with so many biting incidents that she was in danger of expulsion from child care. By getting to know the family, the teacher ruled out aggressive parenting. After several observations at various times of the day and in various settings, it was determined that Kiki bit her peers when they were physically too close to her, when visitors arrived in the classroom, when the room became too noisy, when tags on her clothes were irritating, and during transitions from the classroom to the big playroom.
>
> Two strategies were used to reduce the biting and help Kiki cope. First, her teachers made Kiki's environment more comfortable for her by minimizing unexpected disruptions, keeping the classroom volume low, finding a quiet haven in the big playroom for Kiki, cutting tags out of her clothing, and keeping peers from invading Kiki's personal space. Second, they focused on giving Kiki communication tools to

protect herself from overstimulation. They taught her how to put her hands over her ears and say, "It's too loud," and "Please move away." By modifying her environment and teaching Kiki to meet her own needs, the biting stopped and Kiki developed adaptive coping skills.

Child Temperament

In any given situation, a particular temperament characteristic might be helpful or detrimental. For example, a toddler like Kiki who is sensitive in the tactile and auditory areas might feel pleasure and benefit greatly from sitting on the cozy lap of an adult quietly reading a textured animal book and eliciting animal sounds. The noisy crowd at a parade, however, might easily overwhelm that same sensitive toddler.

Another aspect of temperament is adaptability (Thomas & Chess, 1977). Some children embrace change and novelty as if they were embarking on an adventure, while others resist change through protest or withdrawal. Remember, just as we have goodness-of-fit between the temperament of the child and the temperament of the adult, we must also consider the goodness-of-fit between the child's temperament and environmental demands that support or impede her ability to function in that environment.

Health and Developmental History

A child's health history and developmental history also contribute to his learning and behavior tendencies. Premature birth, low birth weight, and birth complications are known to contribute to developmental delays that may not be immediately apparent. Similarly, many children whose mothers used substances while pregnant or who were born addicted to cocaine, alcohol, methamphetamine, or other substances demonstrate learning, developmental, or behavior problems (American Pregnancy Association, 2008). Early health challenges such as food allergies, multiple surgeries, acute or chronic illnesses, or head injuries can interfere with emotional well-being or impede the development of social competence. Sometimes challenging behavior can be attributed to a child's history of multiple ear infections that have led to speech and other delays.

When a child has suffered a recent illness, we may observe regression in one skill area or another, as can be seen in the following example:

Jackson had adjusted well to Ms. Dianna's classroom. He was friendly and playful with peers and cooperative with staff. His cognitive and language skills were right on target for his age. Around his third birthday, he was hospitalized for pneumonia with a high fever and missed three weeks of preschool while recovering. When he returned to school, he was quiet and had difficulty expressing himself, as though he had lost words and the relationship skills he had previously mastered. With patience and support on the part of Ms. Dianna over the next several months, Jackson regained these skills and social connections.

Several mental health and neurological conditions have manifestations in outward behavior. A child with attention deficit hyperactivity disorder (ADHD) is likely to display a short attention span, distractibility, poor impulse control, excessive activity level, difficulty delaying gratification, and low persistence. Some children with ADHD do not display hyperactivity and impulsivity and, because their behavior is not disruptive, their developmental needs can be overlooked. If the child's attention and related issues are seriously impeding his ability to learn and to function in the classroom with ordinary support, you may consider referring the family for further evaluation.

Similarly, children on the autism spectrum (ASD) often display behaviors that reflect difficulties with social and emotional functioning. If a child demonstrates significant impairments in social interaction and communication skills, shows repetitive stereotyped movements, and has a narrow range of interests, and if these difficulties impede his relationships, development, or day-to-day functioning, the child should be referred for further evaluation. Keep in mind that unless you are a mental health or medical professional, you may not diagnose or use the terms *ADHD* or *autism* or suggest any other clinical condition. Instead, you should provide detailed and specific information about the behaviors of concern in your referral. If a child has been diagnosed with a health or mental health condition, it is important for you to collaborate with the professionals who are treating him so the expectations and strategies used are consistent in all environments.

Environmental History

Environmental history refers to the child's *past and current experiences*. It is essential to know the child's environmental history because events in his life can support or impede his social–emotional development and behavior. The first issue to consider is whether the child has experienced a trauma or significant loss. If trauma is recent or ongoing, the child may be in danger and the professional should intervene by calling child protection authorities to ensure his safety.

History of trauma is also relevant because a pattern of trauma or chronic stress in the early years has been found to disrupt brain development, making a child prone to hypersensitivity and hyperreactivity (Perry, 1995; Schuder, 2004), as reflected in the following scenario:

Dom's first four years, when his parent's were still married, were filled with upheaval. His father was playful and fun when he was sober, but when he drank, he became violent. His parents divorced when he was four and his father moved to a neighboring state.

Ms. Keisha, Dom's kindergarten teacher, described him as "ready for a fight at all times." If a child bumped into him, Dom would kick or hit the other child. Dom often told Ms. Keisha that the children were being mean to him. Because Ms. Keisha knew about Dom's history of trauma and stress, she was able to provide the safety, security, and reassurance Dom needed to be able to reinterpret these situations in a more accurate and benign manner.

Witnessing violence, especially chronic violence as experienced by Dom, has been shown to interfere with children's mastery of developmental milestones. Chronic, irresolvable stress that exceeds a child's ability to cope, such as that associated with abuse, severe poverty, homelessness, and untreated parental mental illness or substance abuse can be considered "toxic stress" (Harvard, 2012). Toxic stress alters the developing brain and nervous system in ways that keep the child's *fight-or-flight* response on high alert at all times and inhibits development of higher-order cognitive processes such as logic, problem solving, planning, and academic learning. Toxic stress also increases a child's risk of developing posttraumatic stress disorder, depression, anxiety, and conduct problems (Osofsky, 1995; Rossman, Hughes, & Rosenberg, 2000; Lieberman & Van Horn, 2005).

Not all children exposed to chronic and severe stress have such dire developmental consequences. Some children demonstrate remarkable resiliency to stress and trauma. Child characteristics such as high intelligence and positive mood have been shown to increase resilience. However, one of the most critical protective factors in the face of severe stress is having a secure attachment relationship with an attuned, responsive caregiving adult (Siegel & Hartzell 2003; Harvard, 2012).

Even when stress is not traumatic, it can affect a child's behavior. Moving to a new home, the birth of a sibling, and a parent's new job are all positive changes that nonetheless are stressful for young children. It is helpful to consider what types of stress the child has experienced in the past and what stressors may be occurring in the present.

Sometimes stress involves disruption to the child's attachment with the primary caregiver. When a parent is sick, requires hospitalization, faces military deployment, or travels for work, a child might experience grief and loneliness that lead to changes in behavior. As an adult, you may be familiar with grief, loss, or separation because of your own life experiences. Your memories of those experiences can guide your efforts to support the child. This was the case for Melanie in the following story:

> Recently, Melanie's student Leo lost his favorite aunt. It brought back memories for Melanie. When she was eleven, her beloved grandmother suddenly passed away. She was devastated. She remembered the attempts people made to comfort her. Some people said, "Grandma is in a better place." Others told her to remember how many other people are still around to love her. Even her best friend tried to cheer her up and distract her from her grief. Melanie felt terribly alone and frustrated that nobody understood or permitted her to feel her pain.

As a kindergarten teacher, Melanie's memory of that experience guided her as she helped Leo cope with his loss. Melanie knew that Leo needed the opportunity to feel and work through his own grief. She remembered how she would have liked to have been supported and was able to offer Leo the support he needed.

Family Dynamics

The dynamics in a child's family often contribute to how he behaves and interacts with others. **Family dynamics** refers to *the quality and nature of relationships within the family—that is, how people relate to one another.* Families differ in many ways. Some have happily united parents, while others have parents who fight every day. Some children have divorced parents who communicate well, while others are coping with the stress and confusion of conflict, custody disputes, and visitation issues.

Frequently, grandparents or other relatives are a child's primary guardians for a variety of reasons. It is important for early childhood professionals to have a general idea of why guardianship was awarded to someone other than the biological parents. That reason may impact the child's functioning and behavior. For example, the early years of a child whose parents struggle with substance abuse or mental illness are often fraught with inconsistency, emotional unavailability, or even danger. A child whose parent is incarcerated is likely to be a child who has experienced trauma and loss. When the parent of a young child has died, it is helpful to know the circumstances around the death. How old was the child? Was the death sudden or did it follow a lengthy illness? What was the nature of their relationship before the death? How are the surviving adults coping? How did they discuss the death with the child? Each of these factors can impact the child's adjustment to the loss.

Family members can be a wellspring of information about the child's circumstances. When we inquire, however, we must be sure to demonstrate a nonjudgmental attitude and a great deal of sensitivity, as demonstrated by Margie in the following example:

Donnie had been in Margie's class for a few months. Initially charming and outgoing, Donnie was showing increasing anxiety as the winter holidays approached. The other children were eagerly crafting holiday gifts for their parents, but Donnie was unenthused and very quiet. When his grandmother arrived to pick him up, Margie asked her if they could chat privately for a few minutes.

MARGIE: "Today, I noticed that Donnie didn't have his usual enthusiasm when the children made holiday crafts for their parents. I was wondering if there is any information you could share that would help me understand his feelings so I can give him the support he needs."

DONNIE'S GRANDMOTHER: "Well, actually, his mother has been in jail for the past year, and Donnie doesn't know if he will be able to see her during the holidays."

MARGIE: "Oh, thank you. That helps me understand what he's going through. Do you have any thoughts or suggestions about how I can best comfort him during this difficult time?"

Margie was careful not to judge or give advice, but instead, she described the child's behavior and warmly and gently asked about the circumstances so she could best support the child.

Family Expectations

It is also helpful to consider each family's expectation of the role of the early learning program. The following three examples illustrate the wide range of assumptions families have regarding the purpose of the early education setting:

Roxy is the busy working mother of four active children. The neighbor who had been babysitting Joshua moved away and Roxy needed child care right away. Roxy heard that your program is a safe, reliable place for three-year-old Joshua to spend his time while she works and his siblings attend school. If he learns something, well, that's fine, too.

Nicole, the principal of the local high school, comes from a long line of educators. She likes the fact that your program is nationally accredited, but she is frustrated that you don't send four-year-old Mollie home with homework and completed worksheets. Nicole thinks *learning through play* is another term for *babysitting*. She thinks you should do more teaching.

Rocco wants his seven-year-old son Vinnie to play. At your parent-teacher conference, Rocco expresses dissatisfaction with the fact that Vinnie is learning to write paragraphs so young. He fears that Vinnie will become stressed if he experiences such demands.

There are as many parental expectations as there are parents. As an early childhood professional, it is essential to welcome all ideas and concerns expressed by families. It is also important to be able to explain to them the following:

- Why you are using particular methods
- What theories underlie your selection of those methods
- How specific practices fit within your early education philosophy

By bridging your educational approach with the families' expectations, you will strengthen the parent-teacher partnership so critical to children's success.

LOOKING IN THE MIRROR...

Consider the children and families with whom you have worked.

Think about a child whose sensory processing pattern poses a challenge for you:

- What steps can you take to improve that child's functioning?

Think about a child whose health, developmental, or environmental history seems to contribute to challenging behavior:

- How can you use your knowledge about the child's background (including stress) and family dynamics to address his behavior and support his social and emotional development?

Think about a family whose expectations differ from your own:

- What steps can you take to come to a common understanding and an effective working relationship with that family?

DEVELOPMENTALLY APPROPRIATE GUIDANCE

Early childhood experts agree that classroom expectations and learning activities must be developmentally appropriate for the participating children (National Association for the Education of Young Children, 2009; Bredekamp & Copple, 1997). Expectations and activities in the social and emotional domains are no exception. Just as we would not expect a four-year-old with motor delays to jump rope consistently well, we cannot expect a four-year-old with delays in impulse control to keep his hands to himself when something stirs his interest. Yet we often feel frustrated with children's inability to demonstrate impulse control and other social and emotional skills. While our frustration is understandable, we cannot let it impede our ability to think strategically about how to support the development of those skills.

Young children seek to understand the world in multiple ways and thus require a variety of instructional and guidance strategies. For example, play is vitally important to the development of the whole child and perhaps the most natural vehicle for learning in young children (NAEYC, 2009; Bredekamp & Copple, 1997; Stone, 1995; Paley, 2004). So an essential goal is to find engaging play-based activities individualized to support the unique social–emotional needs of each child. Although there may be cultural differences in the specific ages at which targeted skills are expected to emerge, and preferred approaches to building those skills may vary on the basis of culture, our efforts to promote social and emotional skills must be developmentally appropriate for all children.

But how can we determine what is developmentally appropriate for any given child? Developmental milestone charts can give you rough guidelines for developmentally appropriate expectations for a group of children of a certain age.

For individual lesson planning, developmental screening instruments can provide a clearer picture of the unique strengths, weaknesses, and needs of each child.

Milestones of Typical Development

Many developmental milestone charts are available to guide families and professionals in establishing expectations and selecting activities and materials for a group of children. Social and emotional skills develop at different rates among children of the same age, and in many areas, the *normal* range is fairly broad. Nonetheless, when you are familiar with expected developmental milestones in all the developmental domains, you will be more confident that your expectations are appropriate for the children in your program. (See Figure 4.1, Web Resources for Developmental Milestones.)

Developmental Screening and Assessment

To ensure that activities are developmentally appropriate for each individual child, early childhood programs should have a regular system for measuring developmental skills in all domains, including the social–emotional domain (Squires & Bricker, 2007). **Developmental screening** is *a procedure used to determine if a behavior pattern is aberrant enough to warrant further evaluation and intervention.* Without a screening tool, we generally rely on our instincts and experiences to determine developmental skill levels. With such subjective judgments, accuracy can be compromised, and it can be awkward to discuss concerns with families and make a case for referral. Several research-based screening instruments are available from which to choose (Drotor, 2008). Such instruments, when used as an integral part of the early childhood program, not only facilitate communication with families but also provide a basis for comparison over time of the child's development in several skill areas. The Ounce of Prevention Fund has compiled a highly recommended summary of the importance of developmental screening and offers guidelines on how to select and use a screening instrument (McCann & Yarbrough, 2006).

FIGURE 4.1
Web Resources for Developmental Milestones

This resource for developmental milestones is provided by the CDC and emphasizes early identification of developmental delays to provide prevention and early intervention services.

The Whole Child: ABCs of Child Development from the Corporation for Public Broadcasting at pbs.org/wholechild/abc
PBS focuses on four domains: physical development, social and emotional development, thinking skills, and communication skills.

Learn the Signs, Act Early from the Centers for Disease Control and Prevention at cdc.gov/ncbddd/actearly

When developmental screening reveals that a child's functioning is outside the expected developmental range, further evaluation may be necessary. An **evaluation** is a *detailed procedure conducted by a specially trained professional, such as a psychologist or an occupational therapist, to determine the child's unique profile of strengths, weaknesses, and intervention needs. The evaluation allows the specialist to develop a comprehensive individualized plan for remediation or treatment.* The results of an evaluation typically include recommendations for the regular caregiving adults (e.g., parents and teachers) that will address the needs identified in the evaluation and reinforce the treatment or remediation program.

Uneven Development

In addition to variance between children, skills are often mastered unevenly within a given child. Some skill areas will be more advanced than the child's chronological age and some less advanced. (See Figure 4.2.) Your challenge is to determine the specific pattern of strengths and weaknesses in each child so that you may offer appropriate activities. The benefits of screening go beyond determining the need for formal intervention. Screening can also help educators and families identify the child's specific skill areas most in need of support in the school and home settings.

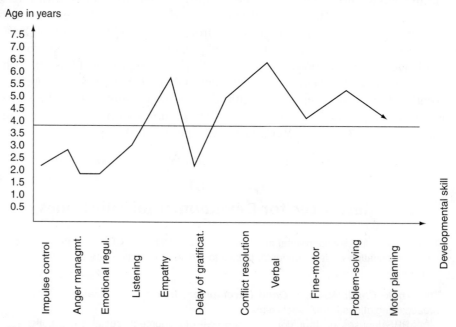

This fictional example of a four-year-old child's social and emotional skills by age illustrates the uneven nature of development. (This example is not based on a standardized instrument.) Janice Englander Katz

FIGURE 4.2 Uneven Skill Development

Even in typically developing children, uneven skill development can pose challenges, as the following descriptions illustrate:

> Three-year-old David can easily transition from active outdoor play to the quiet structure of story time because he can regulate his impulses and activity level. On the other hand, David falls apart when working at the easel and cries inconsolably when his picture isn't just right. He needs support in dealing with disappointment and mistakes.

> Ciara is very empathic and is the first one to comfort other children when they are hurt, yet she is often the one who hurts them with her long, lanky legs and constant motion. She needs support in the areas of personal space and impulse regulation.

> Andre is a keen observer who patiently waits his turn for snack and circle time. His teacher, though, cringes at the sound of Andre's constantly whining voice when he helplessly tells on his classmates for every little thing. Andre needs support in developing ignoring skills, a more appropriate tone of voice, and effective communication skills.

David, Ciara, and Andre have wonderful strengths, such as self-regulation, flexibility, empathy, and impulse control. But when their *behavior* is bothersome, can we assume that the children are willfully choosing to act that way? Are these three children disturbing the teacher on purpose, to get under her skin, or is there another explanation?

All behavior has meaning, including *challenging behavior*. **Challenging behavior** refers to *actions on the part of the child that are disruptive, offensive, dangerous, or destructive.* The early childhood professional must become a detective to figure out what underlies challenging behavior. It is puzzling to see a bright, articulate, upbeat five-year-old, so capable of thoughtful conversation, throw himself on the floor in a fit of rage when he loses a game. What is it that interferes with a child's functioning or causes one social or emotional skill to lag behind his other skill areas?

Knowledge, Skill, or Will?

Before addressing the child's behavior, look carefully to see if the challenging behavior reflects a need for *knowledge, skill building*, or the *will* to behave in a certain way. A **knowledge need** occurs when the *child does not know and* *might not be expected to know how to behave appropriately in a given situation.* For example, a three-year-old who has no siblings and has never been in a group setting might not be expected to know about waiting, cooperation, taking turns, or following a schedule when he begins preschool. Similarly, a kindergartener might not know that he must be quiet in a school library.

A common reason for challenging behavior is that the child is lacking one or more social or emotional skills. A **need for skill building** exists *when the child clearly knows what is expected but lacks the skill to behave in the appropriate manner consistently across situations.* For instance, four-year-old Ricky *knows* he is supposed to sit quietly during story time, but he has *not yet mastered the skills* of regulating his excitement or controlling his impulse to touch the children around him. Six-year-old Sarah knows she is supposed to share the blocks, but she lacks the cognitive flexibility to accept that she cannot use all of the blue rectangles and must find another solution.

From my many years in the clinic and early childhood classrooms, I have compiled a list of essential life skills (Figure 4.3), the mastery of which greatly enhances a person's relationships and well-being. Most difficulties in social or emotional functioning of children and even adults are the result of underdevelopment in one or more of these skills. Peer conflict, class disruption, and caregiver

---

FIGURE 4.3
Essential Life Skills

Read the list of **essential life skills** several times until you know them. Then when teachable moments arise, you can make a lasting difference in the personal and social development of the children in your care by helping them progress in the development of these skills.

Personal Skills

Delaying gratification	Responding to teasing
Dealing with your anger	Ignoring
Dealing with other people's anger	Accepting constructive criticism
Dealing with embarrassment	Accepting no
Dealing with failure	Awareness of own/others' body language
Dealing with disappointment	
Dealing with frustration	Thinking ahead
Coping with fear	Distracting
Accepting consequences	Dealing with contradictions
Recognizing feelings in oneself	Dealing with a false accusation
Admitting wrongdoing	Focusing and sustaining attention
Being honest	Persistence
Being optimistic	Knowing appropriate time and place

Social Skills

Joining in	Voice volume
Introducing yourself	Using humor
Starting a friendship	Saying "no"
Maintaining a friendship	Being assertive, not passive or aggressive
Starting and ending a conversation	
Understanding the feelings of others	Apologizing
Treating people how you want to be treated	Asking permission
	Expressing an opinion
Saying "thank you"	Expressing affection
Offering help	Giving reasons
Asking for help	Convincing others
Compromising/negotiating	Giving information
Taking turns	Expressing feelings
Sharing	Giving emotional support
Resisting negative peer pressure	Giving advice
Respecting personal space/proximity	Avoiding gossip
Listening carefully	Giving constructive criticism
Getting to the point	Tone of voice
Staying on topic	Not interrupting
Making a request	Giving a compliment
Agreeing/disagreeing	Receiving a compliment
Eye contact	Formal/informal language
Manners	Giving a complaint effectively

stress can be reduced when we focus on helping children develop essential life skills. When you keep in mind that social and emotional skills mature in a progression, the same way cognitive and motor skills develop, you can remove your own frustration from the equation and focus instead on fostering the specific skills that need support. The list is far from complete but is intended to remind us to be intentional about promoting these competencies in children.

The following scenario exemplifies how a teacher can use the list of essential life skills to address a typical peer conflict:

Caleb stood behind William at the top of the spiral slide. Caleb grabbed William's shoulders, turned him around, and shouted, "*C'mon! Move!*" William instantly responded with a swift kick to Caleb's shin. Caleb yelped. Luckily, Ms. Margie had witnessed the whole altercation and said, "Boys, come here, please."

Ms. Margie: "Caleb, tell me what happened."

Caleb: "William kicked me."

Ms. Margie: "William, you kicked Caleb. Can you tell him why?"

William: "'Cause you grabbed me and got close to my face and screamed real loud. That made me mad!"

Ms. Margie: "So when Caleb grabbed you, got close to you, and was loud, it made you mad and you kicked him?"

William: "Yes!"

Ms. Margie: "Caleb, what made you decide to grab William and yell in his face?"

Caleb: "He was going too slow. He wouldn't hurry and I wanted my turn."

Ms. Margie: "You wanted him to move faster so you could have your turn? It's hard to be patient, isn't it? William, what would you like Caleb to do differently next time he wants you to hurry?"

William: "He could say in a normal voice, 'Hurry up, William!' He doesn't have to grab me and yell."

Ms. Margie: "Caleb, do you think you could do that next time? Use his name without grabbing and ask politely?"

Caleb: "Yeah, next time."

Ms. Margie: "Caleb, how did you feel when William kicked you?"

Caleb: "It hurt! It made me mad."

William: "Well I was mad, too!"

Ms. Margie: "What would you like William to do differently next time he is mad at you?"

Caleb: "He could just tell me he doesn't like what I did and I'd stop."

Ms. Margie "Can you do that William? Can you tell Caleb with words without hurting him?"

William: "I can try."

Ms. Margie: "Good, now let's act out the situation the way you said you'd like it to go."

Through this simple discussion and role-play, the boys recognized that they had alternative choices for dealing with challenging situations. Ms. Margie acknowledged Caleb's difficulty with waiting patiently and prompted William to offer Caleb an alternative way to get someone to move faster. Caleb, in turn, gave William suggestions about handling his anger in ways that don't hurt people. Ms. Margie then gave them the opportunity to practice the new skills before returning to play.

Caleb needs to work on the essential life skills of respecting people's space, keeping his hands to himself, using an appropriate tone of voice, and waiting patiently. William needs to work on managing his own and other people's anger. When the boys returned to play, Ms. Margie stood ready to acknowledge their efforts at patience, anger management, and the other skills.

Young children are not very sophisticated when explaining their reasons for noncompliance. "I want it!" implies that a child has not yet mastered the skill of dealing with disappointment or compromise. "I don't want to!" suggests that the child has not yet mastered the flexibility to stop doing what he is enjoying and instead do something that is required. Before we assume that the child is willfully disobedient, we must be sure he has the knowledge and skills to behave appropriately. Remember that children's skill development may be uneven. In addition, children may be inconsistent in their use of an emerging social or emotional skill, especially when the skill is new or when the child is tired or stressed. Be sure to address knowledge and skill-building needs before assuming that the behavior is a child's unwillingness to cooperate. An excellent source of skill-building activities that is organized by age and developmental domain is *Ages & Stages Learning Activities,* by Elizabeth Twombly and Ginger Fink (2004).

When we are sure that the child *knows* what behavior is expected and has demonstrated *skill* in that area across situations but continues to behave in a contrary manner, we may be looking at a problem of **will**, *a determination, desire, or motivation to behave in a certain manner.* A **problem of will** is *an active choice on the part of the child to defy expectations or authority.* This is a matter of motivation. Why would the child choose to defy a command or rule? Before we can address the behavior, we have to understand what motivates and sustains it.

Analyzing Challenging Behavior

When your earnest detective work uncovers evidence that the child has actively made a choice, a willful decision to behave in a manner contrary to rules, a functional behavior assessment would be helpful to apply.

A **Functional behavior assessment (FBA)** is *an organized effort to understand the function that a child's difficult behavior is serving in order to decide the best way to address it.* A functional behavior assessment can be enhanced with parent and teacher ratings and interviews that provide useful information. Another component to FBA is **functional analysis (FA)**, *a specific procedure where a child is observed directly in a variety of situations on multiple occasions, using clearly defined behavior indicators, that reflects a running account of* **a**ntecedents, **b**ehaviors, and **c**onsequences (ABCs) (Bijou, Peterson, & Ault, 1968). In FA, the observer must look at what led up to or triggered the behavior (antecedents), the intensity and duration of the behavior, and what followed the behavior (consequence). Functional analysis may be more time consuming than parent and teacher behavior ratings, but it yields very accurate and specific information. The best way to understand the child's behavior is to use both indirect (FBA) and direct (FA) methods of information gathering (Alter, Conroy, Mancil, & Haydon, 2008).

For young children, the analysis of the challenging behavior must be done in the context of the child's sensory preferences and his developmental levels in many domains. It is also helpful to consider his knowledge of expected behavior and his ability to perform those behaviors in different settings under various circumstances. Given that information, the functional analysis begins with consideration of the **antecedents**, *the events or triggers that preceded or stimulated the behavior*. Please see Figure 4.4 for guiding questions about behavior antecedents.

When a child is hungry, tired, or upset, previously acquired skills can seem to disappear. It is important to try to understand the basis for this regression and support the child's efforts to work through the difficult situation.

It is also essential to define the behavior very clearly. For example, a child can disobey actively and defiantly by saying, *"No!"* He can disobey passively by ignoring the request or saying, "in a minute" without doing the task that was requested. In a similar vein, "aggressive behavior" should be clearly defined. Do we mean physically hurting by hitting, kicking, biting, or scratching? Or do

---

FIGURE 4.4

Guiding Questions to Determine the Antecedents of Behavior

- When is the behavior most likely to occur and in what setting?
  - Does it occur at the same time every day?
  - When certain people are present?
  - During transitions?
  - With more or less structure?
- Who is the authority figure or caregiver?
  - What are the relationship style and temperament of that adult?
  - What is the nature of the attachment and relationship history with the adult (warm or critical)?
- What immediately precedes most occurrences of the behavior?
  - When a specific peer is involved?
  - When she doesn't get what she wants?
  - When told to wait?
- Is the trigger internal?
  - Did she just remember her parents' argument before school?
  - Is she hungry or tired?

FIGURE 4.5
The Meaning of the Behavior to the Child

- What does the current situation mean to the child?
- What problem is the child trying to solve through this behavior?
- What is the child trying to accomplish or communicate?
- Why now?

we mean name-calling, humiliating, or threatening with words? A clear definition of the behavior improves the accuracy of our analysis and the effectiveness of our interventions.

Outward behavior is generally a child's solution to a problem or a way to communicate a need. To determine the function the behavior is serving for the child, we need to observe closely, keeping in mind the questions in Figure 4.5.

We must also consider the usual consequences that motivate the child to repeat the challenging behavior. By observing what happens after the behavior occurs, we can determine the environmental variables that reinforce it. To get this information, it is useful to ask the questions in Figure 4.6.

By carefully analyzing the antecedents and consequences of a child's behavior, we are better able to determine effective strategies for addressing the needs of that child. When we know, for example, that unstructured situations are particularly difficult for a child, we can be sure to provide additional structure, guidance, and support to preempt negative responses. When we discover that a child's defiant behavior toward an adult is followed by something rewarding to him, such as peer approval or adult attention, we can alter those consequences.

FIGURE 4.6
Guiding Questions to Determine
the Consequences of the Behavior

- Does she get what she wants?
- Does she get rewarded in some other way, such as sent home from preschool where she and mother watch TV together?
- Does the behavior lead to outcomes that result in attention?
- Does the behavior lead to outcomes that relieve her from punishment, such as provoking the adults to argue?
- Does the behavior result in uniting adults who usually disagree?
- What consequences can I provide that will address the underlying problem and reduce occurrences of undesirable behavior?

LOOKING IN THE MIRROR...

Picture a child who you know well. Use Figure 4.2 to think about that child's pattern of strengths in the social and emotional domain. Draw a line across the figure to represent the child's chronological age. Compare that child's development in the skill areas listed under the bottom line and connect the dots as shown in the sample:

- In what skill areas does the child function at or above his age level?
- In what skill areas does the child function below his age level?
- What strategies can you use to support the skill areas in which he shows weakness?
- In what ways can you use his strengths to support the development of his weaker or emerging skills?
- What factors do you need to consider in reducing the unwanted behavior if his skills appear to be adequate and his challenging behavior appears to be willful?
- What strategies can you use to reduce the unwanted behavior?

Developmentally appropriate guidance requires that we look at the social and emotional development needs of each child and tailor our approach to his or her existing strengths and weaknesses. Sometimes a child simply needs information about appropriate expectations in a given setting. At other times, the child's behavior tells us that he needs support in one or more specific skill areas. And sometimes we need to address the child's motivation to behave in a certain manner. This comprehensive analysis enables us to find strategies that meet the individual needs of each and every child. Young children, with their relatively limited life experience, also have a limited repertoire of coping skills. Ultimately, the best outcomes will come from an approach that targets developing specific skills with positive behavior support and takes into account the antecedents and consequences of the behavior (Stoiber, Gettinger, & Fitts, 2007).

Summary

Each child comes from his own individual set of developmental competencies and circumstances. You can glean useful information about how to work with any child when you explore such individual factors as sensory preferences, temperament, family dynamics, and health and environmental history. In addition, recognizing developmental variability between children and within a given child will enable you to determine if the child lacks the knowledge of expectations or needs to work on developing specific skills. Finally, exploring the circumstances that lead to or result from challenging behavior will allow you to modify the environment in ways that promote social and emotional competence.

Review and Apply

1. Using the concepts presented in this chapter, describe the factors you must consider to individualize social and emotional learning experiences for each child.

2. Todd plops down between Dale and Kyle, who are in the middle of a card game of Fish. "I wanna play! Give me some cards." The boys tell him that he can play the next game, but Todd grabs several cards from the pile.

   a. What essential life skills can you target with Todd to help him interact more effectively with his peers?

   b. Brainstorm several strategies you could use to promote Todd's development of those skills.

chapter 5

Contextually Informed and Culturally Appropriate Guidance

"I'm the boss of me! Except when Grandma comes to school, then she's the boss of me."

—Reggie, Age 4

After reading this chapter, you should be able to

▶ Describe the contextual factors that influence expectations for children and explain how those factors affect children's behavior.

▶ Describe the ways culture shapes expectations for children's learning and behavior.

▶ Compare and contrast individualistic versus collectivist cultural values and beliefs as they relate to child guidance practices.

▶ Apply strategies for resolving conflicts with families resulting from cultural differences.

Is it OK to steal? Is it OK to lie? These moral questions seem simple at first glance, but with more information, we find they can be rather complex. What if we are talking about stealing a medicine to save a person's life? What if telling the truth will break someone's heart and serve no positive purpose? How is it that we know right from wrong?

Just as we have to take other information into account when we make decisions, so it is with children. How does a child, with his limited life experience, know what behavior is appropriate in any given situation? Appropriate behavior depends on many factors, including **context**, *the circumstances that surround the behavioral expectations,* and **culture**, *the array of values and teachings stemming from the child's family and community.* When we guide our young students in the social–emotional domain, we must remain aware of the significant influence of contextual demands and the importance of culture.

CONTEXTUALLY INFORMED GUIDANCE

Most children have experienced inconsistent expectations. Children vary in their ability to generalize a rule from one situation to the next, and this is made more complicated because different adults in different moods in different settings at different times ask children to behave in different ways! It is important to take context into account when we lay out expectations for social and emotional behaviors in young children.

Expectations in Context

Expectations for children's behavior depend on many variables, including location, time of day, and the presence of specific people. It's a wonder that children can navigate all the different sets of expectations in their daily lives. We must be very intentional when we establish those expectations and especially clear when we convey them to young children.

"Use your inside voice." "Slow feet, please, until we get to the playground." All day long, we ask children to consider the context of their actions. We expect them to behave differently inside versus outside. Running, jumping, climbing, and shouting are desirable activities on the playground but can be dangerous or disruptive in the classroom.

To help children feel comfortable practicing their emerging skills, it helps to set up our classroom to be a risk-free environment. For example, learning materials should be appropriate for the age and developmental level of the children and organized for easy access. Activities and materials that challenge children but ensure some level of success can promote skills and confidence. And it is best to try to balance novel (new) and familiar materials so that children's curiosity can be stimulated but they also feel safe.

Children function best when they can count on consistency and predictability. When a routine is disrupted, such as with the arrival of a classroom guest or a field trip, we typically expect children to adapt. And yet, dealing with change is difficult for some children. They require additional support and patience from the caregiving adults.

Even within the same setting, different adults may have different expectations. Some adults are more flexible and tolerant, while others are firmer and less yielding. Neither of these response styles is right or wrong, and children may find more comfort from one style than the other. Your challenge is to balance flexibility and consistency. For example, Mark, who has difficulty sharing, knows from experience that you and the children expect him to let others play with a toy he brings from home. One particular day, his grandfather gave him a new set of race cars and you know that he will not want to share them. At free playtime, when Mark brings out the cars, you decide to gently guide the children to choose another activity.

It is also important for us to remain aware of our own emotional states so that our expectations for the children do not vary on the basis of our mood. If you were feeling generous and patient yesterday, you might have overlooked a child's class disruption or made a playful joke out of a child's backtalk. Today, even if you are feeling stressed and annoyed, the child will expect the same level of patience and humor that he got yesterday when he behaves that way today. From one day to the next, the rules and expectations should not change unless the circumstances can be articulated to the children. In the case of Mark, you might explain that these cars were a special gift. As complex human beings in the context of a complex world, this consistency can be very difficult to deliver.

The home and school settings most likely differ in terms of behavioral expectations and consequences. A typical early childhood classroom is a group setting with shared materials, whereas the home environment generally has fewer social requirements such as sharing and taking turns. The school environment is often more structured than home, with specific locations and specified times for particular activities. Consequences also may differ between school and home, as the following scenario illustrates:

> When Jeff took the ball from Brynne, she pushed him down and stepped on his hand. Ms. Rossman asked Brynne what she thought might happen if she treated Jeff that way. She expected Brynne to acknowledge that Jeff might get hurt and not want to play with her. Instead, Brynne said, "I'll get spanked with a spoon?" Ms. Rossman was shocked. She would *never* hit a child, and school policy strictly prohibits physical discipline. Brynne was simply anticipating consequences based on her experiences at home.

For this reason, it is important to know about parenting style and discipline practices of the families of your students.

Ecological Systems Theory

In addition to contextual influences within the program setting, we must always remember that children live within the context of their families and families live within the context of neighborhoods and communities. Urie Bronfenbrenner, cofounder of Head Start, looks at a child's development within the context of the system of relationships that form his or her environment. Bronfenbrenner's Ecological Systems Theory defines complex layers of environment, each

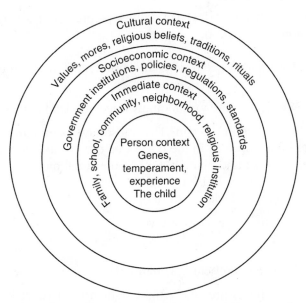

FIGURE 5.1 **Ecological Systems Theory** *Source*: Based on Bronfenbrenner, U. (1979). *The Ecology of Human Development: Experiments by Nature and Design.* Cambridge, MA: Harvard University Press.

having an effect on a child's development, including the child's own biology (Bronfenbrenner, 1979). Please see Figure 5.1.

A child's development is fueled and steered by the interaction between factors in the child's maturing biology, his immediate family/community environment, and the societal landscape. Changes in any one layer will impact the other layers, as can be seen in Dylan's story:

> Late one evening, the county sheriff delivered an eviction notice to Dylan Gole's recently unemployed parents. Dylan arrived at school the next day stressed and tired, resulting in irritable whining and aggression toward peers. Ecological Systems Theory would point out that the downturn in the economy resulted in Mr. and Mrs. Gole's job loss. Their unemployment impacted their ability to pay rent, which, in turn, resulted in their eviction. Being evicted at any time is demoralizing and stressful, but the stress is acute when it happens suddenly in the middle of the night when options are limited. The all-night stress in the Gole family kept Dylan awake and resulted in his difficulty coping the next day.

To understand a child's development and behavior then, we must look not only at the child and his immediate environment but also at the interaction of events in the larger environment. Fortunately, Ms. Keisha had established a warm, trusting relationship with Dylan and his parents, so it was not difficult for her to gather more information:

KEISHA: "Dylan, you seem tired and bothered today. Were you up late?"

DYLAN: "We slept in the van. Mommy cried and Daddy was mad."

KEISHA: "You slept in the van? That must have been hard. If you need to be by yourself in the quiet area or you need to rest, we can get your cot and blanket, OK? You just tell me."

At pick-up time, Keisha weighed her words carefully when Mrs. Gole helped Dylan with his coat.

KEISHA: "Hi, Mrs. Gole. How are you?"

MRS. GOLE: "I've been better."

KEISHA: "You've been better? Tough day?"

MRS. GOLE: "Things are really tight right now. I don't know if Dylan told you we were evicted last night and the shelter was full, so we drove around for hours and slept in the van."

KEISHA: "What a difficult situation."

MRS. GOLE: "Hopefully, something will open up this afternoon. We're looking for a small apartment until my husband or I can get back to work."

KEISHA: "I'll be sure to give Dylan extra support during this difficult time. He took a nice long nap today and woke up feeling a little better than he did this morning. Please let me know if there is anything you'd like me to do to help him deal with this."

In earlier chapters, we discussed the role that your own stress can play in your daily interactions with children and possible ways to manage that stress. Stress is an inevitable part of life for children as well. As Ecological Systems Theory would suggest, stress at any level can influence the child's developmental path. By maintaining open lines of communication and warm relationships with families, we can usually get information about the context of a child's behavior, and that information can help us provide the support he needs.

Part of that context is the culture in which the child is being raised. A final underlying principle in promoting social–emotional development is the importance of knowing, respecting, appreciating, and honoring the diversity of cultures in early childhood settings. We refer to those responses as **cultural competence**.

CULTURALLY COMPETENT GUIDANCE

Culture is *a shared system of meaning, which includes values, beliefs, and assumptions expressed in daily interactions of individuals within a group through a definite pattern of language, behavior, customs, attitudes, and practices* (Maschinot, 2008; Christiansen, Emde, & Fleming, 2004; Emde, 2006). Cultural competence refers to the ability to interact respectfully and effectively with individuals from a variety of cultures and backgrounds.

You are the product of your cultures. *Cultures*, the plural, reflects that your shared system of meaning can be defined by many variables that describe you:

- Gender
- Race
- Religion
- Generation/age
- Marital status
- Sexual orientation
- Educational level
- Socioeconomic level
- Region of the country in which you live
- Country of origin and circumstances of immigration

Individuals, families, and organizations have cultures that may differ in any or all of these dimensions. For example, a woman who came with her family from Guatemala to the United States as a child in 1975, became a citizen, went to college, and settled in San Francisco may have a shared system of meaning that is very different from a woman who came from Guatemala with little education in 2012 to escape poverty and settled in a small rural town in Indiana. Both are women from Guatemala, but they differ in generation, circumstance, educational level, and more. One cannot assume that just because they are both women from Guatemala that they are categorically alike in their pattern of language, behavior, customs, attitudes, and practices.

Although within an ethnicity or religion or gender there may be well-researched cultural patterns, we must be careful not to stereotype a whole group of people on the basis of those sampled. The two women from Guatemala might very well share some characteristics that are often seen in Latina women, but those similarities cannot be assumed. The key is to be aware of the influences of your own culture, acknowledge your biases, recognize and suspend your stereotypes, open your mind, and get to know people as individuals who bring with them a variety of cultural influences. From time to time, you will encounter conflicts influenced by your cultures and those of the families with whom you work. Later in the chapter, we discuss strategies for working through cultural conflicts.

As the author, I acknowledge that I have formed my theories and practices in ways that are consistent with my own cultures and experiences. I am a middle-class, middle-aged, college-educated, Caucasian, Jewish, married woman from the Midwestern United States. I appreciate that the reader and the children in his or her care may come from very different backgrounds than mine. The children, families, teachers, and students with whom I work have brought with them a vast array of cultures and the rich blessing of diversity. By keeping my mind open, listening carefully, and sometimes making embarrassing mistakes, my quest for cultural competence continues every day.

The Scope of Cultural Diversity in Early Childhood Classrooms

According to the 2010 U.S. Census, approximately 53 percent of children under age 5 in the United States are White/Non-Hispanic. Forty-seven percent of children under age 5 are characterized as Black/African American, American Indian/Alaskan Native, Asian, Native Hawaiian/Pacific Islander, Hispanic, or two or more races (U.S. Census Bureau, 2011). About 20 percent of school-age children in the United States speak a language other than English in their homes. Between 14–16 percent speak Spanish in their homes (Espinosa, 2010; Reyes & Moll, 2006). So it is quite likely that you, as an early childhood professional, will work with children who come from a variety of cultural backgrounds and that those backgrounds will differ from your own. Some communities have significant numbers of immigrants from

LOOKING IN THE MIRROR…

Consider your cultural background:

- What is your ethnicity or country of origin?
- Under what circumstances did your family (or you alone) arrive in this country?
- If you know other people from your country of origin, how are you similar and how are you different from them in your beliefs and practices?
- How has your gender influenced your experiences and your thoughts and feelings about yourself?
- How has your sexual orientation influenced you?
- Do your religious beliefs affect your decisions and practices?
- How do those religious influences differ from those of your friends, coworkers, or students?
- Have you moved from one region of the country to another, such as from the South to the Midwest or from the East Coast to the West?
- If so, did you notice differences in the ways people behave?
- If not, do you have preconceived ideas about how people from other regions behave?

Answering these and related questions is an important step in understanding the role your culture plays in your current interactions and activities.

one specific country for reasons such as geographic proximity, refugee acceptance, migrant work, and more. If you work in a community with a predominant cultural group that differs from your own, it is critically important for you to learn the cultural themes unique to the dominant immigrant group.

The United States has been called a *melting pot*, implying that those who are native to this land and all those who have immigrated here have blended or eventually should blend together into a relatively homogeneous stew. The melting pot symbolizes the notion of assimilation or integration, where immigrants seek to adopt the values, beliefs, language, and customs of the land to which they have arrived. The United States has also been called a *salad*, suggesting that all the various peoples retain their distinct national or cultural flavors. A salad symbolizes the notion that immigrants preserve the characteristics of their homeland. The families of the children in our programs can be anywhere on the continuum between assimilation and preservation, and we must be careful not to assume the place of any individual or family on that continuum.

In *The Changing Face of the United States*, Maschinot presents seven concepts that can help us understand culture in the context of working with an increasingly diverse population of children and families (Maschinot, 2008). Maschinot's ideas are described and slightly modified as follows:

1. **Cultures are complex networks, not descriptive lists:** Cultural sensitivity is a person's genuine attempt to understand another person's beliefs, not simply having rote knowledge about traits or customs that may characterize the person's cultural group.
2. **The notion of *cultural scripts* helps define culture: Cultural scripts** are *the combination of elements that forms the way a person views the world, thinks, and behaves*. Cultural scripts often guide how we solve problems and face challenges, including those in our work with children and families.
3. **Cultural scripts are powerful motivators of behavior, even if people are unaware that they have them:** Because our own cultures are often outside our awareness, we may behave in certain ways "just because that is the way things are done."
4. **We rarely question our own cultural scripts:** Our own view of the world, to us, is an undeniable reality; at the same time, the people with whom we work experience *their own view of the world as universal reality*. Discrepancies between the two worldviews can and often do cause tension. If you are part of the prevailing or mainstream culture, it might be difficult to overcome your perception that your worldview is reality and is more accurate than the worldview of someone else. This perception is often reinforced and remains unchallenged by the prevailing cultural community.
5. **Cultures are dynamic:** Individuals draw on several cultural models to respond to a given set of circumstances, such as those you considered about your own culture in your self-reflection earlier in the chapter.
6. **Culture and Ethnicity are two different things:** Here, **ethnicity** refers to *a family's country of origin*. It is an important cultural variable, but you have many other cultural variables that influence your beliefs and practices.

7. **Knowing your own cultural scripts and determining the cultural scripts of the families with whom you work are prerequisites to understanding the notion of culture:** Because cultural scripts often lie below the level of awareness, we must be sensitive, open, and nonjudgmental in attempts to learn the culture-driven beliefs and practices of the families with whom we work.

Based on Maschinot, B. (2008). *The Changing Face of the United States: The Influence of Culture on Early Child Development.* Washington, DC: ZERO TO THREE.

Culturally Shaped Behaviors, Expectations, and Practices

In our everyday interactions with young children, we must remain aware of the culturally influenced behavior patterns, expectations, and practices of children and families that differ from our own. The following scenarios exemplify potential culture-driven differences:

> Four-year-old Jatan was carried to his first day of preschool in the arms of his father. Mr. Singh inquired about the lunch routine so that he could be sure to come and feed his son.
>
> Cecilia insists that 14-month-old Jaqueline is potty trained. All the adult needs to do is hold and carry the toddler in order to feel her body's signal that it is time to use the potty.
>
> Wally Miller's family does not celebrate holidays or birthdays. Mr. and Mrs. Miller want you to make other arrangements for Wally when the class celebrates a birthday.

In most early childhood programs in the United States, four-year-old children are expected to eat independently, toilet teaching does not begin until the child is around two, and birthdays are occasions to celebrate. So, who is right and who is wrong? Of course, the answer is neither. In many cases when the family's cultural practices differ from those of the professional, it stems from differences in underlying values. Mr. Singh comes from a culture that values nurturing and closeness over independence. Cecilia's background is one where physical contact is highly valued and children are constantly held, facilitating communication between the adult and child. The Millers practice a religion that does not observe birthdays and holidays.

Janet Gonzalez-Mena, in her meticulous investigation entitled *Diversity in Early Care and Education: Honoring Differences,* summarizes several themes in which cultural differences may play themselves out in the early childhood arena. While these concepts are sometimes presented as categorical, either/or distinctions, Gonzalez-Mena is careful to point out that real differences in these areas fall somewhere on a continuum (Gonzalez-Mena, 2008, pp. 67–68). She also reminds us that even within a given culture, individual families may differ in the manner in which a given variable is expressed. It is useful to consider the dimensions discussed in the upcoming sections when we reflect on ourselves and the families with whom we work.

Individualist vs. Collectivist Cultures

Researchers distinguish between cultures that emphasize individualism and those that emphasize collectivism. **Individualistic cultures** *encourage children to think for themselves, empower them to solve their own problems, promote independence in personal care, and welcome their expression of thoughts and feelings. High value is placed on autonomy and independence.* Praise for accomplishments and affirmation of children's uniqueness are common in individualist cultures (Gonzalez-Mena, 2008; Maschinot, 2008; Pena & Mendez-Perez, 2006).

In **collectivist cultures**, the *child is seen first and foremost as a member of the group, and individuality and autonomy are de-emphasized. The goal is* inter*dependence, where a child's uniqueness is primarily for the benefit of the group, not the child himself.* Therefore, possessions are shared among the group. Qualities such as helpfulness, cooperation, and being a team player for the betterment of the group are highly valued. Teaching and socialization of all the children are the responsibility of all the adults.

Around the world, the United States is among the most individualistic cultures. Hofstede surveyed people in 53 countries about various sociological topics (Hofstede, 1991). The United States emerged with the highest rating in the promotion of individualism. Asian and Latin-American countries scored highest on interdependence (Maschinot, 2008). In view of the influx of immigrants into the United States from many countries that highly value interdependence, it is essential for professionals to appreciate both sets of values and create environments that maintain a balance on the dimension of independence and interdependence.

Many excellent publications are available that describe cultural themes that are characteristic of specific ethnic, racial, or religious groups (Espinosa, 2010; Gonzalez-Mena, 2008; Hofstede, 1991; Maschinot, 2008; Reyes & Moll, 2006). For example, Linda Espinosa describes specific and distinct values, beliefs, and customs that researchers have observed in Latin-American, Asian-American, and African-American families. For our purposes, cultural themes are presented as general frameworks without reference to specific populations because of the wide variability of behavior patterns observed among individual families even within population groups.

Cultural Differences in the Classroom

In the next four chapters, we will explore major social and emotional skill areas that are important for all young children to grow and thrive. Each of these discussions will be influenced by cultural values. Families and professionals may eagerly support some of the principles and strategies presented because they jibe with their own cultural values. Others may be less welcoming of these concepts on the basis of their cultural backgrounds. The aim is to establish a balance between the values inherent in individualistic cultures that emphasize *in*dependence and autonomy, and collectivistic cultures that emphasize *inter*dependence and community. All young children in the United States will benefit from developing comfort and competence in both areas because America's native peoples and the majority of immigrants come from collectivistic cultures but must function in a predominantly Anglo-American individualistic society (Maschinot, 2008). The degree to which a given early childhood program tends to lean toward one end of the spectrum or the other depends on the orientation of the decision makers and the local community.

The distinction between individualistic and collectivistic cultures is relevant in countless day-to-day events in the early childhood classroom. Food preparation and service, for example, can promote independence, interdependence, or aspects of both. Are children in your program served food, or are they engaged in the process of preparing and serving food for the group—even at a young age? Is food served on individual plates or family style?

Cultures also differ in the degree to which they value independent thinking and expression of opinions. How do you feel about children having the belief that they can take charge of their lives and their activities? Here are different reflections three professionals shared at a recent workshop:

EUGENIE: "I am shocked by the sassy mouth on little Bella! Four years old and you would think she's queen of the universe. 'Miss Eugenie, I don't want that one....I want the pink one!...I don't like the choices for centers today....I think we should have the puzzles out.' That little girl thinks she owns the place. She needs to do what *I* tell her to do! I'm in charge! I'm her elder!"

McKENZIE: "I think your Bella sounds delightful. She could become a very powerful leader. She knows what she wants and knows how to assert herself to get her needs met. It's the kids who need help on every little thing who bug me. They are always asking for direction and needing to follow the other kids. They can't seem to think or do anything for themselves."

REMBERTO: "I don't mind when kids look to each other for feedback. It helps them understand what is expected of them to be part of their community of learners. We are all in it together, and if children find comfort in asking for help or direction, it just means that they want to belong to something larger than themselves."

Each of these teachers is expressing a preference or a set of expectations that is consistent with his or her cultural values. None of them is wrong, but they are very different from each other.

> # LOOKING IN THE MIRROR...
>
> - Do you think children should have choices and be encouraged to express and act on their preferences, or should they adapt to what is presented to them?
> - In what circumstances should they be encouraged to think and act independently?
> - In what circumstances should they be expected to adapt?
> - Are there families with whom you work who encourage behaviors that differ from your values?
> - If so, how do you manage the discrepancy?

Like Eugenie, McKenzie, and Remberto, your answers will influence your expectations and interactions.

Cultural values can also create discrepancies in the desirability or undesirability of external reinforcement such as praise or rewards. Should you praise a child for mastering a self-care skill independently, such as drinking from a cup, toileting, or zipping a coat? While such responses aim to encourage autonomy, in some cultures, praise is reserved only for displays of cooperation and collaboration among members of the group. In the following example, Ms. Bev's use of rewards is met with three different reactions from families:

Ms. Bev has always believed that promoting a child's self-esteem would instill in that child the confidence to do things on his own. She knows that each child develops according to his own developmental timetable, so Ms. Bev individualizes her learning plans to best support the developmental needs of each four-year-old child in her classroom. Jackson, Robert, and Chloe are three children who do well in most skill areas with the exception of solving problems that have multiple steps, such as making a collage or creating a picture book. Ms. Bev decides to use a simple reward system for the three of them. She understands the importance of privacy, so each child keeps a chart in his or her cubby and earns a star for gradual improvement on problem-solving tasks. The parents of the three children have very different reactions to their star charts.

Jackson's parents glow with pride when Jackson earns the maximum ten stars in a week. They have great hopes for Jackson's future, anticipating that he will become a successful entrepreneur or businessman. Each star is a step closer to their goals for their son.

Robert's parents are appalled. Why would you give a child a reward for doing something he should be doing anyway? If the adult says a child should do something and provides the opportunities and resources to do it, then the child should do what is expected. There's no need for silly star charts.

Chloe's parents don't understand why Chloe gets stars for doing things alone when they would prefer that she work together with her peers to solve her problems. They feel that seeking help and working with others builds a sense of community and helps children see that their social connections are more important than their personal needs or accomplishments.

The responses of the parents of Jackson, Robert, and Chloe echo the sentiments of the three teachers, Eugenie, McKenzie, and Remberto described in the context of children's self-determination. Many teachers would not have considered using a star chart because they share the views of Robert's and Chloe's parents. Instead, they may have tried collectivistic strategies to improve problem-solving skills, such as finding a more skilled peer to be a work buddy or encouraging the child to observe others as they model the desired behavior.

Some issues related to play and toys are also tied to culture. For example, if a child brings a toy from home to show her peers, is she expected to let the whole group play with it as community property, or does she reserve the right to choose whether or not she shares? Some teachers use show-and-tell or sharing circles as opportunities for children to develop confidence by standing in the limelight. In contrast, some cultures would find such a practice to be an unwelcome overemphasis on material objects and possessions that is often observed in individualistic societies.

In the United States, with its emphasis on consumerism, some early childhood settings are filled with lots of objects to stimulate learning. Sand tables, puzzles, books, riding toys, stacking toys, sorting toys, art supplies, and musical instruments may be available to engage the senses. Compare these classrooms with those of people-oriented cultures that emphasize human interactions and relationships above material objects. Children are encouraged to look into the faces of other people to learn the meanings of facial expressions and other nonverbal communication. It is through strong relationships that children learn the important lessons in life.

In a similar vein, do you think the environment should be filled with bright colors, background music, and lots of engaging activities? Or should the

LOOKING IN THE MIRROR...

Do you feel that reward charts are effective and desirable ways to build skills in children?

- If so, specify what lessons the child is learning as a result of such a system.
- If not, what is it that you oppose about reward systems?

How would you handle a parent whose views on external reinforcement (like star charts) differ from your own?

LOOKING IN THE MIRROR...

Do you believe that early childhood classrooms should have many toys and objects from which to choose?

- If so, how do you think this abundance benefits the children?
- If not, how do you think children can learn the important skills of early childhood education?
- How many toys and learning objects should be available?
- What kinds of objects and materials would be most beneficial?

environment allow for meaningful inactivity where problem solving happens through quiet meditation (Gonzalez-Mena, 2008, p. 107)? In many societies, time that is left unscheduled and space that is left unoccupied are considered desirable because open time and space allow opportunities for children to explore what interests them, discover for themselves, and create their own meanings.

Cultures also differ on the role and nature of learning through play. Many early childhood educators trained in the United States and Europe are taught to see it as fact that children learn best through play. Learning through play, however, is not universally accepted as the best way for young children to learn. Pressure inspired by high-stakes testing has led teachers in some American preschools to use worksheets and flashcards as methods for teaching letter and number concepts. Throughout the world, the focus of many early education programs has become preparation for the next phase of education rather than the joy of discovery and being in the moment. For example, according to Sir Ken Robinson, a world-renowned expert on education reform, there are increasing numbers of *cram schools* in Japan, where children as young as age 1 begin to prepare for entrance exams to prestigious elementary schools. It is believed that a potential Japanese executive's future is largely determined by the time he or she enters first grade (Robinson & Aronica, 2009).

One result of the emphasis on school readiness in the United States and other societies is that many parents have come to expect concrete work products from their child's preschool day. While observing her child's classroom through a one-way mirror, a parent asked me why the children were "not working." She said, "I thought he'd be learning here, and the teacher is just goofing around with the kids." The children had fabricated cell phones out of wooden blocks and were "ordering tacos" from a classmate who was running a busy restaurant, complete with menus, waiters, and customers. This classroom had countless authentic opportunities for children to write that went beyond the order pads in the restaurant, such as logs for documenting scientific discoveries and graph paper for tallying types of bugs, weather conditions, and the increasing weight of the class gerbil. The mother looked uncertain when I explained the profound social skills, rich literacy skills, and abundant math and science skills that were emerging from the children's elaborate storytelling, character development, documentation, and record keeping. The mother had really hoped for more paper-and-pencil work in her child's early learning experiences because her culture emphasizes observable work products.

Should play and conversation be child-directed or adult-guided? In some cultures, children are not provided playthings to keep them occupied but rather accompany adults as the adults go about their business. Children are expected to learn, not by doing, but by observing adults (Mistry, 1995). Cultures also differ in the nature of talk between adults and young children. In schools in the United States, it is not unusual to find teachers and students engaged in back-and-forth conversations where the adults actively solicit children's ideas, concerns, and preferences. In fact, this very book strongly recommends conversation. A review of the literature suggests that parenting styles that encourage this sort of egalitarian approach to conversation in young children may better prepare children for success in formal education settings (Mann, Steward, Eggbeer, & Norton, 2007). Mutual back-and-forth dialogue between children and adults is a manifestation of underlying socialization goals that encourage autonomy and exploration. These goals are not universal across cultures. Socialization goals such as being cooperative and obedient tend to elicit more directive input from adults (Mann, et. al., 2007; Pena & Mendez-Perez, 2006).

Cultural Differences in Child Guidance Strategies

How do children learn right from wrong? How should they deal with difficult emotions? How should they resolve conflicts? Child guidance strategies are often culturally influenced. For example, the use of time-out is controversial in early care and education settings for several reasons, some of which are culturally based. In individualistic cultures, being in time-out means being separated from the group so that the undesirable behavior is not reinforced by attention. It can also be used to give the child the time and space, separate from the group,

LOOKING IN THE MIRROR...

- From the standpoint of your culture, do you believe that adults should engage in relatively equal conversations with children that give equal validity to the child's opinions and ideas?
- Or do you think that the adults' role is to inform and instruct the child and direct his thoughts and behaviors?
- Do you believe that children learn best by interacting with people and objects?
- Or do you think children learn best by observing the communication and activities of adults around them?

to calm himself down and think about alternative ways to behave (perhaps chill out instead of time-out). This approach suggests to the child that he is in charge of his behavior and has choices to make. In some cultures, children are not given the message that they have choices to make about behavior. In addition, separation from the group can be quite devastating for a child raised in a family where the orientation is collectivistic and the highest value is placed on being part of the group (Gonzalez-Mena, 2008).

Should children be encouraged to cope with conflict or difficult feelings by expressing them directly with words? Or should emotions be contained and conflict be handled indirectly through innuendo and subtle communication? In many American early childhood programs, the approach to emotional regulation begins with adults externally providing support with the goal of having the child develop an internalized sense of control over his or her behavior. In some cultures, however, it is expected that the community will always externally control behavior (Gonzalez-Mena, 2008, pp. 134–135). With such opposing orientations to child rearing, it is easy to see how conflicts can occur in early care and education settings.

Approaching Cultural Conflicts

In early childhood programs, it is inevitable that the cultures of families will at times be at odds with the practices and values of the program. Considering how many cultural dimensions and sets of beliefs exist, it is surprising that cultural conflicts don't emerge more frequently than they do.

There are many possible ways you can resolve culturally influenced conflicts (Mangione, 1995; Keyser, 2006; Gonzalez-Mena, 2008). Effective approaches should always begin with reflection. Reflection requires that we first look within ourselves to understand the underlying beliefs, values, and reasons behind our actions. Then we must reflect open-mindedly on the perceptions, beliefs, and values of the family. It requires that we listen respectfully and without judgment to their concerns and thoughts and feelings. Often, we have to observe the nonverbal communication and also consider what the family is *not* saying. In many cultures, direct verbal expression of opinions is not acceptable, so we must tune into more subtle means of expression (e.g., looking down, looking past the listener, turning a shoulder, speaking in the third person, using metaphors). It is then helpful to restate what you *heard* the family say before you go on to express your point of view. When you do express your position, remember to do so respectfully and be as clear as possible about the underlying reasons for your position. The family may not share your underlying beliefs, so be prepared for disagreement. It is useful to frame any disagreements simply as differing viewpoints, not necessarily right or wrong answers. Try to find common ground by exploring goals that you and the family do share. Then, you and the family can brainstorm to find strategies that you both agree are acceptable ways to attain the shared goals. And finally, be sure to keep the door open for follow-up and further discussion.

Earlier in this chapter, Ms. Bev implemented a star chart to improve children's skills in multistep problem solving. Robert's family was upset about her use of a reward system. Ms. Bev uses the following approach to work through this culturally influenced conflict with Robert's parents:

Ms. Bev: "Thank you for coming to talk with me today, Mr. and Mrs. Lind. I understand that you have some concerns about our star chart. Would you mind sharing your thoughts with me?"

Mr. Lind: "Robert should do what is expected just because he has been told to do it. We don't want him to think that he will get things just for doing what he is expected to do. You are the authority, and if you tell him to do something, he is obligated to do it."

Ms. Bev: "You feel strongly that Robert should do the things I tell him to do because I am the authority figure and that by rewarding him, I'm giving him a different message. You are concerned that rewards will lead him to do things for the sake of getting rewards, not because he simply must do them. Is that what you are saying?"

Mr. Lind: "Yes. It is not necessary to reward him."

Ms. Bev: "OK, I understand. My thought was that he would feel more motivated to work on the skills and feel better about his accomplishment with a little star."

Mr. Lind: "He needs to do what he is told. It doesn't matter how he feels about it."

Ms. Bev: "It is important to you that he does what is expected and his feelings don't really enter into it, is that right?"

Mr. Lind: "That's correct."

Ms. Bev: "I think I understand your point of view. Do you have some suggestions about how I can help motivate Robert to persist on longer, more complicated projects?"

Mr. Lind: "You need to tell him more firmly what you expect."

Ms. Bev.: "OK, I can do that. Perhaps I can give him a pat on the back or a thumbs up when he accomplishes a new skill? Would you be comfortable with that?"

Mr. Lind: "That will be fine."

Ms. Bev: "If you'd like, I'd be happy to meet with you again at your convenience in a few weeks to see how things are going."

In this scenario, Ms. Bev was careful to listen with an open mind to the Linds' concerns, here voiced entirely by Mr. Lind, which might reflect a cultural inclination for the male to be in charge. While Ms. Bev still values the use of external rewards in some cases, she demonstrated respect for the wishes of Robert's family. She proposed a less tangible reward like the social reinforcement of a pat on the back or a thumbs up. The family agreed to this compromise and moved

LOOKING IN THE MIRROR...

- Does your cultural background tend to favor collectivism, individualism, or some combination of both?
- Have you encountered a coworker, colleague or parent whose views about discipline differ from yours?
- What underlying values does your discipline approach emphasize?
- What values does that coworker, colleague, or parent's approach emphasize?
- How could you approach this person to discuss the conflict and work to a resolution?

on. It can be anxiety provoking to enter into conflict-resolution conversations, but they can go a long way in strengthening relationships between you and the family and prevent conflicts in the future.

Summary

When we support social–emotional competence in young children, we must remain aware of the influence of contextual demands and the role of culture. Children live in the context of their families, communities, and society at large. They are subject to stress and challenges just like the rest of us. We need to balance predictability and consistency with tolerance and flexibility. We should also try to balance novelty and familiarity, structured and unstructured experiences, and whole-body movement and quiet, restful activities.

We must keep in mind the pervasive influence of culture in the decisions we make every day. We should consider the roles played by our ethnicity, religion, gender, generation, and other cultural variables. Some cultures tend to be individualistic, emphasizing independence and autonomy. Other cultures can be considered collectivistic, emphasizing interdependence and community. Most people have aspects of both individualistic and collectivistic cultures, and we can help children develop competence along the whole continuum. As educators, we may find that our culture-driven values and practices are incompatible with the values and practices of the families with whom we work. At such times, it is helpful to reflect on our own cultural values and be open and receptive to the cultural values that underlie the ideas and practices of those families. Through this reflective process, we can increase the effectiveness of our important work.

Review and Apply

1. Describe the ways context and culture influence expectations for children's behavior, priorities for early care and education, and approaches to guidance.
2. A parent of a new child in your program expresses to you that she is uncomfortable with how much chatter and playtime she sees in your classroom.

a. What steps can you take to better understand the basis of her concerns?
b. Applying the concepts presented in this chapter regarding cultural differences in expectations and approaches, how would you respond to this parent's concerns?

PART 2 SUMMARY

The Guiding Principles

Promoting social and emotional development in the early care and education setting is arguably among the most important responsibilities of the early childhood professional. This task is not simple and requires self-reflection and ongoing consideration of several underlying guiding principles. The process should be relationship based, requiring the professional to put priority on establishing a warm, mutually respectful relationship with the child and parents. The process must also be individualized to align with the unique needs, preferences, skills, and challenges of each child. In addition, the process must recognize and accommodate the developmental differences among children as well as developmental variability within a given child. The professional must also recognize the importance of contextual variables in children's social–emotional functioning and development. And finally, the process must appreciate the particular culture of the child and family.

part 3

· ·

Building Emotional Competence

Part 1 focused on the importance of promoting social and emotional development, described reflective and parallel processes, and explored the qualities in ourselves that influence the ways we approach our work as early educators. Part 2 examined five guiding principles educators must always bear in mind when supporting social and emotional development in young children. In Part 3, we consider the essential emotional competencies that children need to master as they grow and develop.

Self-regulation and autonomy are qualities long associated with academic and personal success. These personal competencies interact and feed on each other as children grow and learn. Each of these skill areas has a complex developmental pathway and relies on both the inborn nature of the child and supportive elements in the environment.

chapter 6

Supporting Self-Regulation Skills

*"Sometimes a dragon comes out of me
with fire and messes everything up
and I can't get him back in the cave."*

—DALE, AGE 5

After reading this chapter, you should be able to

▶ Define self-regulation and describe its components.
▶ Explain the influence of sensory processing on children's outward behavior.
▶ Identify behaviors that can result from difficulty with attention regulation.
▶ Explain how improving children's emotional awareness, emotional management, and emotional expression skills can lead to better functioning and outward behavior.
▶ Describe differences in the development of self-regulation capacity due to temperament, brain development, and attachment relationships.
▶ Identify practices and strategies that promote self-regulation in the classroom.

In a series of studies between 1968 and 1974, Walter Mischel and his colleagues at Stanford University tempted each of 653 preschool children with a delicious marshmallow. Each child was told that he could eat the one marshmallow in front of him right away, or if he waited until the adult came back into the room, he could have two marshmallows. The children sat with the marshmallow in front of them, often struggling and squirming, for up to fifteen minutes in their efforts to await the bigger reward. Some of the children gave in to temptation and licked, nibbled, or outright ate the single treat. Others were able to delay their gratification and were rewarded with twice the deliciousness several minutes later (Mischel, Ebbesen, & Zeiss, 1972; Mischel, 1996).

In follow-up studies a decade later, researchers found correlations between how long those preschool children waited and measures of their academic and social competence as teenagers. Results suggested that the preschoolers who successfully delayed gratification and waited for the bigger reward demonstrated better verbal skills, were more rational and attentive, and were better able to deal with frustration and stress as teenagers than those who did not wait (Mischel, Shoda, & Peake, 1988; Mischel, 1996). The preschool children who were able to come up with their own waiting strategies tended to have significantly higher ratings of cognitive, self-regulatory, and coping competence as well as higher SAT scores as teenagers (Shoda, Mischel, & Peake, 1990).

The Stanford marshmallow experiments provide a strong case for the importance of self-regulation in predicting social and academic success as children grow. The ability to delay gratification is one of several components of self-regulation. What exactly do we mean by *self-regulation?*

DEFINING SELF-REGULATION

Self-regulation is *the ability to monitor and manage one's thinking, attention, feelings, and behavior to accomplish goals* (Thompson, 2009). The development of self-regulation entails a child's increasing ability to control bodily functions, manage powerful emotions, and maintain focus and attention (Shonkoff & Phillips, 2000). We see examples of self-regulation when an upset child calms himself, when children take turns playing with a popular toy, and when an energetic child returns from the playground and quietly sits down to read. In a nutshell, self-regulation refers to the many processes by which people exercise control over their functions and inner states. Most broadly, "Self-regulation is essential for transforming the inner animal nature into a civilized human being" (Vohs & Baumeister, 2004).

Self-regulation is not the same as self-control. Impulse and emotional control can be difficult for children whose temperament gives them more to control. Emotionally passionate or highly active children have to work harder than their more mellow peers to self-regulate. But some children tend to put forth excessive control over their impulses and emotions. Children whose temperaments or early experiences inhibit them from trying new experiences—those who are shy or reticent—might be reluctant to learn through exploration. This child is easy to overlook because his behavior is not disruptive. Alternatively, a child may be intensely fearful of change or unfamiliar people and situations. It is very important to address the self-regulation needs of these children. Research suggests that shy toddlers who had high levels of self-control were more socially withdrawn and less socially competent than their peers. Those with high self-control and an exuberant temperament were rated as more socially competent. The researchers concluded that healthy self-regulation means knowing when to exert control and when to loosen up (Tarullo, Obradovic, & Gunnar, 2009).

What does it take for a child to demonstrate self-regulation? Scientists describe a complex and interrelated set of executive functions that are necessary for the development of self-regulation. **Executive functions** refer to *higher-order cognitive activities necessary for adaptive and goal-oriented behavior that exert control over basic sensory, attention, emotional, and behavioral processes* (Raaijmakers, et al., 2008). Executive functions include response inhibition, attention control, planning, flexible thinking, and problem solving. These processes involve integration of functions throughout the brain but occur predominantly in the prefrontal cortex, a part of the brain that is not fully developed until early adulthood.

This chapter will focus on the components of self-regulation, its developmental process, and influences on its development. Through self-reflection and discussion of targeted strategies, we will explore ways to promote children's executive functions so vital to self-regulation.

COMPONENTS OF SELF-REGULATION

Four components of self-regulation that are necessary for healthy development are sensory, attention, emotional, and behavior regulation.

Sensory Regulation

Sensory regulation refers to *the ability to take in, modulate, and organize sensations to engage in the task at hand* (Williamson & Anzalone, 2001). Everything infants know, they take in through their seven senses. (See Table 6.1.) The images they see, the sounds they hear, the feel of objects and the movements of their bodies all combine to create a mosaic of sensory experience. Infants integrate that input into a primitive understanding of the world. As they grow, children develop the ability to process more and more complicated information both from their sensory environment and their own mental constructions. In this regard, when we observe a child's outward behavior, we are witnessing the effectiveness of his sensory processing. To understand that behavior, it is useful to consider *sensitivity* and *reactivity*, which were introduced earlier in our discussion of temperament (Williamson & Anzalone, 2001).

All day long, we are bombarded with sights and sounds and other sensory input. **Sensitivity** refers to a person's *capacity to take in and process sensory input*. How much sensory stimulation is enough and how much is too much?

TABLE 6.1 • The Seven Senses

Outer Senses	Sensory Organ	Experience	Example
Auditory	Ears	Sound	When Kyle hears his favorite song, he relaxes.
Visual	Eyes	Vision	Cindy does not like the dark.
Tactile	Skin	Touch	Marlie can't stand itchy fabric.
Olfactory	Nose	Smell	Strong odors upset Cal.
Gustatory	Tongue	Taste	Robin loves tangy food.
Inner Senses			
Vestibular	Inner ear	Balance, body in relation to gravity, equilibrium	Bobby loves the feeling of spinning and then trying to walk.
Proprioception	Muscles and joints	Movement, orientation of body in space, rate and timing of movements	Pele wobbles and almost falls when stepping on an escalator.

Based on Williamson, G., & Anzalone, M. (2001). Sensory Integration and Self-Regulation in Infants and Toddlers: Helping very young children interact with their environment. Washington, DC, USA: ZERO TO THREE: National Center for Infants, Toddlers, and Families.

At what point do we feel the most contented, and at what point do we begin to feel overwhelmed?

Sensory threshold refers to *the point of detection of sensory input in a given person at a given time* (Williamson & Anzalone, 2001). How loud does music have to play before you can hear it clearly? How bright does the room have to be for you to be able to see the details of a picture? If you need the music to be at a much higher volume than your friend, you are said to have a high sensory threshold and lower sensitivity in the auditory modality. The children in your care will also differ in their levels of sensitivity. It is essential to recognize this variability as you set your expectations and interact with children, as can be seen in the following three examples:

You call Jackson's name three times before he slowly turns his head to look at you, despite normal hearing. During an art activity, Jackson has more glue on his face than on his paper, but he doesn't appear to notice. On the busy playground, a child accidentally knocks Jackson to the ground, which doesn't seem to faze him. Jackson has a high sensory threshold, or low sensitivity in the tactile, auditory, and proprioceptive modes.

Unlike Jackson, when Marcie enters the busy big playroom, she clings to you with her hands over her ears and whimpers, "It's too loud." Balls are flying and dinosaurs are chasing jungle animals on tricycles. Marcie buries her head in your lap. She is highly sensitive to auditory stimulation.

In contrast to Jackson and Marcie, Jared loves to swing, the higher the better. He jumps off the swing and twists in the air. He spins and spins until he dizzily falls down, laughing the whole time. Jared has a high threshold for vestibular and proprioceptive stimulation and seeks more and more stimulation until he is satisfied.

Reactivity refers to a person's *level of response to sensory input*. It is what a person *does* in response to stimulation. Children vary a great deal in how reactive they are to sensory stimulation. When stimulation exceeds the comfort level of a child with low reactivity, he may react by cowering in a corner, spacing off into a daydream, or even falling asleep. A more highly reactive child might bite and hit, scream and cry, or run from the room. Some children, like Marcie (described earlier), respond by retreating, perhaps quietly closing their eyes, or turning their head. Other sensitive children, like Dale in the following example, respond very intensely or with exaggerated movements:

Each morning at 10:15, Dale begins to whine. He knows that at 10:20, his class goes to the big playroom where the other children enjoy running, climbing, shouting, throwing balls, and playing monster. Dale wants nothing to do with all that. When you finally cajole him down the hall and into the playroom, he hits and pushes his classmates who get too close, and he tries to run out of the room. Dale is highly **sensitive** and highly **reactive**.

Some children who have a high sensory threshold seek stimulation just to attain a level of comfort, like Jared in the earlier example. They climb on counters, poke their friends, wiggle and squirm, make noises, or talk incessantly. This sensory-seeking behavior may be evident in any or all of the seven modalities. The following true story is about two siblings who differ significantly in this area:

Kalyani, the mother of four-year-old Molly and two-year-old David, describes her children as follows: "Molly's favorite sound is the vacuum cleaner, especially when she can hold the vibrating handle. She likes to wear corduroy, eat hot sauce, and play bouncy horse on my lap. As a baby, she went from crawling to running and climbing and hasn't stopped moving since. David, on the other hand, hides in the closet when we turn on the fan. He will only eat his spaghetti plain and won't eat anything crunchy or textured. He refuses to go near a swing set. Anything new or slightly different throws him into a frenzy." Kalyani is puzzled by the sensitivity and reactivity differences in her two children. Molly needs a great deal of sensory stimulation to feel comfortable, and she seeks it from a variety of places in her world. David is easily overstimulated and fearfully withdraws from sensory stimulation.

Molly has a high sensory threshold with which she copes by stimulation-seeking activities. David has a low sensory threshold, meaning he is highly sensitive, and he copes by sensory avoidance.

Effective **sensory processing** requires *the ability to organize sensations from the body and the environment and put them to adaptive use* (Ayres, 1979). When trying to understand what underlies a child's challenging behavior, a great deal of information can be gleaned when we consider her sensitivity, reactivity, and the effectiveness of her sensory processing.

Young children typically do not have the freedom to select settings and activities that are compatible with their levels of sensitivity and reactivity. The adults in their lives, such as parents and teachers, generally determine their environments and activities. When we tune in to the sensory processing attributes of each child, we are able to modify their experiences in ways that increase their effectiveness. These adaptations can include providing quiet spaces and down times for highly sensitive children and creating opportunities for sensory stimulation and gross-motor play for those who are less sensitive. We can guide highly reactive children to find effective ways to cope with their feelings of sensory overload.

Variability in sensitivity and reactivity explains why at an amusement park, some people enjoy the gentle, predictable merry-go-round and others prefer the roller coaster. As adults, our interests, hobbies, and career choices are often influenced by our sensitivity and reactivity. Bungee jumpers, off-road racers, firefighters, and action photographers perhaps have high sensory thresholds (low sensitivity) and high reactivity characterized by stimulation seeking. The selection of more subdued activities and careers, such as librarian or book-keeper, may reflect high sensitivity and low reactivity. You have opted to teach young children. Always keep in mind that your sensitivity and reactivity influence how you cope and interact with children.

LOOKING IN THE MIRROR...

To better understand sensory regulation in children, it helps to reflect on one's own sensory experience:

- How sensitive and reactive are you?
  - Do you like music soft or loud?
  - Do you like dim lights, bright lights, flashing strobe lights?
  - Do you prefer bland food or hot, spicy food?
  - Do you prefer the feel of wool or cotton fabrics?
- When sensations exceed your comfort level, is your reactivity level high (you want to shout or run out of the room) or low (you try to avoid the stimulation and get quiet or inhibited)?

Attention Regulation

Attention is a general term that refers to *one's level of alertness and ability to focus selectively on a desired sensory stimulus.* **Attention regulation** is *the process of focusing selectively on the task at hand, resisting distractions, and sustaining focus for the length of time necessary to complete the task* (Williamson & Anzalone, 2001). Over the early education years, demands for attention regulation increase. Children's attention-regulation skills evolve right along with their developmental advances in other domains.

At birth, infants are able to attend to selected stimuli. Research suggests that infants are hardwired to look at faces and, in fact, show early preferences for the face of their mother and the sound of their mother's voice (Walton, Armstrong, & Bower, 1998). Infants' attention is also drawn to novelty, a tendency clearly tied to learning. For more information on how infant learning and interests are measured, please see Figure 6.1.

An important milestone in the development of attention regulation is **joint attention**, *the manner in which two or more individuals simultaneously attend to a common or* goal *object* (Grossberg & Vladusich, 2010). You can see joint attention in action when you sit with an infant or toddler and enthusiastically point to an object as if to say, "Look at this!" Most babies will look at the object to which you are pointing. Joint attention is important for many aspects of development, including that of theory of mind. **Theory of mind** is *a set of beliefs a person develops to describe, explain, and make predictions about other people's knowledge, beliefs, and behavior based on inferences about their mental states* (Boyd & Bee, 2010). Theory of mind has

FIGURE 6.1
Measuring Infant Learning and Interest

One way developmental scientists study infant learning takes advantage of infants' preference for novelty. The approach involves a preference technique called habituation/dishabituation (Kaplan & Werner, 1986). During a **habituation/dishabituation procedure**, the researcher shows the baby an object and observes the baby's focus and any of a number of physiological functions (heart rate, brain waves, etc.). When the child looks away from the object, habituation is said to have occurred because that stimulus has become familiar and is no longer interesting. When the second object is shown, dishabituation is said to occur when the baby looks at the object and physiological reactivation occurs (heart rate and brain activity increase). For example, the researcher shows the infant an image of a puppy. Initially, the baby looks intently at the puppy and measurable increases occur in heart rate and brain activity. After a few exposures to the puppy, the baby looks away and physiological responses decrease, signifying that habituation has occurred. It is assumed that the puppy is no longer novel and therefore no longer interesting. When a different image appears in front of the baby, perhaps a picture of a kitten, she will look again and physiological reactivation, or dishabituation, occurs. Through this paradigm, we are able to ascertain what babies find worthy of attention. The very process is informative in that very young infants demonstrate the ability to regulate their attention according to their needs (human connectedness) and interests (novelty).

been linked to competence in the cognitive, social, and emotional domains (Carlson, Moses, & Claxton, 2004; Van Hecke, et. al., 2007). Children on the autism spectrum have been found to have deficits in both joint attention as infants and theory of mind as preschoolers (Toth, Munson, Meltzoff, & Dawson, 2006; Baron-Cohen, 2001).

As toddlers attempt to master important tasks of language, cognition, self-care, and social development, their demands for attention regulation increase. During the second and third years, as children realize that objects and actions can be represented by words, their attention is drawn to the links between objects and the words for them. A literal naming explosion takes place. Through interactions with more experienced language users, toddlers attend to the manner in which words are put together to convey complete thoughts and learn to express themselves in ways consistent with the sentence structure of their community's language.

The attention requirements of a toddler are linked to other cognitive advances as well. Emerging narrative memory, symbolic processing, and temporal reasoning are cognitive skills that enable children under age 3 to recall and relate events from the past and create simple dramas. Emerging spatial-mathematical skills allow them to stack blocks, nest objects, sort shapes, and piece puzzles together. Learning self-care tasks like toileting, dressing, and washing contributes to the young child's sense of self and competence. Erik Erikson refers to this stage as "autonomy versus shame and doubt," wherein successful attainment of these cognitive, personal, and social competencies is considered critical for the child's healthy psychosocial development (Erikson, 1993). It is no wonder, then, that such tasks consume the attention focus of children in this very busy and productive age range. Although novelty is still a magnet for attention, children are increasingly able to stay focused and persist in activities that engage their interest and build their sense of autonomy.

Sitting still and sustaining attention for story time or circle time can be very difficult for children under age 3. Such organized group time provides an important opportunity for children to learn how to be part of a community with a shared purpose. It is important to remember, however, that sitting quietly in a group and focusing on a single task is not particularly natural for very young children, whose preference is to be actively *doing*. A few minutes of circle time is generally long enough for children under age 3.

Preschool and kindergarten settings demand longer and longer spans of attention. Children in this age range are expected to engage in multistep projects, some of which occur over a series of days (like studying how a plant grows). Their games require more intensive focus and specific attention to relevant aspects of the task. In the following scenario, we can see the challenges of selective attention faced by four-year-old Gregor as he plays pick-up sticks:

Twenty sticks of multiple colors lay in a pile. Gregor, Megan, and Liam pick up one stick at time, hoping not to disturb the other sticks in the pile. When Liam touches a well-placed red stick, Gregor gets upset. He wants to be the one to pick up the red sticks, despite their placement in vulnerable spots. He is focusing on an irrelevant aspect of the task, stick color. During Megan's turn, Gregor picks up the tube that held the sticks and pretends he's a pirate with a periscope. He walks around the room calling, "Arrgh, Matey" to his classmates and misses his next turn at pick-up sticks.

Gregor also has difficulty resisting distractions during quiet reading time. He picks up a tattered copy of a bug encyclopedia and pulls a loose string from the binding, which detaches the binding from the pages. On his way to where the tape is kept, he stops to admire the morning's art drying on the rack. He then remembers his blue sparkles and goes to find them in his art box to show his teacher. In his art box, he sees his new scissors, and so on.

Gregor's difficulties are not uncommon in preschool but become increasingly debilitating as school demands intensify. Children like Gregor struggle to focus and sustain their attention to the relevant aspects of a task.

As adults, we also vary in our abilities to sustain and focus attention in the face of distractions. At any given time, we may have several tasks competing for our attention, especially when working in an early childhood setting. Each child needs something from us. We have schedules to follow, paperwork to complete, and lessons to plan. While we're doing all that, we may be thinking about the demands of our own families.

It is a wonder that we can focus on any task long enough to finish it. But it was not always that way. Over the years, most of us have failed to give an important task the proper level of attention and have suffered such consequences as an overdrawn checking account, a lower grade, or a missed appointment. The important thing to remember is that attention regulation is a skill that is harder for some people to master than others. As early childhood professionals, we can empathize with those challenges and must patiently nurture the attention-regulation skills of the children in our care.

Emotional Regulation

Every day, we hear news stories about people committing violent acts out of jealousy or rejection. We have all observed drivers with road rage and the tirades of frustrated shoppers. We strive to be happy but sometimes suffer disappointment, hurt, grief, and despair. It can be challenging to deal with difficult emotions in a manner that is effective, or at least not detrimental. **Emotional regulation** refers to *one's ability to inhibit, enhance, maintain, and modulate emotional arousal to accomplish one's goals* (Eisenberg, et al., 1997). Research suggests that emotional regulation has as many as eight basic emotional skills:

- Awareness of one's emotions
- Ability to recognize others' emotions
- Use of emotional vocabulary
- Capacity for empathy and sympathy

- Distinction between internal feelings and external expressions
- Adaptive coping through self-regulatory strategies
- Awareness of the role of emotions in relationships
- Emotional self-efficacy, or sense that one is capable of coping (Saarni, 1999)

These emotional-regulation skills tend to cluster into three areas: emotional awareness, emotional management, and emotional expression. Each of these skills is an important element of our capacity to regulate emotions and becomes more sophisticated and differentiated as we mature. For example, a toddler's awareness of his emotional state and corresponding emotional vocabulary generally starts with "happy," "sad," "angry," and "scared" (or, more playfully, "glad, sad, mad, and scared"). With more life experiences, children discover variants of each of those emotions. Happy can be silly, pleased, or excited. Sad can be disappointed, hurt, rejected, ashamed, or lonely. Anger subsumes feeling frustrated, jealous, insulted, annoyed, and irritated. Finally, scared can include anxious, nervous, alarmed, and terrified. Children as young as three can begin to recognize subtle differences in emotions and the words that describe them, so it is important for adults to provide those words when children struggle with difficult emotions. In the classroom described next, four-year-olds are provided the tools to recognize and communicate a rich array of emotions:

Ms. Darla knelt down beside tearful Maddie to ask why she was crying.

MADDIE: "Tara says she's not my friend because she's Lonna's friend and Lara's friend."

MS. DARLA: "It sounds like you feel left out."

MADDIE: "Nobody wants to play with me."

MS. DARLA: "I bet that makes you feel lonely."

MADDIE: "She said I can't come to her birthday party."

MS. DARLA: "You feel disappointed about that, don't you?"

Richard threw his puzzle on the floor and stomped his foot.

RICHARD: "I can't do it! I hate puzzles!"

MS. DARLA: "Richard, that's a hard puzzle. It looks like you feel frustrated!"

RICHARD: "Puzzles are dumb."

MS. DARLA: "Sometimes we want to give up when we can't get it right. It's hard to keep trying when we feel discouraged."

Ms. Darla uses a reflective approach by labeling the child's emotions with words she herself might use under similar circumstances. In Ms. Darla's class, by virtue of her consistent modeling, the children learn to recognize their emotions and those of others.

Managing difficult emotions involves the use of physical and cognitive strategies that become more effective as a result of brain development. Emotions are processed in a midbrain region called the limbic system and involve stimulation of the sympathetic nervous system. The **sympathetic nervous system (SNS)** is *the part of our autonomic nervous system that enables us to mobilize the body's resources under stress. The sympathetic nervous system governs the fight-or-flight response, characterized by increased heart rate and force of contraction, dilation of the pupils, reduced digestion, and other physical changes* (Silverthorn, Garrison, Silverthorn, & Johnson, 2009). Earlier in human evolution, our SNS enabled us to run from threatening creatures or fight for our survival. In modern days, it serves the important function of mobilizing us into action when we perceive a threat or face heightened stimulation. It is a part of the nervous system that is quite active during a temper tantrum, an anxiety attack, or a good cry. The fight-or-flight response flips on all at once, like a light switch.

In contrast, the **parasympathetic nervous system (PNS)** *enables us to calm down, relax, and rest.* It complements the SNS in self-regulation. Sometimes referred to as the **relaxation response** (Benson & Klipper, 2000), the PNS can be activated when we take slow deep breaths, relax our muscles, meditate, or think about peaceful images. As opposed to the trigger-switch fight-or-flight response, the PNS works more like a dimmer switch, slowly and gradually. We can help children who are upset calm down by acknowledging their emotions and gently encouraging them to take a few deep breaths, tighten and relax their fists, get a drink of water, and count to ten.

To understand how to help a child calm down, consider a time when you were upset and somebody tried to comfort you. In the following example, imagine how you would feel if you were Jane:

> Jane had always wanted to be the director of a child care center. She started as a classroom aide and worked her way up to lead teacher by attaining her bachelor's degree and developing a reputation as a loyal and conscientious worker. She has taken on increasingly more complicated administrative tasks when Francine, the director, is away from the center. When Francine announced her retirement, Jane and other staff applied for the director position. With her credentials and work history, Jane knew she was the top candidate.
>
> Monday morning two weeks later, Francine entered Jane's classroom and introduced Marta, a woman who just moved to town and was hired to be the new director. Jane was shocked. Her heart was pounding, her hands were shaking, and she felt like throwing up. She ran out of the room and began sobbing in the staff lounge.
>
> Peggy, another teacher, heard Jane's sobs and came in to comfort her. Jane poured out her heart and described her disappointment. Peggy responded, "Oh, don't let it bother you. It's not that big a deal. Marta seems really nice. She is the logical choice because she has business experience. Be reasonable." It took all of Jane's power not to throw a coffee cup at Peggy.

Have you ever tried to be logical when you are upset? Logic requires activation of the prefrontal cortex, the brain area that lets us inhibit reactions and reason through problems. Jane's pounding heart and other physical symptoms clearly indicate that her SNS was activated, diminishing her capacity for logic at the moment. It was made worse by Peggy's comments that invalidated Jane's emotions and minimized the importance of this devastating event.

Like Peggy and Jane, sometimes our responses to children unintentionally heighten the intensity of their emotional arousal:

> Ricky wanted to play outside with the other children, but his mother forgot to send boots and mittens. Several other four-year-olds were staying in for the same reason. Rivers of tears streamed down Ricky's disappointed face. In efforts to support him, Ms. Mallory said, "Don't cry, Ricky, there will be other days to play outside. Look, lots of the other children are staying inside, too."

Although trying to be supportive, in effect, Ms. Mallory is diminishing the meaningfulness of something that is extremely important to Ricky. Just like Jane, Ricky needs to hear that his feelings are valid. He needs to know that Ms. Mallory appreciates his distress. Both Ms. Mallory and Peggy would be more effective in comforting if they were to join Ricky and Jane in their pain by acknowledging the meaningfulness and intensity of the disappointing experiences before offering another perspective or solution.

The importance of this emotional connection is evident even in infancy. The infant's ability to regulate his emotional state depends on the caregiver's level of attunement to that state. Developmental scientists demonstrate the crucial role of caregiver attunement to emotional regulation by using the still-face paradigm (Tronick, et al., 1975). In the still-face paradigm, mother and baby sit face to face. In the first step, mother and baby actively engage in a synchronous back-and-forth exchange of gazing, smiling, and interacting. The baby mirrors the emotional state of the mother, who mirrors the emotional state of the baby. Next, the mother looks away, and returns to look at the baby, but this time keeps her face completely still, showing no emotion and not responding to the baby's bids for interaction. Research consistently finds that in the absence of the synchronous attunement on the part of the mother, the baby tries several strategies to reengage the mother and after a short time becomes emotionally distressed, shows increased negative emotion, fusses, squirms, and reduces gaze, as if giving up (Mesman, van IJzendoorn, & Bakermans-Kranenburg, 2009; Adamson & Frick, 2003). When mother returns to her synchronous interaction with the baby, the baby soon returns to a calm, positive state.

The still-face paradigm reminds us that, from the very beginning, people need to feel emotionally understood to maintain a state of contentedness. So before we can expect a person to regulate her emotional state, we must communicate through words or gestures that her feelings are valid and understood.

Behavior (Impulse) Regulation

The most frequent concerns expressed by early educators involve children's outward behavior. An entire industry has formed around addressing **challenging behavior**, *conduct that is disruptive, dangerous, or otherwise interferes with a child's functioning, learning, or relationships*. As previously described, self-regulation requires optimal sensory processing, sustained and focused attention, and emotional management. Challenging behavior can result from difficulties in any or all of these components, but some skills are specific to behavior regulation.

One of those skills is **impulse control**, *the ability to resist the inclination to act immediately without consideration of other behavior choices or possible consequences*. It involves inhibiting the impulse to do one thing and, instead, stopping to think about what is most appropriate or needed (Thompson, 2009).

Impulses can be physical, aggressive, or verbal, as can be seen in these classroom scenarios:

> Five-year-old Gail proudly walked to her cubby to get the fragile ceramic doll her mother carefully placed in a padded box for show-and-tell. The doll's velvet dress proved to be impossible for Delaney to resist touching. Delaney acted on the impulse to reach out and feel the delicious fabric, and the doll fell to the ground in pieces.
>
> Robby and Dan were building a city with large cardboard brick blocks. Each was working on a different tower when Robby's tower collapsed and toppled Dan's. Dan punched Robby without considering the potential consequences of his aggressive impulse or the fact that the toppling was unintentional.
>
> Mrs. Dorn was explaining to the first-grade class how to use the new classroom microscopes. Cole interrupted to explain that his brother has a microscope to look at germs. Ronald commented that he had a germ that caused a sore throat, which prompted Cole to tell the class that he once had a sore throat, too. Cole and Ronald disrupted the class with their verbal impulses without considering consequences or the needs of others.

These behaviors should be interpreted as children's ways of saying they need additional support in learning to control their physical, aggressive, and verbal impulses.

A related skill in the area of behavior regulation is **delay of gratification** or **deferred gratification**, *the ability to postpone immediate satisfaction for the sake of future consequences* (Shoda, Mischel, & Peake, 1990). Recall the four-year-olds in the Stanford marshmallow experiments. The promise of a larger reward was enough for some children to resist the single treat that lay before them. Many children, however, struggled unsuccessfully with the waiting task and gave in to temptation. Delay of gratification is necessary for successful mastery of many vital interpersonal skills, such as sharing, negotiating, and compromising. Taking turns and waiting for everyone to be served before eating also require delay of gratification. A child who postpones fun activities to first complete work is demonstrating delay of gratification. These important delay skills in Mischel's young subjects were largely responsible for their future social and academic success as teenagers.

It should be noted that the components of self-regulation do not work in isolation but rather interact in complex ways to enable a child to successfully manage internal and external stimulation and responses. For example, strong attention regulation appears to protect children with high levels of dispositional anger from developing behavioral and emotional problems in middle childhood (Kim & Deater-Deckard, 2011). Delay of gratification, an important aspect of behavior regulation, was found to correlate significantly with the emotional regulation skill of coping with frustration and stress (Shoda, Mischel, & Peake, 1990). Similarly, behavioral inhibitory control tends to correlate with the development of theory of mind (Carlson, Moses, & Claxton, 2004).

EXPLAINING DIFFERENCES IN SELF-REGULATION CAPACITY

With so many components involved in self-regulation, it is understandable that considerable variability is present among individuals in the development of this competence. This variability can be explained by innate variables, such as temperament and brain maturation, and by experiential factors, such as early relationships and guidance strategies.

Temperament

Research suggests that some attributes of temperament are evident before birth. Very active fetuses often grow to be very active children and have a higher likelihood of being labeled *hyperactive* by parents and teachers (Accardo, et al., 1997). Because temperament is evident so early in life, one could assume it has a genetic component. Indeed, when we consider the temperaments of the children with whom we work, we can often see similarities in one or both of their parents. This is true for ourselves as well. We can often see in ourselves qualities that are present in our parents or our own children. The following story illustrates the inheritance of temperament dimensions that impact self-regulation from one generation to the next:

> Four-year-old Harley has not stopped moving since his mom was six months pregnant with him, according to his exhausted mother. He loves to climb on *everything*. At his second birthday party, he broke his arm diving wildly from the spinning merry-go-round at the park. He constantly talks, grabs, touches, and cranks the TV to its highest volume, flailing his arms and legs to his own rhythm.
>
> Harley's mother used to needlepoint and write poetry but now cries herself to sleep. His father, a test pilot for the army and motorcycle

enthusiast, thinks his wife exaggerates the problems. Harley has a highly active and reactive temperament with a high sensory threshold for auditory, vestibular, proprioceptive, and tactile stimulation. It is likely that he inherited his temperament from his father, who apparently has found socially acceptable ways to channel those same qualities in himself: flying jets and riding motorcycles.

The adults in Harley's world can help him by directing him to activities where those qualities are beneficial, such as gymnastics or soccer, and supporting his efforts to function effectively in environments where the qualities are detrimental. While we cannot change a child's innate temperament, we can guide him in coping effectively with environmental demands and provide opportunities for him to express his intrinsic nature.

Brain Development

It might be hard to remember a time when you did not have the capacity for focused and sustained attention, emotional regulation, impulse control, and delay of gratification, but there was such a time. As infants and toddlers, we had some primitive self-regulation skills but depended largely on our caregivers to help us regulate sensory input, emotions, and behavior. Brain development is a protracted process that begins at two weeks gestation and, when it comes to self-regulation functions, continues into adulthood.

One way to understand the developing brain is with a simple model using our hand. Make a fist with your thumb tucked into your palm and your fingers folded over your thumb (Siegel & Hartzell, 2003). The middle two fingers represent the area right behind your eyes. The back of your hand corresponds to the back of your head. The center of your wrist is the top of the spinal cord. The center of your palm is the **brainstem**, the part of the brain that *develops first and regulates the sleep-arousal cycle and fight-or-flight response.* Your thumb tucked into your palm symbolizes the **limbic** structures, which *mediate emotion and motivation.* The very top part of your thumb represents the **anterior cingulate** that *helps allocate attention and coordinate what we do with our thoughts and bodies.*

An *essential brain area for self-regulation* is the **prefrontal cortex**, represented by the front of your fingers to your fingernails (Thompson, 2009; Tarullo, Obradovic, & Gunnar, 2009). This important brain region does not finish developing until a person is in his mid-20s, so it is no wonder that young children, especially those with active temperaments, have trouble controlling their impulses. Part of that structure, the **orbitofrontal** cortex, represented by your two middle fingernails, is positioned *to connect virtually all the essential brain processes involved in self-regulation: the brainstem (arousal and attention), the limbic system (emotions and motivation), and the frontal cortex (reasoning and logic)* (Siegel & Hartzell, 2003; Tierney & Nelson, 2009).

Although great variability is present in brain maturation and self-regulation development among children of the same age, those variations are fairly stable across childhood. A preschooler who demonstrates good emotional regulation will likely be a high school student with good emotional regulation. This does not mean that a child's brain development is an immutable force beyond the influence of environment. While it is true that brain development in utero is largely under genetic control, barring malnutrition or toxins, most development that occurs after birth is experience dependent and defined by gene-environment interactions (Tierney & Nelson, 2009). It is up to caregiving adults to ensure that the young child's environment supports healthy brain development.

Brain growth involves a process of **neurons,** or *nerve cells*, connecting to other neurons across a **synapse,** the *space between neurons*. When a person is subjected to any experience, especially recurring experiences, synaptic connections are formed and learning occurs. The quality of those experiences determines the nature of those connections and what will be learned. Repeated traumatic or hostile experiences result in greater development in the limbic system and diminished development of the prefrontal processes involved in effective problem solving (Perry, 1997; Zeanah, Nelson, Fox, Smyke, Parker, & Koga, 2003). In contrast, positive experiences characterized by secure relationships and attuned attachment promote healthy development of the brain areas responsible for executive functions and healthy integration of arousal, attention, and emotions (Tierney & Nelson, 2009). Always remember that the positive and negative experiences we provide play a vital role in the structural and functional development of the brains of young children.

Attachment and Supportive Relationships

The quality of a child's primary attachment relationships is a critical variable in her development of self-regulation. The infant is completely dependent on her parents for temperature regulation, maintenance of comfort, and protection from overstimulation. When she is secure in her attachment, she and her caregiver share the regulation of her sensory and emotional states. With consistently repeated occurrences of **co-regulation**, or *sharing of emotional regulation*, the child becomes able to regulate her own internal states. When the attachment relationship is absent, inconsistent, or of poor quality, the development of self-regulation is impeded (Colle & Del Giudice, 2011; Calkins, 2011).

Several additional relationship factors contribute to mastery of self-regulation as the child's circle of caregivers expands to

include teachers and others. When we respond sensitively and refrain from dismissive, critical, and punitive responses, we are promoting in the child self-awareness and **self-efficacy**, *a sense that one's actions matter and that one can have an effect on the world*. The emotional climate at home and in the classroom, with manageable demands and constructive adult-child conversations about managing emotions, also contributes to the development of self-regulatory skills in children (Thompson, 2009).

PRACTICES TO PROMOTE SELF-REGULATION IN THE EARLY CHILDHOOD SETTING

Competence in self-regulation depends on supportive relationships, as described earlier. Daily routines and classroom environments that are predictable and secure promote self-regulation. Beyond those basics, it is helpful to take advantage of the many skill-building opportunities that emerge from everyday experiences. Providing the experiences, support, and encouragement that help very young children learn to self-regulate is a critical element of quality care and education (Gillespie & Seibel, 2006).

Creating a Supportive Classroom

Although novelty and surprise can stimulate interest and provide excitement, there is something reassuring about knowing what to expect. Children depend on a healthy balance of novelty and predictability to thrive and grow. It is the certainty inherent in predictable routines that enables children to regulate their own internal states and handle new experiences as they emerge. The four-year-olds described in the following example know what to expect and so can manage their impulses effectively:

Angie *really* wants the animal floor puzzle that Donnie is assembling. She knows that free play will last for twenty more minutes and is confident that she will have plenty of time when he is finished.

Yummy macaroni and cheese sits steaming in front of Yolanda, but she waits. Yolanda knows that all children must first be served and that the class will say a poem and take a deep breath before eating.

For children who cannot yet read, a picture schedule is an effective device to ensure that children know routines.

Many commercial products are available for making pictorial schedules. It is more fun and results in more buy-in, however, to photograph the children engaged in various activities and have them create a picture schedule themselves.

It is also helpful to use concrete materials and symbolic reminders to facilitate self-regulation. It is not always easy for young children to keep track of their arms and legs. When children are expected to remain in a particular area, such as during circle time, each child can have his own carpet square that defines his spatial boundaries. Footprints or shapes can be taped or painted on the floor to remind children where to stand when lining up. A common example of a symbolic reminder is the use of the terms *inside voice* and *outside voice* to promote regulation of volume. *Slow feet* reminds children to regulate their bodies while walking. Showing children to put their finger on their lip and their other hand on their hip (*lips and hips*) creates an easy way for children to remember to keep their hands to themselves and their mouths quiet when necessary.

One playful approach is to imagine with a child that she has a dimmer switch on her tummy. When her arousal, emotional, or activity level is too high, we can remind her to turn it down by rolling the switch counterclockwise. The dimmer switch gesture can be used discretely as a reminder to calm down. Of course, the child can turn up the switch when higher arousal is appropriate.

Using Targeted Self-Regulation Activities

One of the most important ingredients of self-regulation is self-awareness. We can help children become observers of their internal states by sharing our inferences about their inner states. For example, when you observe children engaged in a conflict, help them negotiate and give them the language that describes their own and the other's inner experiences. "Jack, you seem frustrated that Robyn got to the easel first. It is hard to be patient while you wait. What can you say to Robyn so she knows you want it?" Or, "Robyn, I see that you are enjoying the easel. Remember, Jack is very eager to use the easel, too." By labeling their emotions, they become increasingly self-aware of the myriad emotions they feel and the various means by which they can manage them. It is important to be intentional about building emotional vocabulary and incorporating the idea of regulation in everyday conversation.

It is also useful to be intentional about modeling our own coping experiences, as can be seen by Mr. Carl:

> Mr. Carl and four children share stories at lunch. Trenton talked about playing in the big scary waves at the beach. Mr. Carl followed Trenton's lead and described a time in his childhood when he played in waves and lost his footing. He explained how frightened he felt and how he worried he might not make it back to shore. He finished his story by describing his relief in knowing his dad was right beside him to help.

By sharing a narrative from his past, Mr. Carl enables children to see that difficult emotions are normal and can be managed.

> Later that day, Jillian told Mr. Carl that she would *not* put away her crayons until her picture was done, despite the fact that the children were lining up to go outside. Mr. Carl knelt beside Jillian and said, "I see that it is important to you that you finish your picture and I wish we had more time. But it's also important to the children that they go out and play. Look, they are all excited to go and are getting frustrated because they have to wait while we figure this out. Somebody will feel disappointed either way."

Mr. Carl acknowledged his feelings, Jillian's feelings, and the feelings of the other children. In doing so, he helps Jillian recognize that her behavior choices impact other people in ways she may not have considered. Because all of the children heard the words *excited, important to you, frustrated,* and *disappointed,* they are more likely to use those words in the future to describe their own emotions.

Everyday conversations can also be used to guide children on how to handle difficult emotions. Children enjoy telling stories about their lives and hearing stories about the lives of others. As we participate in this sharing of narratives, we can point out the emotional components of the experiences as well as the ways the characters in the stories cope with those emotions.

Circle time provides another excellent opportunity to explore self-regulation concepts. Teachers can select specific books or create unique puppet plays that target self-regulation issues, as Mr. Carl does in the following example:

> Matt's mother told Mr. Carl, "Today has been one disaster after another. We woke up late and Matt couldn't find the book he wanted for school. Hunting for it nearly made us late, so we didn't have time

to make the pancakes he had hoped for and he had to settle for cereal. Then he heard his father and me argue, and we left without Matt getting his dad's hug. We arrived here at school, and his buddy Josh is absent. What a day!"

Mr. Carl decided that a perfect book for story time would be *Alexander and the Terrible, Horrible, No Good, Very Bad Day*, by Judith Viorst *(1972)*. As he recounted each of the many miseries suffered by Alexander in the story, Mr. Carl stopped to talk with the children about similar experiences they have had and ideas they might have for Alexander to cope with the mishaps on his very bad day. It was during that story that Matt began to share his woes about the events in his own day. His classmates' sympathy helped him regulate his emotions.

Tools to promote self-regulation can be found in common childhood games and materials. Many games require attention regulation and impulse control. The game of "I Spy" is so simple, it can be played anywhere at any time. It requires children to selectively focus their attention on one attribute, such as color, shape, or letter and guess what the leader has in mind. To be successful at the game of "Memory," a visual attention card-matching game, the child must concentrate on each player's activities and resist the impulse to flip over just any card. "Follow the Leader" requires that children watch the leader carefully so they can imitate the action precisely.

Gross-motor games such as Duck-Duck-Goose, Simon Says, and Red Light-Green Light require listening, waiting, and resisting the impulse to commit one action in favor of the appropriate action. Board games are also useful for developing impulse control, frustration tolerance, and emotional regulation. In some popular children's games, the player can get very close to the goal and then land on a square that requires the child to go back to the beginning. These disappointing experiences can be quite difficult for some children who will need extra support in their efforts to cope. As children get older, games such as checkers and chess are useful for building strategic thinking and planning skills.

When children are riled up, for example, returning from recess or when a guest arrives, a *whisper song* can bring the level of arousal down and increase calm in the classroom. You can begin by singing a familiar song at the volume already present in the room. Children inevitably join in when they hear their favorite songs. Then tell the children we will sing the next verse in a whisper, and, finally, we will only mouth the words. This simple strategy effectively brings the volume and energy in the room to a manageable level.

To teach children the relaxation practice of deep breathing, have them lie on their backs holding a stuffed animal on their tummy. Ask them to breathe in deeply and watch the animal rise, rise, rise; then slowly let their breath out and watch the animal gently sink. Another enjoyable approach is to hand each student an imaginary balloon and say, "OK, very quietly and slowly, we will blow up our balloons as big as we can on three big breaths. Ready?" Model three deep inhales and slow exhales into the *balloon* while monitoring and coaching their technique.

Recognizing Challenging Behaviors as Opportunities to Promote Self-Regulation

Try as we might, we cannot always protect children from difficult experiences, like sensory overload, rejection, frustration, or disappointment. We also cannot prevent every impulsive or aggressive act or temper tantrum. Such is the stuff of life. But when these events occur, we must be deliberate in how we help children cope so that lasting positive changes can occur.

When we reflect on our responsibilities as early educators, we can see that promoting self-regulation is undeniably among the most important. So why do we often feel annoyed when children behave in a manner that suggests their self-regulation skills are lacking? We generally don't feel annoyed by underdeveloped literacy or number skills. Why, then, is poorly regulated behavior considered an incidental inconvenience? Perhaps we should look at emotional outbursts and impulsive or aggressive behavior differently: Such *misbehavior* is an opportunity to teach an essential life skill. It is simply a piece of *information* about the child's capacity for self-regulation. This perspective was introduced in an earlier chapter in the context of individualized guidance. Here, we will focus on challenging behavior as an opportunity to promote self-regulation.

When we reframe challenging behavior as information about a child's skill level in a certain area, we begin to solve the puzzle of how best to promote the underlying skill. We begin by acknowledging the child's feelings and thoughts, thereby improving his self-awareness. Then we can explore with the child the consequences of his behavior choice, including its impact on other people. This conversation enables the child to acknowledge that other people have needs and desires that may conflict with his own, an important aspect of theory of mind. That insight often propels a child over age 3 to consider negotiation and compromise. Conversations about choices and consequences do help children under three build impulse control and empathy skills, but children this young typically do not yet have the cognitive capacity for compromise.

Once the child has been able to express his feelings, thoughts, and motivation for the *misbehavior* in a supportive context, he can be guided to see it as a problem to be solved, as in the following example:

> Five-year-old Tessa grabbed the puzzle piece out of Dale's hand because it was likely to fit the section on which she was working. Dale squealed and messed up Tessa's completed work. Ms. Marla observed the kerfuffle and recognized the need for some guidance in self-regulation.

TESSA: "Dale messed up my puzzle!"

DALE: "Tessa grabbed my piece!"

MS. MARLA: "Tessa, you really wanted the piece Dale was holding to finish your section. Dale, how did you feel when she took that out of your hand?"

DALE: "I was mad!"

MS. MARLA: "Dale, what would you have wanted Tessa to do instead?"

DALE: "She should ask me for it."

MS. MARLA: "Tessa, could you do that? Could you ask him next time instead of grabbing?"

TESSA: "Yes."

MS. MARLA: "Tessa, how did you feel when he messed up your puzzle?"

TESSA: "Mad and sad because I worked hard on that!"

MS. MARLA: "You were mad and sad when he decided to mess up your hard work. What would you want him to do or say instead?"

TESSA: "He could ask me to give it back. He didn't have to mess it up!"

MS. MARLA: "Dale, it is OK to feel mad. Do you think you can do what Tessa asked if you get mad like that again? Use words and ask for it back?"

DALE: "Yes."

Opportunities like this occur dozens of time a day in early childhood settings. After Ms. Marla acknowledges the inner states of the children, she guides the children in a reflective process of problem solving. She encourages them to generate alternative solutions or behavior choices. When we present problem-solving steps as distinct decision points, children come to realize that *they* are in charge of their actions and not at the mercy of their impulses. Please see Table 6.2 for a description of problem-solving steps.

Another important aspect of emotional regulation is awareness of *triggers*. A **trigger** is *an object or event that stimulates emotional arousal*. Triggers can be internal, such as having an idea, feeling hungry, or remembering somebody's harsh words. An internal trigger in the preceding example was that Tessa saw a particular puzzle piece in Dale's hand and she had the idea that it would fit. Triggers can also be external, like being teased, hit, or told no. For Dale, Tessa's grabbing the puzzle piece was a trigger. Dale's messing up the puzzle

TABLE 6.2 • Problem-Solving Steps

Problem-Solving Step	Description	Example
Identify the problem.	Define the situation as a problem to be solved.	Ella wants the red ball, but Don had it first.
Generate solutions.	Help the child brainstorm possible ways to solve the problem or accomplish the goal. It is important not to evaluate *good* or *bad* solutions.	Ella says, "I can grab it; I can call Don a name; I can ask him to give it to me when he's done; I can tell the teacher...."
Generate potential consequences of those solutions.	Evaluate the potential consequences in the context of desired goals.	"What would happen if you grabbed it? Yes, Don might be upset. Would he let you have the ball? No? What would happen if...?"
Pick the best choice.	Select the choice most likely to achieve the desired goals with the fewest negative consequences.	"It sounds like asking him to give it to you when he's done might work, and nobody would get in trouble."
Evaluate effectiveness and modify selection.	If the choice did not accomplish the goal, review choices.	"So he said no? What were some of your other choices?"

was a second trigger for Tessa. Like Ms. Marla, we can help children identify their triggers.

A concept related to problem solving involves the distinction between a reaction and a response, as explained in Chapter 1. A **reaction** is *an immediate action that follows a triggering event.* Dale's instant reaction was to mess up the puzzle. A **response** is *an action following a triggering event that results from*

LOOKING IN THE MIRROR...

We all have events that irk us, and it is helpful to be in tune with our own triggers. Whining, tantrums, and defiance are child behaviors that often trigger emotions in teachers.

- What child behaviors trigger frustration or other difficult emotions in you?
- What behaviors on the parts of parents are triggers for you?
- Are there job requirements, regulations, or policies that are frustrating or irksome triggers for you?
- What strategies do you use to deal with those child behaviors, parent behaviors, or pro-grammatic annoyances?

Self-awareness regarding our triggers enables us to be intentional in how we cope.

thoughtful consideration of possible choices and their potential consequences. With Ms. Marla's help, Dale and Tessa were able to come up with more effective responses for solving their problem. Ms. Marla was very deliberate about using the word *decide* when referring to Dale's behavior. *Decide* and *choose* are words that indicate a person has control over what he will do to solve a problem. The distinction between **reaction** and **response** is also important as we consider our own behavior as professionals. When we are aware of our own triggers and recognize that we can choose how to respond rather than impulsively react, we can be more intentional.

Children under age 4 may lack the cognitive and language capacity to benefit fully from this multistep problem-solving approach. Nonetheless, it is never too early to use words such as *choice, decide,* and *happen.* With guidance, very young children can learn about the impact of their behavior on others, as seen with the toddlers in this scenario:

> When Jack bit Meg and she cried, his teacher said, "Look at what happened to Meg's arm when you bit her. It is red. She feels sad because her arm hurts. Let's get Meg some ice so her arm feels better."

Quantifying Emotions

We can also help children understand that all anger is not the same. Sometimes we are a little angry and sometimes we are ready to explode. The Anger Scale in Figure 6.2 is a useful tool to help children measure the level of emotion they are feeling. A child as young as three can recognize that she has more control over her behavior when her anger is at Level 2 than at Level 5. The first step is

FIGURE 6.2 Anger Scale

to explain the Anger Scale to children when they are calm, using examples from your own life or those of the children's. You can ask children to tell you about situations that led them to feel the various levels of anger. In a group discussion or individually, children can brainstorm ways that they can handle their feelings when they are at Level 3 or 4 or 5. Then, when a child is in the throes of an angry outburst, you can use this common language to guide effective responses, as Mr. Carl does in the following scenario:

> During circle time, Mr. Carl told the story of when, as a child, he wanted a toy and his mother would not let him have it. He explained that he felt very angry. He held up the Anger Scale and pointed to Level 5, like a volcano erupting. He asked the children to share stories about when they felt as angry as Level 5. The children took turns describing their actions when they were that angry and explored the consequent events. They brainstormed other choices they could have made that would have had better consequences. The group decided that at Levels 4 and 5, the top priority is to calm down by using deep breathing, getting a drink of water, squeezing and relaxing their muscles, counting to ten, or going to the quiet area. At lower levels, the children felt that they could try other strategies, such as talking about their feelings or drawing pictures.
>
> Later that day, Roger was upset because Jay wouldn't get off the fire engine. Mr. Carl asked Roger to point to how angry he was feeling on the scale and what he thought he needed to do to handle his feelings.

The Anger Scale can be adapted for other emotions. An Anxiety Scale or a Sad Scale can help children comprehend that emotions can be examined and behavioral responses can be actively selected.

Providing Outlets

People vary greatly in their preferred emotional outlets. Some people feel better when they talk or write about their experiences and feelings. Others favor physical activity, like dancing or running. Still others prefer artistic expression such as drawing, painting, sculpting, or making music. It is important for children to have an array of acceptable outlets available so when their emotions are aroused they have the means to self-regulate. Emotional expression goes hand in hand with emotional regulation. In later chapters, we will explore strategies for emotional expression that take coping style and preferences into account.

LOOKING IN THE MIRROR...

As an adult, how well do you delay gratification?

- When you have to wait in line at the bank or store, are you content to entertain yourself while you wait, or do you feel impatient and stressed?
- How can you guide children to use effective strategies to help them wait?
- What strategies do you use to resist temptation, like controlling the impulse to bite your nails or break a diet?
- How can you guide children to use strategies to control their impulses?
- When you are upset about a child's behavior, what strategies can you use to regulate your emotions?
- How can you guide children to use strategies to regulate their emotions?

Summary

When we reflect on our own journey of self-regulation development, we begin to comprehend the complexity and challenges that characterize this life-long process. Reflecting enables us to empathize with the difficulties faced by young children as they grapple with regulating their arousal, sensory input, attention, emotions, and behaviors. Children differ from one another in self-regulation capacity because of differences in their temperaments, brain maturation, and relationship histories. When put in this context, we can reframe their challenging behavior as opportunities to target specific self-regulation skills. The strategies described in this chapter are intended as suggestions or guidelines only. Each of us brings to our classroom a multitude of strategies from our own experiences and reflections that enable us to create environments, relationships, and activities that foster self-regulation in children.

Review and Apply

1. Describe the components of self-regulation and explain how temperament, brain maturation, and attachment relationships support or impede the development of self-regulation.
2. Kindergarteners Kai and Niki argue loudly, each asserting that *she* had the xylophone first. They began pushing each other and playing tug-of-war with the instrument.

   a. What are the underlying skills for which the girls need more support?
   b. Using the strategies discussed in this chapter, how would you help the girls resolve their conflict?

chapter 7

Fostering Autonomy: Wonder, Confidence, and Motivation

"I'm a kid, so I don't know very much, but I know that I wonder about everything."

—Tyrell, Age 6

After reading this chapter, you should be able to

- ▶ Explain why autonomy is important for children's development.
- ▶ Identify the three components of autonomy and describe the interplay among them.
- ▶ Explain how autonomy contributes to success in school and life.
- ▶ Describe how certain temperament dimensions, relationships, and other experiences contribute to differences in autonomy.
- ▶ Create strategies and practices to promote autonomy and its components in the early childhood setting.

"Me do it!" was Jessica's first sentence. When she wasn't digging for bugs on the playground or burrowing under piles of leaves, at age 2 Jessica was climbing on the kitchen counter to help herself to a banana. Her parents stayed nearby to keep her safe, but they supported her sense of adventure. Now in kindergarten, she "reads" to the class, theatrically describing the pictures and adding details that she creates from her imagination.

Jessica seems to have a drive for **autonomy**, *the ability to think for herself and govern her own decisions and direction.* She has the three fundamental qualities that underlie autonomy: wonder, confidence, and motivation. Some children like Jessica seem to come into the world booming with wonder, teeming with confidence, and bubbling over with motivation. Our job with those children is to guide their drive for autonomy into safe and positive channels. Other children are less eager to dive in and take charge for a variety of reasons. Our role with these children is to encourage and bolster the underlying qualities of wonder, confidence, and motivation that will support their developing autonomy. In the following scenario, Ms. Keisha prompts Javon's nascent sense of autonomy:

Javon watched his classmates as they eagerly unpacked the microscopes. "Let me see! Let me see!" the children shouted as one after another slipped premade slides under the scopes.

MS. KEISHA: "Javon, would you like to see what's on the slides?"

JAVON (LOOKING AT HIS SHOE): "I can't. There are too many people."

MS. KEISHA: "Yes, there are a lot of people. I wonder why they are so excited. Should we take a look?"

JAVON: "I guess."

MS. KEISHA: "OK, let's get in line behind Brandon so we can check it out. What do you think Brandon can see in that microscope? I wonder what it looks like?"

JAVON: "I don't know."

MS. KEISHA: "I don't know either, but what do you think it might look like? Can you guess what could be on that slide?"

JAVON: "It might be a bug. I don't know. It might be black."

MS. KEISHA: "Maybe. It might be a black bug. I don't know for sure either, but we'll find out soon. OK, it's our turn."

JAVON: "Wow! It's a fly's wing! I didn't know fly wings had little rectangles."

KEISHA: "I wonder if all fly wings have rectangles. How could we find out?"

Keisha recognized that Javon lacked the confidence and motivation to seek out new information and act on any sense of wonder that may be hiding inside. Keisha inspired Javon's autonomy by modeling her own wonderings and the steps she was taking to satisfy her curiosity.

THE IMPORTANCE OF AUTONOMY

Developmental psychologist Erik Erikson (1902–1994) devoted his life to understanding how children and adults grow socially and emotionally. Erikson's Psychosocial Stage theory of development says a great deal about the emergence of autonomy and its component parts. Erikson proposed that people go through a series of eight crises, or social tasks, throughout their lives, and the resolution of those crises is necessary for healthy development (Erikson, 1993). Table 7.1 shows Erikson's Psychosocial Stages. Erikson's first four stages are most relevant to the discussion of autonomy.

During the first year, according to Erikson's theory, infants learn that the world is safe and the people in their world will predictably meet their needs. This discovery assumes the infant is in healthy attachment relationships with her primary caregivers. With successful resolution of this Trust vs. Mistrust stage, the child will gain the sense that she can have an impact on the world and can get her needs met. During the second and third years, the child's new cognitive capacities enable her to pursue goals, express her needs and ideas directly, and make choices. Her physical skills allow her the mobility necessary to explore her surroundings and master self-care skills, such as toileting. Successful resolution of the Autonomy vs. Shame and Doubt stage results in a sense of independence or autonomy.

Erikson's third proposed stage, occurring between ages 3 and 6, is called Initiative vs. Guilt, characterized by a child's newfound abilities to assert himself and organize multistep activities around a goal. Successful completion of this stage results in an increasing sense of purpose. And fourth, Industry

TABLE 7.1 • Erikson's Psychosocial Stages

Age	Stage	Outcome	Example
Birth–1 year	Trust vs. Mistrust	Hope	Maggie knows that when she is upset, Mommy will comfort her.
1–3 years	Autonomy vs. Shame and Doubt	Independence	Billy takes a book off the shelf and sits down to look at pages.
3–6 years	Initiative vs. Guilt	Purpose	Billy proudly finishes a challenging puzzle.
6–12 years	Industry vs. Inferiority	Competence	Maggie writes a play for herself and her friends to act out for their parents.
12–18 years	Identity vs. Role Confusion	Fidelity	Bill, a math lover, gets a job as an intern for an accounting firm.
18–30 years	Intimacy vs. Isolation	Love	Bill and Maggie fall in love and get married.
30–late adult	Generativity vs. Stagnation	Care	Bill and Maggie balance childrearing with their accounting and law practices.
Late adulthood	Ego Integrity vs. Despair	Wisdom	Bill and Maggie retire and start a foundation for the community.

Based on Erikson, E. (1993). Childhood and Society (2nd ed.). New York: W. W. Norton, Inc.

vs. Inferiority, characteristic of children from six to twelve years old, is the stage when children master more sophisticated skills in their areas of interest. Successful resolution of this stage is said to result in a sense of competence. Research confirms that most children around the world progress more or less through these stages and supports the notion that wonder, confidence, and motivation work in concert in the development of autonomy, though the terms to describe the process may differ slightly.

Cultural Considerations

It should be noted that in some cultures, autonomy is not valued as highly as it is in the American culture and, in fact, might be discouraged in young children. The United States was founded on principles of individual freedom and responsibility. The Declaration of Independence expressly states the following:

> We hold these truths to be self-evident, that all men are created equal, that they are endowed by their Creator with certain unalienable Rights, that among these are Life, Liberty and the pursuit of Happiness.

Our national script declares that we are free to take our happiness into our own hands and urges us to do so. In many cultures, however, other values take precedence over autonomy, such as responsibility to the community and interdependence among its members. We must always keep in mind that some families might not encourage self-direction and independence, and we must respect the values of the families represented in our programs. With that caveat, we explore the development of autonomy and its three important ingredients.

COMPONENTS OF AUTONOMY: WONDER, CONFIDENCE, AND MOTIVATION

What do you wonder about? Do you wonder how things work? Do you wonder why people do the things they do? Do you wonder about the meaning of life? These questions have inspired brilliant engineering feats, philosophical theories, religious beliefs, and innumerable works of art. **Wonder** is *a feeling of surprise and awe caused by something unexpected, unfamiliar, or inexplicable.* When we wonder, we are compelled to explore so that we can understand the world better. Wonder is like curiosity with a dash of amazement.

Wonder is a universal experience that can be seen in babies from the very beginning. A newborn is fascinated by the objects that cross his visual path and is particularly in awe when those objects are human faces. As soon as he is physically able, he will reach for objects so he can learn about their shape and texture. He will crawl under and over obstacles to learn about relationships among objects and eventually he'll climb and run to discover more.

Another important ingredient of autonomy is confidence. **Confidence** refers to *the belief in oneself and one's abilities or power*. For a child to be willing to explore his world or do things on his own, he must believe that his actions will make a positive difference. Evidence suggests that a child's **self-theory**, or *belief about himself*, is extremely important in determining whether he tries new things and persists in difficult tasks (Dweck, 2000). Children are more likely to approach challenging tasks when they are **mastery-oriented**—that is, *when they believe that their success on a task is within their control and that with effort, their skills will improve*. Mastery-oriented children believe that intelligence is not fixed and they have the power to increase it. In contrast, some children are **helpless** in their orientation. They *believe that a person's innate intelligence determines success or failure on a task, and that one has a certain unchangeable level of intelligence and there is nothing he or she can do to change it*. Mistakes and setbacks are considered failures of the person due to not having enough intelligence as opposed to indications that the person must put forth more effort (Dweck, 2000). The different responses of five-year-olds Jared and Julie illustrate this distinction:

> Jared, Julie, and Marc were playing Memory with a pack of forty animal cards. The children took turns turning over two cards at a time to see if they matched. At the end of the game, Julie had three matches, Jared had three matches, and Marc won handily with fourteen matched pairs.
>
> Jared crossed his arms, furrowed his brow, and stomped his foot, "I'm so dumb. I hate this game. I can't play it!"
>
> In contrast, Julie looked at the small stack of cards that she had earned and said, "I'm going to have to pay more attention. Maybe I should watch more carefully when you guys turn over your cards. I'll have to work on that."

Is Marc smarter than Julie and Jared because he won the game? Or did Marc concentrate harder and pay more attention to the task at hand? Jared's helplessness relates to his belief that the outcome of the game depends on his innate intelligence, or lack of it. Julie believes that her effort and concentration were the problems and that she can improve by using the strategy of watching the other players as they turn over cards. Julie has the confidence to know that her actions matter and that she can improve. Jared's defeat diminishes his confidence because he believes that there is nothing he can do to improve his performance.

It is interesting to note that praising a child's intelligence or work product has been found to hinder self-confidence in children. Research suggests that praising a child's *effort* and strategic thinking is more likely to build confidence and motivation than praising the child's intelligence or his finished product (Dweck, 2000; Dweck, 1999; Bronson & Merryman, 2009).

This finding leads us to the third ingredient necessary for a child's developing autonomy: motivation. **Motivation**, or **mastery motivation** refers to *a* *psychological force that stimulates an individual to attempt independently, in a focused and persistent manner, to solve a problem or master a skill or task that is at least moderately challenging for him or her* (Morgan, Harmon, & Maslin-Cole, 1990; Hauser-Cram & Mitchell, 2009). Just like with wonder, children are innately motivated to explore the world and master new skills. *When a person is purely motivated by the sheer pleasure of learning or doing*, like most children are from the start, we refer to it as **intrinsic motivation**. In contrast, **extrinsic motivation** refers to *one's willingness to apply himself to a task* only *with the promise or expectation of an external reward*. How we respond to a child's pursuit of tasks can inspire or diminish his intrinsic motivation.

Carol Dweck and her colleagues have conducted several experiments in which children performed tasks and were either praised for their intelligence ("You got *x* correct; you must be smart."), for their effort ("You got *x* correct; you must have worked really hard."), or for their finished product, with no praise for effort or intelligence. Children who were praised for their effort were significantly more likely to take on increasingly challenging tasks. Children who were praised for their intelligence were unwilling to take on more difficult tasks, presumably because setbacks or task failures were taken personally and were perceived to be a reflection on their intelligence. In other words, if they perform poorly, it must be because they are dumb. Only the children praised for their effort demonstrated the motivation to pursue more challenging endeavors (Dweck, 1999).

Ms. Denise understands the benefits of acknowledging a child's effort and strategies instead of a seemingly immutable trait like intelligence, as can be seen in the following scenario:

> Six-year-old Barry brought to class an intricate birdhouse he fashioned with craft sticks and toothpicks. Clearly, he had spent a great deal of time on his project. Ms. Denise and the children were impressed. Rather than tell Barry that he is a terrific woodcrafter or how nice was the birdhouse, she said, "Wow, Barry! It looks like you spent a lot of time working on the details of that birdhouse. How did you know how to make that?" Barry beamed with pride and explained his strategy of beginning with the inside details and then putting the craft-stick siding around it. Inspired by Ms. Denise's line of inquiry, the children took turns asking Barry about the design and other phases of his construction. By focusing on Barry's strategies and effort, all of the children got the message that thinking, planning, and putting forth careful effort are highly valued activities.

Over the past several decades, countless articles in popular magazines have advised parents and teachers to be very generous with praise, stickers, and other rewards. Awards Day in elementary schools can last hours because every child has to get some sort of award for just about everything. Many classrooms have star or point charts where children can earn points and cash them in for small prizes. They are encouraged to accumulate external rewards. Inevitably, a class has an impulsive child or a bored child with incomplete work who is publicly humiliated by her lack of points because the chart is posted for all to see. Sometimes such children can earn a consolation prize for committing an act that implies very low expectations, such as the "nice friend" award.

An insightful eight-year-old recently described the token economy at her school. In this token economy, the second-graders earn funny money for achievement or appropriate behavior. With their earnings children may buy prizes. They also "lose money if they are bad." When asked if anyone in the class was "bad," she listed four "bad children" who rarely earn or keep money for prizes. Already in second grade, their peers and teachers have pegged these children as "bad children" and more than likely that is how they see themselves. At best, such reward systems replace children's intrinsic motivation with extrinsic motivation. At worst, they crush motivation altogether. Two excellent expositions on effective motivation strategies and the negative impact of global praise and external rewards are *Mindset* (Dweck, 2006) and *Nurture Shock* (Bronson & Merryman, 2009).

Interplay among Wonder, Confidence, and Motivation

How do wonder, confidence, and motivation work together to contribute to autonomy? Wonder is universal and innate, as described earlier. For a child to pursue the quest for knowledge propelled by wonder, he must have the belief that he is capable of mastering the task of discovery. When a person

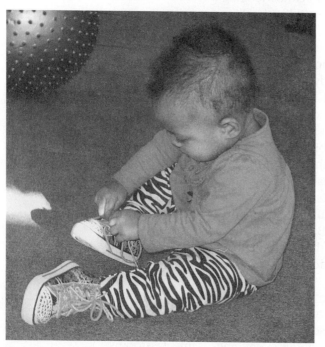

wonders about something and believes that he lacks the ability to learn about it, he is unlikely to try. This sense of hopelessness hinders his motivation. This idea can be described as, "If I believe that my efforts to discover something won't make a difference, why should I even bother? If I have the belief that discovery and mastery are within my power, I will be motivated to find ways to satisfy my curiosity." Unfortunately, many children have lost their sense of autonomy—their intrinsic wonder, confidence, and motivation—before they even begin elementary school. Just count the times each day that you hear a young child say, "I can't," and " I don't know," without pursuing an answer. In this chapter, we discuss ways to encourage autonomy and its three essential ingredients.

HOW SUCCESS IN SCHOOL AND LIFE DEPENDS ON AUTONOMY

All the ingredients of autonomy, a sense of wonder, confidence, and motivation, are necessary for children to succeed in school and in life. According to Pam Schiller, a leading expert on school success, two of the most important qualities a child needs to succeed in school are confidence and curiosity, here used synonymously with wonder. Confidence enables children to overcome obstacles they encounter and find new ways to solve problems. Curiosity drives intellect and encourages exploration, experimentation, and more wonder (Schiller, 2009). Child mental health expert Bruce Perry describes a path that brings a child from his initial curiosity through exploration and discovery, to the pleasure of mastery of new skills, which builds confidence and ultimately leads to greater curiosity and more exploration (Perry, 2001). Every step along this path increases autonomy.

Even before elementary school, a child's pursuit of new learning and work completion require self-direction and self-governance. For example, to tackle a simple puzzle, a child must be confident enough to apply known concepts such as shape and color to the task at hand. She must believe that her actions will make a difference to justify putting forth the necessary effort. To complete multiple steps, she must have the confidence to know that by doing so, she will reach the desired goal. All new learning requires confidence and motivation, especially when the material is not intrinsically interesting to the child.

School success also requires a certain amount of **creativity**, *the ability to generate new ideas or combinations of ideas to solve problems or develop new forms.* Creativity requires taking risks, and risk-taking depends on confidence. In this sense, the child must be confident that the new idea has merit, that it might possibly fail, and that if it fails, she can cope and/or come up with something else. Her ability to try out her ideas and rethink them if they don't succeed is considered cognitive flexibility and is a very important aspect of autonomy. To quote Robert F. Kennedy in his June 6, 1966, address in South Africa, *"Only those who dare to fail greatly can ever achieve greatly"* (Kennedy, 1966).

Autonomy is important in the workplace as well. The success of an organization or company depends on its employees' motivation and abilities to take initiative, think for themselves, and make good decisions independently (Pink, 2009). These skills do not just appear when a person enters the workforce, but rather must be nurtured and supported throughout the childhood years.

Healthy relationships also rely on the components of autonomy. It is through wonder that people are inspired to get to know each other. Relationships are enhanced when people are genuinely interested in each other enough to observe and ask about the other's thoughts, feelings, preferences, interests, talents, needs, and desires. Four-year-olds Clive and Lon provide a good example of wonder, confidence, and motivation in action as they become friends:

> Lon was new to this preschool and Clive had been there since toddlerhood.
>
> CLIVE: "Hi. I'm Clive. You're new here. What's your name?"
>
> LON: "Lon. We just moved to a new house."
>
> CLIVE: "Where did you live before?"
>
> LON: "In Quincy. It's far away. Did you always live here?"
>
> CLIVE: "Yes. I've been at this school a long time. Do you like army guys?"
>
> LON: "Yeah, do you?"
>
> CLIVE: "Yep. Want to go play with them?"
>
> LON: "Yes! Let's go!"

In the absence of wonder, confidence, and motivation, the preceding conversation would never have occurred. Clive autonomously acted on his wonder about the new classmate. He and Lon both felt confident enough to engage in a new friendship and motivated enough to find common ground on which to begin their relationship.

EXPLAINING DIFFERENCES IN THE CAPACITY FOR AUTONOMY

Not all children demonstrate autonomy as well as Clive and Lon. Children vary widely in their ability and willingness to embrace new experiences and relationships. Three factors that explain the variability among children in their level of autonomy are temperament, attachment/relationship history, and experience.

Temperament

If you have ever been lucky enough to work with multiple infants over a period of time, you can attest to how temperament contributes to autonomy. One baby reaches for anything that moves while another watches passively. One thinks that guests are fascinating while another cries. Three dimensions of temperament are particularly involved in the development of autonomy. These dimensions are the child's initial reaction to a new situation (approach/withdrawal), adaptability, and persistence (Thomas & Chess, 1977).

A child's initial reaction to new and unfamiliar situations can be characterized by his tendency to approach the new stimulus or avoid it. Ten to 20 percent of young children appear to have the temperamental bias toward avoidance of unfamiliar situations. Researchers refer to these children as "inhibited to the unfamiliar." In contrast, 30–40 percent of children show a bias toward approaching the unfamiliar, called "uninhibited" (Kagan, 2005). There is evidence that the behavioral inhibition often identified as fear has, at its core, an intolerance for uncertainty rather than fear itself (Kagan & Snidman, 2004). So when you see inhibited behavior, you may consider gently prompting approach behavior by giving the child information about what to expect and imagery cues to reduce the uncertainty in a new situation. For example, you can say to a child who is inhibited about a field trip, "First, we will get our coats like we always do. Then you and your friends will walk in a line to the yellow bus. I will take your hand as we get on the bus, and then you and Cleo will sit in the same seat on the bus because Cleo is your partner. Next, you and Cleo and the rest of us will get off the bus and walk into the museum where a nice man will stay with us while we walk around the museum." This description allows the child to create a visual image of what he can expect in the unfamiliar situation.

A temperament dimension that is similar to initial reaction is **adaptability**, which refers to *how quickly and readily a child adjusts to a new or changed situation*. The child may be either resistant to change or he may easily settle into a new routine. Change is an inevitable part of life, and only about 40 percent of children score high in measures of adaptability (Thomas & Chess, 1977). Change is difficult for so many people that an entire self-help industry has emerged to help people cope with change. Adults who have difficulty with adaptability might enjoy reading *Who Moved My Cheese?*, a delightful guide with useful strategies for coping with change (Johnson, 1998). Again, by giving children information and strategies for adjusting to new situations and activities, you can ease the minds of children who have low adaptability.

Persistence is a temperament dimension that facilitates autonomy and refers to *the capacity to sustain attention to the task at hand for a sufficient amount of time to attain a goal*. Children vary a great deal in the length of time they can sustain their effort and focus to accomplish a goal. Early educators see these differences every day. One child works and reworks and reworks the puzzle pieces until they fit, while his classmate throws the pieces on the floor, finds something else to do, or walks away in frustration. One child painstakingly works to sound out word after word in a story, while another complains, "I can't read this!"

We can modify the environment in many ways to help children whose temperamental qualities result in challenges to autonomy. We discuss possible environmental modifications in the section about promoting autonomy in the classroom.

Attachment and Other Relationships

When an infant is securely attached, he is gradually able to move farther and farther away from the caregiver to explore his environment. The caregiver is considered a secure base from whom the child can venture out to explore and a safe haven to whom he can return for reassurance if he feels uncertain (Powell, et al., 2009). At the same time as he is venturing toward new and interesting discoveries, the securely attached child is looking back at his caregiver. *The act of looking back at the attachment figure for reassurance and approval* is called **social referencing** (Walden, 1991).

Most young children have secure attachment relationships with their primary caregivers (van IJzendoorn & Kroonenberg, 1988). Several types of insecure attachment can also result from inconsistent or unresponsive caregiving. It is beyond the scope of this book to detail those relationships. For our purposes, though, it is important to know that the quality of a child's attachment relationship with his primary caregiver will impact his relationships with other caregiving adults and his confidence to explore.

Young children can have attachment relationships with multiple caregivers, such as grandparents and child-care providers. The feature of those relationships that is most important for secure attachment is emotional responsiveness. When an infant cries, it's his way of saying he has an unmet need. Responsive caregiving means responding to that need as quickly and warmly as possible. As the baby gets older, the caregiver can give him a brief opportunity to try to calm himself before comforting him. It is not the case that going to the child immediately will spoil him, as some believe. In fact, after repeated experiences of having his needs addressed in response to his signals, the child will feel secure in his ability to affect others by communicating and this security will foster his increasing drive for autonomy.

The Role of Experience in Promoting Autonomy

Jessica, described at the beginning of this chapter, exemplifies a child with a strong sense of autonomy. She obviously entered the world with a temperament characterized by high levels of approach, adaptability, persistence, and activity. It can be assumed that she had positive attachment relationships with her primary and other caregivers. With that support, she developed the confidence to pursue the adventures of her *wonders*. The following vignette describes another child, Tilly, who was born with a similar temperament to Jessica's but whose environment was not conducive to promoting her autonomy:

> At five months, a very curious Tilly would often reach for objects and bring them to her mouth to explore their texture and form. Her mother, very anxious about germs, pulled them quickly from Tilly's little hands and told her, "Icky! Don't touch that!" On the six-block walk to child care at age 2, Tilly often stopped to pick a blade of grass growing through the sidewalk cracks or toddle toward the neighbor's flowers for a sniff. Her mother would pull her back to her side, expressing her concern about being late or getting dirty. Tilly was fascinated by the books in her two-year-old room at child care, but her teacher was worried that the children would tear the pages, so they were kept on a high shelf until the teacher had time to read them to the children. The teachers in the four-year-old classroom frequently corrected Tilly for coloring flowers black and cats purple because, after all, the teacher never experienced black flowers or purple cats as Tilly had in her imagination.
>
> The consequences of these early experiences were evident in kindergarten. Tilly's teacher enjoyed taking the children on bug hunts in the forest behind the school, but by age 5, Tilly had been convinced that bugs are "icky and dirty." Countless books about bugs and

every other subject were accessible to the children, but Tilly did not approach those low shelves.

The responses of Tilly's caregivers over time diminished her natural quest for autonomy. A few simple restrictions would not be enough to diminish a child's developing autonomy and, in fact, are necessary to keep children safe. Rather it is a caregiving or teaching pattern of prohibition and restriction that can limit the child's quest for autonomy. A child's life experiences will either reinforce or crush her sense of wonder, confidence, and motivation.

Learning theorist Albert Bandura coined the term **reciprocal determinism** to describe *the interactive forces of person components (cognitive and emotional factors), environmental reinforcers, and behavior on the development of personality*. Reciprocal determinism, according to Bandura, is a key element in personality development, especially with respect to the emerging sense of competence and autonomy (Bandura, 1989). Jessica and Tilly have similar *person components* in that their temperaments were very much alike and they are presumably equally bright. Jessica's environmental reinforcers, in the form of encouragement and permission, served to propel her toward discovery, while Tilly's reinforcers, in the form of restriction and correction, discouraged exploration and discovery. As a result, their behavior patterns, and thus the trajectory of their development of autonomy, were markedly different by as young as age 5.

Children also differ in their level of autonomy because of the relative presence or absence of opportunities for exploration. An environment that is baby proof or child safe is one where potentially dangerous, breakable, or otherwise age-inappropriate items are out of reach and out of sight. When safe, developmentally appropriate items are freely accessible, the child can explore unencumbered by the anxious warnings of caregiving adults. When the environment cannot be so controlled, such as the sidewalk or a neighbor's house, exploration can occur when the adults provide necessary limits, guidance, and support, as can be seen in the following example:

The two-year-olds were taking a walk around the subdivision on a beautiful spring day. After a considerable rain, the blooming flowers were begging to be smelled and the puddles were beckoning the children to splash and frolic. With three teachers for fifteen children, keeping the children safe and dry was a challenge. The children each held the hand of a classmate. Three children who needed extra protection held the hands of the teachers. Ms. Ramona and Jimmy led the group singing a song to the tune of "Hi ho, hi ho, it's off to work I go!" and changed the words to, "Hi ho, hi ho, it's around the puddle I go." When the opportunity to stop for a flower sniff came along, the words became, "Hi ho, hi ho, I love to smell a rose (or petunia or lily)," and the children took turns smelling the flowers.

By turning their temptations into enjoyable opportunities for exploration, the children were assured that they could satisfy their wonder without

LOOKING IN THE MIRROR...

- As a child, were your independent efforts to explore encouraged?
- Did your family and teachers ask what you wondered about?
- In your daily work today, are you encouraged to think independently, or are you expected to follow precise guidelines or standards imposed by others?
- Among your peers, are you more or less likely to be the one who comes up with new activities, adventures, or ideas?
- Among your peers, are you more or less likely to stay close to the routine you know, with the people you know, in the places you know?
- Do you embrace change or resist it?
- What strategies can you use to support a child who is reluctant to explore and try new things?

None of the answers to these questions is right or wrong, better or worse. Reflecting on your answers to these questions, however, will help you plan your approach to supporting autonomy in children. If you are thrilled by novelty and variety, you might find it difficult to motivate a child who is reticent about trying new things. Similarly, if you are reluctant to face change or try new experiences, you may have difficulty understanding a child who is compelled to seek out novelty. Remember, the discrepancy between the child's sense of autonomy and your own can be challenging for both you *and* the child. On the same token, you may be one of the few people who can work effectively with a child whose drive for autonomy matches your own.

reprimand. Early educators can keep a child's intrinsic motivation alive by creating environments and routines designed with their drive for autonomy in mind.

What are you passionate about? In *The Element*, the groundbreaking essay on transforming educational systems, Sir Ken Robinson describes countless individuals whose natural passions and talents were not only untapped throughout their formal schooling years but often discouraged (Robinson & Aronica, 2009). For example, Paul McCartney of the Beatles went all the way through school without knowing he had any musical talent at all and was, in fact, rejected by the Liverpool Choir because he couldn't sing well enough (p. 11). It was only by leaving the limitations of formal schooling that he was able to become one of the most successful musicians of several generations. Formal schooling increasingly focuses on math,

LOOKING IN THE MIRROR...

- What are you passionate about as an adult?
- What talents do you have that your coworkers have never seen or heard?
- When you were a child, were your passions and talents supported and encouraged?
- Are your passions and talents encouraged today?
- How do you encourage the unique passions and talents of the children in your care?

LOOKING IN THE MIRROR...

By looking at the origins of our own doubts and areas of confidence, we can use those insights to guide our interactions with children:

- What factors contributed to your level of confidence?
- When you were young, how did the caregiving adults handle your mistakes?
- Were mistakes seen as opportunities for improvement or character flaws?
- When you made mistakes, were you inspired by the challenge of self-improvement or were you more inclined to give up for fear of repeating mistakes?
- What did your parents or teachers do that increased your sense of autonomy and what did they do that decreased it?
- How can you use those experiences to promote wonder, confidence, and motivation in children?

language, and science at the expense of the arts and other creative endeavors, so as an adult and a professional, you may have to look deep within yourself to get in touch with that little girl or boy inside to rediscover your passions.

Adults vary in the degree of comfort they feel in certain situations. In the early childhood field, for example, it is often the case that teachers feel completely at peace when they are interacting with little children. As parent-teacher conference day approaches or when having to discuss a concern with parents, however, some educators become very anxious. One young and gifted teacher told this author, "I do this work because I love to be with kids and I'm good at it. I'm just not crazy about grown-ups." Like it or not, all little children come with at least one grown-up. Some professionals are perfectly at ease with parents and others are seized with doubt. Some love to speak in front of groups of adults, while others are terrified by the prospect.

PRACTICES TO PROMOTE AUTONOMY IN THE EARLY CHILDHOOD SETTING

With our self-reflection as the backdrop, we now have the opportunity to capitalize on the best from our childhood experiences and discard the practices that were ineffective or counterproductive. We can promote autonomy by focusing on the unique attributes of each child, creating autonomy-friendly environments and experiences, and modeling wonder, confidence, and motivation.

Getting to Know Each and Every Child

Everybody is born with tremendous potential in a limitless number of areas. Every now and then, we hear about a four-year-old piano virtuoso, a fifth-grader with a flawless memory, or a prodigy whose brilliance earned her a

PhD at age 18. But most people have a pattern of strengths and weaknesses that fluctuates closely around an average level for their age. The thing is, we often don't know the limits of a child's capacity in many areas because we simply don't place value on those areas in many early childhood programs.

With the increasing emphasis on testing, it is not uncommon for educators to teach to the standards by which a child will be tested and schools will be evaluated. Many early childhood classrooms have replaced play and discovery experiences with relatively mechanized exercises devoid of creativity, such as worksheets and teacher-directed art. For example, one preschool class learned about ladybugs because the state standards *recommend* they have a unit on insects in the spring. After reading a book about ladybugs, the teacher gave each child one big red circle, four small black circles, and two buttons for the eyes. She dabbed glue on each child's red circle and instructed the children to put the black circles and buttons on the glue. All the *ladybugs* looked exactly the same as they hung on the wall for all to see. The problem is, the children learned nothing about ladybugs. The teacher learned nothing about the children's interests, talents, or passions. Had she read the ladybug story, engaged the children in a conversation about ladybugs, and made accessible the paper, cotton, buttons, glue, scissors, and other material, her wall display would have looked completely different and the learning experience would have been much richer for all. She might have discovered the presence of an entomologist, a surgeon, an artist, or a naturalist in her midst.

Early education should be customized to match the interests (wonderings) of each child. This customization requires a great deal of observation on the part of educators. But beware. Your observations are seen through the lens of your beliefs, expectations, and biases. I have been called in as a behavior consultant many times to help parents and teachers *handle* a child who "does not listen." By "does not listen," we usually mean "does not do what I, the adult, tell him to do." But before discussing what the child is *not* doing, I ask what the child actually *is doing* instead. Here are some of the common responses, with the consultant's observations in parentheses:

"He is unraveling the carpet during circle time." (He is studying how fibers are woven to make carpet.)

"He dumps out the glue and it gets all over." (He is learning about quantity, gravity, and viscosity.)

"He is walking aimlessly around the room." (He thinks best when he's moving and likes to explore.)

"He's playing in the block area and that has not been selected [by the teacher] as an open activity." (He wants to create something.)

"He is talking during story time." (He has something to say that's interesting to him.)

Each of these children is doing something that is natural for him, probably more natural than the request made by the adult. Yes, children do

need to learn to follow rules, but perhaps the teacher-selected activities or
circle-time topics are uninteresting and
uninspiring to this child. If you listen
and watch carefully, you will discover
what the child is passionate about, what
he wonders, and what motivates him. If
you redefine his "disruptive" or "uncooperative" behavior as "a piece of information about what moves the child,"
you may be able to customize learning experiences to optimize the child's
potential. If the behavior is disruptive,
your role is to acknowledge the meaningfulness of the behavior and help the
child find opportunities to fulfill his curiosity or pursue his desired activity in a
more appropriate way.

Providing Experiences That Promote Autonomy

At each age and developmental level, we can create an atmosphere and offer
activities that support confident exploration. Infants explore objects by putting them in their mouth, shaking them, banging them, dropping them, and
otherwise moving them to learn about their properties. Toddlers like to carry
and push objects. They like to climb in, on, under, and through obstacles.
Preschoolers are fascinated by how objects and concepts fit together. So for
every age level, safe, clean, and developmentally appropriate materials need to
be accessible so children can explore autonomously.

    Early childhood classrooms should be filled with opportunities for children to
engage in activities that stir their wonderings. For example, peek-a-boo is the ulti-
mate *wonder* experience for babies. Piaget would tell us that peek-a-boo is a measure of a child's increasing awareness of **object permanence**, or *knowing that an
object exists even when it is out of sight* (Piaget, 1972). For a young infant, when
an object leaves his line of sight, it's as good as gone. By seven months, when an
object is hidden, like when you put your hands in front of your face, the baby is
fascinated by its disappearance and delighted by its reappearance when you move
your hands away and say "peek-a-boo." Infants and toddlers can seemingly play
peek-a-boo forever, so we can create a variety of hiding-and-finding games to support this universal wondering.

    Young children also need opportunities to get messy in safe ways so they
can discover the pros and cons of approaching certain attractions. It only takes
one mouthful of sand for most children to realize that it's a bad idea to eat sand.
Teachers of young children often pour the glue, paint, and sprinkles themselves
to avoid a big clean-up job and a waste of materials. This inclination makes

sense, but keep in mind that a good way for a child to learn about appropriate quantity is to let him use too much and then have to work with a mess, clean it up, and not have enough for next time.

We promote autonomy when we offer children choices of how they can spend their time. The choices should not be unlimited because that would be overwhelming for most children. In the following scenario, Ms. Marcia engages the entire group of four-year-olds in the decision about the activities from which they would like to choose:

MS. MARCIA: "Children, we have 45 minutes before lunch. What are some of the things you'd like to do? Doug, you have your hand up."

DOUG: "We need to finish our village, so we need the blocks and the railroad tracks."
Several classmates nodded.

MS. MARCIA: "Yes, you've been working on that for a long time. What else, kids?"

EVAN: "We need the kitchen center because we have our pizza restaurant."

MS. MARCIA: "Oh, yes, the pizza! Other areas?"

PAOLO: "I'd like to paint."

MS. MARCIA: "I bet a few of you would like to paint. Sounds good. Is there anything else, or does that sound like enough?"

DOMI: "How about the sand table? We haven't done that in a while."

MS. MARCIA: "Class? The sand table?"
They all nodded.

MS. MARCIA: "OK, so we have blocks, tracks, kitchen, paint, and sand table. Is that the right number of activities? Is it too much or do we need more?"

SEVERAL CHILDREN: "That's enough."

MS. MARCIA: "OK, now go for it!"

The children dispersed and moved toward their preferred activity. Eight children approached the sand table and began to argue about who got there first.

It is often the case that that when you give young children choices, conflicts will arise. These challenges provide perfect opportunities to engage the children in genuine conflict resolution and problem solving. One very meaningful strategy for promoting autonomy is to create or take advantage of genuine problems to negotiate and solve. In the preceding example, the children found that eight children would be too many to be at the sand table at the same time. Ms. Marcia expected that result:

MS. MARCIA: "Hmm. I see that all eight of you would like to play at the sand table. Is that going to work?"

CHILDREN: "No. That's too many!"

MS. MARCIA: "So all of you would like to play here, but eight is too many. How many children would be the best number here?"

RANDI: "We usually have four and that seems good." The children nodded.

MS. MARCIA: "So who should be the four?"

DOMI: "I should go first because it was my idea."

MS. MARCIA: "Kids, does that sound fair to you?"

CHILDREN: "I should go first, too!"

MS. MARCIA: "So, lots of you think you should go first. Have we solved our problem?"

CHILDREN: "No."

MS. MARCIA: "But the idea that some go first and some go later is the idea of taking turns. Do we like the idea of taking turns?"

CHILDREN: "Yes."

MS. MARCIA: "How can we decide?" The children shrugged their shoulders. Ms. Marcia thought they could use some guidance. "Sometimes it works well when the people who wait for the second round get a longer turn. What do you think of that idea?" Everybody seemed to like that idea.

Several children said they would rather wait for the longer turn and went to play elsewhere. Three children stayed for the first round at the sand table.

Many aspects of Marcia's classroom approach promote autonomy. First, the children selected the activities from which they would choose. Second, the children created a genuine problem for themselves, and Ms. Marcia, tempting as it was, did not solve the problem for them but, instead, guided the children to solve the problem themselves. Third, she gave them the opportunity to make decisions that might not work and then figure out why they didn't work and what to do about the remaining predicament.

Finally, the children in Marcia's class are obviously given a variety of opportunities for long-range projects, such as the design of an elaborate village that they could revisit and the establishment of a pizza restaurant. Many other activities can involve complex, multistep learning processes that occur over time. Two such activities might be growing plants from seeds and observing the metamorphosis of a caterpillar into a butterfly (or a tadpole into a frog). Projects that last days or weeks increase children's level of engagement in the process of learning (Hyson, 2008; Helm & Katz, 2011).

Modeling the Language of Autonomy

When we use reflective language in the presence of young children, we model an essential skill that can guide their interactions with the world for the rest their lives. Earlier in this chapter, we described the ways Ms. Keisha drew Javon into exploring with microscopes by modeling the language of wonder. Initially, he was reluctant to approach the task, but Ms. Keisha's enthusiasm and wonder motivated him to try. He often said, "I don't know." Rather than leave it at that, Ms. Keisha persisted by saying, "I don't know either, but what do you think?" Javon was able to see that his thoughts were meaningful and valid even if he didn't know the answer, which increased his confidence and motivation.

When you think aloud through a problem, you demonstrate multiple ways of handling life's ups and downs and that a person may choose from alternatives. It is OK and even recommended that teachers ponder aloud about minor issues, as Ms. Donna does in the following vignette:

> "We just got back from the butterfly park and it would be fun to read about butterflies. We have three butterfly books but only five minutes before lunch. The one you children have enjoyed over and over would take much longer to read than five minutes. We could read part of it now and finish it later. Or we could read the shorter book and finish the whole thing. What are your thoughts?"

Classroom Management vs. Promoting Autonomy

A child-directed classroom is one that promotes autonomy and independent thinking. This experience can be intimidating or uncomfortable for a teacher who believes that he or she needs to be in control of the children's activities, learning, and behavior. It can get messy and it can be unpredictable. Children need choices and it is helpful to limit the number of choices given to children to a level that is comfortable for you. Sometimes teachers offer young children the opportunity to solve their own problems or resolve their own conflicts, and the results are remarkably unsuccessful. For example, in the sand table experience described earlier, the children might have pouted, demanded, or become physical with each other. It is tempting at these times for the teacher to take over and declare a solution. On the contrary, it is more productive to slow the process, break it down into more manageable parts, and support the children's emerging negotiation skills with more targeted scaffolding. With repeated experiences of this kind, children soon learn to manage themselves effectively and autonomously. This approach is not easy for many of us. It takes as much practice by the teacher as it does by the children.

Summary

Autonomy is important for success in school, relationships, and life. The three ingredients of autonomy—wonder, confidence, and motivation—interact continuously to enable children to engage in increasingly complex experiences with more and more independence. Every child enters the world programmed to wonder and discover. It is our responsibility as early educators to support that discovery and not diminish it with our efforts to direct, control, and standardize. By creating opportunities for children to experience the world in their own ways, make decisions, solve problems, and make mistakes, we are promoting autonomy. When we find this to be difficult, it means we must reflect on the source of our discomfort and provide slower, more deliberate, and more targeted support so that the children can succeed in managing themselves.

Review and Apply

1. Describe how biological and experiential factors contribute to the three components of autonomy.
2. Taylor refuses to play in the sandbox, will not go down the slide, and follows you like a shadow on the playground.

a. What information do you need to understand Taylor's reticent behavior?

b. What strategies can you use to increase Taylor's sense of autonomy and its ingredients of wonder, motivation, and confidence?

PART 3 SUMMARY

Building Emotional Competence

Children need to be able to bring an optimal level of arousal and enthusiasm into play to grow and thrive. These are the skills of emotional competence: self-regulation and autonomy. To interact effectively with the world, a child must be able to cope with sensory input, pay sufficient attention to important tasks, manage the emotions that come with life's ups and downs, and behave in ways that meet his needs without interfering with the well-being of others. Some children need more support than others in accomplishing these self-regulation goals because of their unique temperament profile, brain maturation, and experiences. By recognizing that self-regulation skills develop in a progression like any other skill, we can tailor a child's experiences to support the emergence of these vital capacities and strengthen them through targeted activities.

Self-regulation is only part of the emotional development story. Children need the wonder, the motivation, and the confidence to explore their world. These are the ingredients for a sense of autonomy. Babies are hardwired to wonder and programmed to discover new things. Our role is to encourage this natural tendency by creating safe and authentic opportunities for exploration and discovery. We must resist the temptation to solve their problems for them and not get drawn into mechanistic approaches to teaching that squelch their sense of wonder. It is competence in these two sets of emotional skills that will propel them to greater and greater heights throughout their lives.

part 4

· ·

Reflective Support of Social Skills

· ·

"No man is an island entire of itself; every man is a piece of the continent, a part of the main."

—John Donne, Meditation XVII (1839)

· ·

In the discussion about culture, we explored distinctions between individualistic and collectivistic ways of life. In truth, these dimensions are on a continuum with greater or lesser emphasis depending on circumstances. In Part 3, we looked at essential emotional skills, and in Part 4, we will explore important social skills, including empathy and communication. But again, the distinction between emotional competence and social competence is not clear-cut. Social skills and emotional skills are mutually dependent. Children cannot acquire self-regulation or autonomy in the absence of supportive relationships, and their social competence is enhanced or hindered by their mastery of emotional skills.

chapter 8

Promoting Empathy and a Sense of Community

*"You can be my partner so I can show you everything
so you know just what to do. That way, you'll have a
lot of fun here. I got your back."*

—CALVIN, AGE 5, TO NEW CLASSMATE

After reading this chapter, you should be able to

▶ Define the concept of empathy and sense of community and describe how they are linked.
▶ Explain why empathy is important for effective living.
▶ Describe how biological, maturational, and experiential factors contribute to the development of empathy and sense of community.
▶ Create strategies and practices to promote empathy and sense of community in early childhood settings.

Mia and Leah were cousins enrolled at Greentree Child Development Center at the age of six weeks. They found comfort in each other's presence and preferred to play beside one another rather than alone. As toddlers, just as surely as they shared joy and humor, they shared distress. If Mia cried at a transition, Leah's cry followed seconds later. If Leah stumbled and bumped her elbow, Mia immediately showed anguish. When one child was comforted, the other stopped crying, too. But Mia and Leah were not the only toddlers who felt the emotions of others. In fact, over the course of most days, countless instances occurred of toddlers offering sad peers their bunnies or mimicking the silliness, suffering, or defiance of their classmates.

When Mia, Leah, and their classmates were five years old, they could be seen helping each other with buttons, describing the emotions of a new and frightened student, and patiently supporting the emerging reading skills of a less advanced peer.

By second grade, this group of children had organized and planted a community garden. They grew peppers, tomatoes, and many other crops, which they sold to family and friends in the fall. They all agreed that the proceeds from the sale of their crops would go to the local food bank to help those in their community who were less fortunate.

Is there something special about the children at Greentree Child Development Center that made them such caring and supportive citizens? Did something in particular about how they were nurtured at home lead to their warmth? Did certain practices at Greentree promote kindness? The answer to all three questions is, "Yes." There are factors related to innate qualities in children, to family child-rearing approaches, and to school/center philosophies, policies, and practices that contribute to children's competence in empathy and sense of community.

DEFINING EMPATHY AND SENSE OF COMMUNITY

Empathy refers to a person's *emotional response stemming from appreciation of another's emotional state and is similar to what the other person is feeling* (Lapsley, 2011; Eisenberg & Fabes, 1990). It can also be defined as an *affective (emotional) response that is more appropriate for another person's situation than one's own* (Hoffman, 2000). According to Daniel Siegel, empathy involves the capacity to create "mindsight" images of other people's minds, or "you-maps," and see situations from another's point of view (Siegel, 2011). For example, your coworker enters the room in distress because her beloved dog has been missing for two days. Though you've never had a dog, you are nearly moved to tears by her anguish and can feel her fear and anxiety. Your emotions mirror hers and most of this is experienced below the level of consciousness. This emotional experience is empathy.

Similarly, Mia, Leah, and their classmates demonstrated strong empathy that developed and changed in nature over the years. As toddlers, their empathy took the form of relatively unregulated mirroring of the emotions exhibited by their peers. By kindergarten, their empathy led them to behave in ways that reduced the suffering of one another. By the time the children were eight years old, their empathy inspired action for the betterment of their classroom community and their community at large.

A concept related to empathy is sense of community. **Sense of community** refers to *a feeling of belonging, that members matter to one another and to the group, and a shared faith that members' needs can be met through their commitment to being together* (McMillan & Chavis, 1986). Sometimes the word *community* is used to distinguish one geographical area from another, such as the east-side neighborhood of a city. Sometimes community is used to connote commonalities among people, such as the Jewish or Muslim community or the Greentree School community.

McMillan and Chavis (1986) proposed that "sense of community" has four essential elements. The first element is **membership**, *the feeling that one belongs within the boundaries of a group.* Membership implies that some people are in and other people are outside the group. This element is a powerful motivator and source of anxiety in young children, as evidenced by the very common yet devastating threat, "You can't come to my birthday party!" Group members have a stronger commitment to the group when they feel that they have made a greater investment in the group. That higher level of commitment leads to greater cohesiveness, which, in turn, increases its members' motivation to live up to the expectations of the group (McMillan & Chavis, 1986, p. 10).

The second element of sense of community is influence. **Influence** reflects *a person's belief that he has an impact on the activities or the success of the group, and the group has an impact on his behavior or well-being.* In other words, each member matters to the group and the group matters to each member. It also implies that conforming to group expectations is important and strengthens a person's standing in the group. In a group of four-year-olds, the element of influence can be heard in the familiar pleas, "He cut in line!" and "She didn't put away her blocks!" Even four-year-olds sense that the behavior of one group member impacts the lives of the other members. The influence of a member on a community and the influence of a community on a member operate concurrently and bilaterally (in both directions).

The third element is **fulfillment of needs**, *the understanding that associating with the group will meet the needs of its members.* Members prioritize their needs in ways that are consistent with the group. This ordering is how groups develop a shared system of values. In the early childhood classroom, need fulfillment translates into behavior that, depending on what is reinforced, can result in a community atmosphere that is supportive and respectful, aggressive and competitive, or something in between.

Shared emotional connection is the fourth element necessary for promoting a sense of community and relates to *the intensity, frequency, importance, and desirability of the interactions with the group.* The greater a person's investment of time, energy, and other resources, the stronger is his emotional connection, which, in turn, strengthens the group (McMillan & Chavis, 1986, pp. 10–14). When group members engage in meaningful projects together, their shared emotional connection strengthens their sense of community (Katz, 1994; Helm & Katz, 2011).

To understand how these elements of sense of community work together, we look at two kindergarten classrooms:

Every morning, Keisha greets each child with a caring smile and a warm conversation. The children excitedly relate the events of their lives and feel assured they have an attentive audience in Keisha. Sometimes, they interrupt each other, as children naturally do. At these times, Keisha says, "Please hold that important thought. We'd like to hear it, but Billy is telling us about his new puppy. Let's listen to Billy's story." Each child knows that he is an important member of the classroom community. If they squabble over a toy, Keisha brings the children together to discuss how they will negotiate and resolve their issue. Each child knows he or she plays an important role in the long-range projects of the group, such as the playground mural or the class orchestra.

Each morning, Pauline busily organizes her planned materials as children funnel into the room. She looks up to acknowledge the occasional parent who approaches her, but many of them prefer to communicate with her by slipping notes in the box she placed near the door for that purpose. It feels more comfortable to them than approaching Pauline with a concern. The children argue over toys, and when the volume begins to bother Pauline, she intervenes. She asks, "What's the problem here? Who had it first?" The children argue their case and have differing accounts, so she takes the toy away until a witness comes forward to tell what he or she saw. In circle time, Pauline asks the children to raise their hands to answer her questions about the weather or letter sounds. If they are incorrect, she says, "No, that's not it. Does anyone know the right answer?" After a few days, the same two or three children shoot their hands up in the air while the other children otherwise occupy themselves, often disturbing their classmates. They have learned how to compete for attention, even if the attention is negative.

The differences between the sense of community in the classrooms of Keisha and Pauline are significant. Keisha inspires feelings of worth in each and every child through her interest in their stories, her assurance that their thoughts and ideas are worthy of respect, and her creation of group activities. She uses words like *we* and *let's* and provides opportunities for the group to solve problems. In contrast, Pauline creates an atmosphere of emotional distance felt by children and parents alike. Her suggestion box practically screams, "Don't talk to me!" By solving the children's problems rather than guiding them through the process of negotiation, she diminishes their motivation to work together to resolve conflicts. In fact, children are reinforced for telling on each other. She discourages their attempts at discussion and rewards only the correctness of the answers. As a result, many of the children find other ways to interact and compete for attention by disrupting the class and bothering each other.

The Link between Empathy and Sense of Community

Do children with greater empathy also have a greater sense of community? At first glance, it would seem that a person who is in tune with the emotional states of others would naturally be someone who is committed to a group of people. On closer examination, however, it appears that having empathy is necessary but not sufficient for having a sense of community. Goleman (1995), in discussing "emotional intelligence," states that individuals with a talent for reading people's emotions and thoughts make good team players, dependable spouses, and good friends or business partners, all indications of a sense of community. Gardner (1999), however, prefers the term *emotionally sensitive* to describe a person with strong empathy skills who uses them for the betterment of others. It is possible to be skilled at reading people but to use those skills in an exploitative and antisocial manner. This quality is not empathy. It is self-serving manipulation. Empathy is an emotional connection to the inner experiences of others that leads a person to feel connected to them. As such, empathy is a necessary part of having a sense of community but must be accompanied by prosocial motives and a commitment to the betterment of others or the group (Gardner, 1999, pp. 118–119; Goleman, 1995, pp. 206–207).

WHY EMPATHY IS IMPORTANT

Empathy is one of the most important skills a person needs to succeed in life (Goleman, 1995; Siegel, 2001; Siegel & Hartzell, 2003). A good deal of research links empathy to conscience and confirms that empathic distress motivates **prosocial behavior** (Hoffman, 2007; Lapsley, 2011; Kochanska, Forman, Aksan, & Dunbar, 2005). **Prosocial behaviors**, *voluntary behaviors intended to benefit others,* include helping, taking turns, sharing, and comforting others (Eisenberg, et al., 1997). **Antisocial behaviors** are behaviors *that show disregard for and violation of the rights of others* (American Psychiatric Association, 2000). Antisocial behaviors include theft, bullying, deceitfulness, irresponsibility, fighting, lack of remorse, and reckless disregard for the safety of others. Early antisocial tendencies have been shown to persist into adulthood, often with serious negative consequences for the individual and society (Caspi, et al., 1996; Moffitt, et al., 2002). Similarly, prosocial tendencies that emerge in the early years have been shown to continue through adolescence and beyond with positive outcomes later in life (Hyson & Taylor, 2011). With stakes so high, it is critically important for early childhood professionals to support the development of empathy and get young children on a prosocial path.

DEVELOPMENT OF EMPATHY AND SENSE OF COMMUNITY

As is the case with most emotional and social skills, biological and environmental variables interact as they influence development.

Biological and Maturational Influences

Human beings are genetically predisposed for empathy, and this inborn quality has several expressions that develop over the early years (Schore, 1994; Hoffman, 2000; Goleman, 1995; Siegel, 2001). In the previous example of Leah and Mia as babies, when one baby was upset, the other was upset. When one was soothed, the other became calm as well. Infants can use emotional expressions and signals of others to regulate their own emotions. By her first birthday, a baby is aware that "minds can be interfaced," that is, she can "hold in mind the mind" or inner states of another person (Lapsley, 2011). She can detect fear or disapproval on the face of a caregiver and alter her own emotional state as a result. A caregiver's frown or look of alarm is enough to stop a baby in her tracks. By 20 months, the toddler can label some emotional states of others, such as "Daddy sad." By age 2, the child can even make causal statements about another's emotions (Lapsley, 2011). A two-year-old might be heard to say, "He fall down. He's sad."

New York University developmental scientist Martin Hoffman proposes five distinct modes by which empathy is aroused. The first three are preverbal and involuntary, which suggests that humans are built to feel, sometimes quite strongly, other people's emotional experiences (Hoffman, 2007). First, **motor mimicry** is *when a child spontaneously imitates the facial, vocal, or postural expression of distress in another person, which results in a feeling of distress in the child.* This spontaneous change was observed in the example of Mia and Leah, each of whose distress triggered distress in the other. Motor mimicry can be explained by the recent discovery of **mirror neurons**, where *the neural firings (signals between nerve cells) in the brain of an observer occur in the same brain areas at the same rate as they do in a person who is experiencing the emotion herself* (Hoffman, 2007; Siegel, 2011). Imagine that you are comforting your coworker who lost her dog. If we used electrons to measure your neural activity and that of your friend, we would see similar brain activation in both of you. Some children on the autism spectrum show dysfunction of the mirror neuron system and also exhibit diminished capacity for empathy and theory of mind, highlighting the link between these processes (Oberman, et al. 2005). See Figure 8.1 for further discussion of mirror neurons.

The second mode of empathic arousal is **classical conditioning**, *in which the child observes signs of distress in another person such as a caregiver, and the*

FIGURE 8.1
Mirror Neurons

Neuroscientists in Italy in the mid-1990s were studying the brains of monkeys. Using electrodes, the scientists discovered that when a monkey watched another monkey eating a peanut, the observing monkey's premotor cortex fired (showed electrical activity) in exactly the same manner and location as the monkey eating the peanut. They determined that *mirror neurons* enable monkeys to virtually get into the minds of other monkeys. Subsequent research confirmed that mirror neuron systems are activated in humans as well. When you observe another person reach for a doorknob, for example, your brain completes the act of turning the knob to open the door. Similarly, when you see a person bump his elbow, you *feel* his distress. When you observe a person being humiliated, you *feel* her painful emotions. The mirror neuron system is now considered to be the root of empathy.

Source: Based on Siegel, D. J. (2011). *Mindsight: The new science of personal transformation.* New York: Bantam Books. pp. 59–61.

child pairs her own distress with that of the caregiver. For example, when the caregiver feels anxious or frightened, her body may stiffen and that stiffening is transferred to the child. The adult's facial expressions and posture become the conditioned stimulus. In the future, simply the facial expression or posture can result in distress in the child.

The third mode is **direct association**, *in which one sees a person in a difficult situation that stirs memories of a similar situation from his own life and feels distress for that person.* Direct association might be seen when a child who has previously felt anxious about starting at a new school can feel the anxiety of a new child just starting in his class. As described by Hoffman, these first three modes often occur at an unconscious level and are quite characteristic of young children (Hoffman, 2007).

The two higher-order modes require symbolic thinking and language. **Mediated association** is *when a more experienced person points out and names the emotion experienced by another,* for example, "Look how lonely Charles feels." The final mode proposed by Hoffman is **role- or perspective-taking**, *the ability to create an image in one's mind of the thoughts, feelings, and needs of another* (Hoffman, 2000). We often promote this mode of empathic arousal when we say, "How would *you* feel if Charles told *you* that he doesn't like *you*?"

Hoffman proposes that children develop empathy by progressing through five stages that are consistent with their neurological and cognitive development. Infants are only minimally able to differentiate themselves and their emotions from those of others. By the time they are three years old, they are well able to perceive that other people have inner states that differ from their own. A child of this age is often capable of relieving a victim's distress by actions that are comforting to the victim, not simply comforting to himself. Hoffman describes that change as a transition from empathic distress, which is governed by one's own strong emotions, to sympathetic distress, which is more focused on the victim's distress as separate from one's own. (See Table 8.1.)

People are also hardwired and have a fundamental need for social connection (Schore, 1994; Cassidy & Shaver, 1999; Siegel, 2001). Developmental scientists have found that the infant's typical fixation with the mother's face is related to early attachment and its subsequent influence on social connectedness (Walton, Armstrong, & Bower, 1998). The needs for social connection and sense of community are not just characteristic of young children. In our society, where nuclear families are predominant and people often move far from their community of origin, the drive for connectedness persists. People find other ways to link up, as is demonstrated by the enormous popularity of social networking sites. At the time of this writing, Facebook users around the world numbered 845 million, half of whom log on daily, with an average of 80 community pages and 130 friends per user (Facebook, 2011). And the numbers are growing. Approximately half of all Americans report regular use of social media networking sites, double the proportion of just three years ago (AGBeat News, 2011). People join clubs, gyms, service groups, and more just to be part of a community. We have a basic drive to interact with one another.

TABLE 8.1 • Hoffman's Stages of Empathy

Stage	Begins	Description	Example
Global Empathic Distress Reactive Newborn Cry	Birth	The infant responds to the cry of another with as much intensity as if he himself were in distress.	*Mia played quietly in her crib, but began to cry loudly when Leah cried at her mother's departure from child care.*
Egocentric Empathic Distress	11 months	The infant shows distress at another's distress, but his actions are geared to reducing his own distress.	*When Leah was crying, Mia felt distressed and went to the caregiver for her own reassurance.*
Quasi-Egocentric Empathic Distress	1–2 years	The toddler makes helpful advances toward the victim, but assumes that what would help him would help the victim.	*When Mia saw that Leah was upset, Mia brought her own blanket to soothe Leah.*
Veridical Empathy for Another's Distress	2–3 years	Beginning to understand that others have inner states that differ from one's own, the child empathizes more accurately and offers more effective comforting actions, although those actions are still motivated to relieve one's own distress.	*Mia cried when classmate Rochelle tore the picture she was drawing. Three-year-old Leah brought Mia's blanket to her.*
Sympathetic Distress	3 years	An understanding that the victim is separate from oneself, a feeling of concern for the victim, and motivation to relieve the victim's distress, not simply one's own.	*Mia cried when Rochelle tore her paper. Leah talked warmly and gently to Mia and brought her some tape.*

Based on Hoffman, M. L. (2007). "The Origins of Empathic Morality in Toddlerhood". *In* Socioemotional development in the toddler years: transitions and transformations, edited by C. Brownell & C. Kopp, 132–149. *New York: Guilford.*

Experiential Influences

While humans do enter the world genetically programmed to connect emotionally and relate to one another, these capacities can be can be supported or dampened by experience. In previous chapters, we explored the importance of secure attachment relationships in the development of self-regulation, autonomy, and other skills. Again, healthy attachment characterized by attunement and synchrony between caregivers and children emerges as an essential factor in the development of empathy. The absence of healthy attachment relationships correlates with a host of poor cognitive and interpersonal outcomes (Zeanah, et al., 2003).

Take, for example, the still-face paradigm described in an earlier chapter. When the mother and infant interact through reciprocal, synchronous exchanges, it's as if they are emotionally one. When the mother presents an unmoving, impenetrable facial expression, the lack of empathic connection between the two quickly disturbs the baby's emotional state and she seems to fall apart. The still-face paradigm is simply an experiment, but its result can be generalized broadly into other interpersonal relationships with children. The development of empathy depends on regular reciprocal emotional interactions, as can be seen in the following vignettes:

> Full of smiles, three-year-old Lee excitedly brought his completed puzzle to Ms. Jolie, who gave it a dismissive look and said, "Put it away, Lee. We're cleaning up." Lee's little heart sank as he put away the puzzle.

Compare Lee's experience with Ms. Jolie to his experience with Ms. Margie:

> Full of smiles, three-year-old Lee excitedly brought his completed puzzle to Ms. Margie, who bent down to look at it and said, "Wow! Lee! Did you do this puzzle? I bet you worked very hard on it! Thank you for showing it to me." Five seconds later, Margie said, "I know you are enjoying what you are doing, but it's time to put away the puzzles so we can go outside." Beaming with a sense of accomplishment, Lee cleaned up.

With Margie, Lee "felt felt" (Siegel, 2011). They were of one mind and he knew she felt for him the way he felt for himself. With Jolie, there was no melding of minds. What was of utmost importance to Lee was completely irrelevant to Jolie. No empathic connection was made. The emotional bond between Jolie and Lee was much like that of the infant when the mother's face was still. If a child repeatedly experiences such a lack of empathy, he will not only feel poorly about himself but his development of empathy for others will also be hindered. He is learning that his emotional world and the emotions of others are irrelevant.

Scientists have examined the impact of early relationship experiences on brain development. Recall that an infant is born with billions of neurons (nerve cells). Each time a child has an experience, for better or worse, brain chemicals flow to form connections between neurons. These neural connections are the foundation of learning (Tierney & Nelson, 2009; Siegel, 2011). When the bulk of those experiences are positive and supportive, the child learns at a fundamental level that the world is safe. In the absence of such experiences, brain development is disturbed and learning potential is hindered.

The Bucharest Early Intervention Project explored the developmental impact of differing amounts of sensitive interaction with caregivers on children who were orphaned or abandoned and raised in institutions. One group had been institutionalized for the first several years of their lives, one group was institutionalized but placed in foster care or adopted during the first few years of life, and the third group had never been institutionalized. The children who spent their first several years institutionalized were found to have impaired brain activity, a higher rate of psychiatric disorders, and stunted physical, emotional, and cognitive growth, compared to those who were never institutionalized. Children who were removed from institutions and placed in foster care or adopted showed higher IQ scores and other positive gains than those who remained institutionalized. Children in the foster care group fared best when placed in care before age 24 months (Zeanah, et al., 2003; Marshall, et al., 2004; Zeanah C., 2009; Nelson, Furtado, Fox, & Zeanah, 2009; Fox, et al., 2011). The brain has a remarkable capacity to compensate and self-correct for detrimental early experiences, as observed with the Bucharest children in foster care. Such neuroplasticity, however, becomes more limited as the frequency, chronicity, and intensity of negative experiences increase (Bos, Zeanah, Fox, Drury, McLaughlin, & Nelson, 2011).

Attachment experiences matter a great deal in the development of empathy and sense of community, but a team of researchers at the University of Minnesota suggests that there is much more to the story of empathy and other prosocial skill development than early attachment. These investigators found complex interplay between temperament, early attachment experiences, and continued personal and interpersonal experiences through the early childhood and adolescent years (Sroufe, et al., 2005; Sroufe, Coffino, & Carlson, 2010). This finding bodes well for the potential of corrective experiences (Siegel & Hartzell, 2003) and highlights the importance of high-quality, relationship-based early childhood programs, especially when early attachment problems exist.

In addition to the nature of relationships, the messages offered by parents and caregivers regarding the importance of empathy and community also influence how well these principles are incorporated into the child's emerging value system. Families and classrooms vary in the extent to which sense of community or sense of belonging is emphasized. Some families or classrooms have routines in which all members, even the youngest, share in preparing, serving, and eating meals as well as joining in the cleanup. Chores and responsibilities convey that everybody plays an important role in the smooth running of the social group. Some families promote a sense of belonging through shared recreational activities like sports, camping, visiting museums, or volunteering.

In some families, the emphasis is less on the family as a group and more on the individual interests of family members. At a recent parent meeting, one mother explained that her typical week consisted of driving after school to and from gymnastics, soccer, tutoring, piano lessons, drama class, and yoga (for the mom). This particular family only had two children, but they rarely saw each other as a family community because of their extensive activities of individual interest.

In other families, individuals are so preoccupied with personal issues like those related to illness or poverty that they are unable to instill a sense of community/belonging as a priority even when it is something they want. For children from families that do not consistently promote sense of community, the early education program can play a critical role in the development of this important competency.

In high-quality early childhood programs, empathy and sense of community are infused into the minute-by-minute interactions between caregivers and children (Bredekamp & Copple, 1997). The benefits of this approach are noticeable even in the behavior of babies. Indiana University Early Education professor Mary McMullen and her colleagues described the behavior of infants and toddlers nurtured in such settings. These **prosocial babies** show *communications and behaviors that help create a positive emotional climate in the group and that involve reaching out—positive, discernable, outward social expressions on the part of one baby toward one or more other individuals, whether infant or adult* (McMullen, et al., 2009). The authors observed that prosocial babies share several qualities. They were cared for and respected as individuals, were friendly, affectionate, and kind to others and appeared to feel a sense of belonging to their community. The teachers in those rooms were consistent about expectations, modeled warmth and etiquette, and naturally showed respect for everyone in the room, including coworkers, families, and, most important, the babies.

The teacher behaviors described by McMullen and others are ideal for all adults aiming to promote prosocial development and can be enhanced through reflective practices and open communication among colleagues (McMullen, et al., 2009; Jennings & Greenberg, 2009). But what about young children who do not demonstrate empathetic and prosocial tendencies? Hoffman recommends that when a child's motives are in conflict with others or when the child behaves in a manner hurtful to others, caregivers should use an **inductive** approach to guiding the child. Rather than punish the child, in an inductive approach, adults *make explicit the hurtful consequence of the child's action on the other person*. For example, when a toddler pushes another toddler, the adult points to the victim's sad face and says, "Look at Bobby. He fell down when you pushed him. Bobby is very sad because that hurts him. No more pushing." As a result of this inductive approach, the child learns to consider the feelings of others and behave in a prosocial manner out of empathy and morality rather than out of fear of personal consequences. While some may be concerned that such an approach instills feelings of guilt in children, Hoffman and others contend that guilt is an important component of empathic, moral, and prosocial development. With repeated adult inductive guidance, anticipation of guilt deters children from harming others (Hoffman, 2000).

Neighborhood or institutional factors also influence a child's empathy and sense of community. Some urban and suburban areas have a local park or playground where people gather and play. Some communities are connected through a religious institution, co-op, neighborhood association, or club where family members of all ages can find activities that connect them with their neighbors. For some children, these opportunities are not available, so it is important for the early care and education setting to serve this connecting purpose.

Culture also plays a part in a child's sense of community. Earlier, we explored the distinction between cultures that promote interdependency and community and those that promote individualism and independence. Even in very individualist cultures, empathy and community are important, and most societies, families, and classrooms fall somewhere on the continuum between the extremes of interdependency and independence.

PRACTICES TO PROMOTE EMPATHY AND SENSE OF COMMUNITY IN THE EARLY CHILDHOOD SETTING

Education systems have often been compared to machines. In a machine, material goes in (facts and information) and gets processed (explained, discussed, rehearsed, or calculated), and a product comes out (answers on a test, a term paper, a painting, or a song in a recital) (Robinson & Aronica, 2009). What gets lost in such an industrial metaphor is the complex, back-and-forth, interactive dynamic that truly characterizes what happens and should happen in educational settings. The machine metaphor suggests that students are passive recipients of education, not active participants in the learning process. Educational programs using a machine model are less likely to promote cooperation, collaboration, or a sense that each individual is an important part of a larger universe, interdependent, and more effective together (Wein, 2008; Malaguzzi, 1998).

An organic metaphor, such as that used by the Reggio Emilia approach, more accurately captures what should characterize an early education system (see Figure 8.2) (Wein, 2008). An organic metaphor describes a school as a living organism in which all parts are interconnected. Such living systems require sustenance, nurturing, and room to grow. The living classroom organism is dynamic, evolves over time, and has a life of its own. Only together with all the other component parts are creativity and progress possible and likely (Wein, 2008; Malaguzzi, 1998).

So what exactly might such a living, interdependent classroom community look like? How is it laid out? How is time used? What types of activities would we see? What would be the role and expected behaviors of the teacher?

Environments That Support Empathy and Sense of Community

Programs like the Reggio-inspired schools consider the environment to be a teaching and learning instrument. When classrooms are set up with community in mind, children come to value themselves as members of a dynamic community (Edwards, Gandini, & Forman, 1998; Wein, 2008).

SPACE

Early learning environments should be child-friendly, peaceful, and comfortable from a child's eye view. There should be places for

FIGURE 8.2
The Reggio Emilia Approach

Reggio Emilia is a small town in Northern Italy whose approach to education has inspired schools around the world since the early 1960s. The approach considers children to be intellectually curious, resourceful, and full of potential. The curriculum is child directed, and activities are driven by the interests of the children. Reggio schools emphasize the arts, believing that children learn multiple symbolic languages through painting, music, drama, and more. The environment, considered an important teaching partner, is characterized by dramatic play areas, work tables, and places where children can solve problems, interact, and learn to communicate effectively (Robinson & Aronica, 2009). The Reggio approach allows children to acquire skills of critical thinking and collaboration. Reggio approach founder Loris Malaguzzi describes "a hundred languages of learning" and suggests that learning materials and opportunities abound and children are open to and benefit from all of them. For example, a projector (or a sunny window) and a wall are sufficient materials to allow children to explore light, shadows, transparency, and more (Wein, 2008, p. 10; Loh, 2006). Please see Edwards, Gandini, & Forman (1998) for more information.

Source: Based on Edwards, C., Gandini, L., & Forman, G. (1998). *The Hundred Languages of Children: The Reggio Emilia Approach—Advanced Reflections*. Greenwich, CT: Ablex.; Loh, A. (2006, December 1). *Reggio Emilia Approach*. Retrieved September 10, 2011, from Brainy-Child.com: http://www.brainy-child.com/article/reggioemilia.shtml.; Robinson, S. K., & Aronica, L. (2009). *The Element: How finding your passion changes everything*. New York: Penguin Group, Inc.; Wein, C. A. (2008). *Emergent curriculum in the primary classroom: Interpreting the Reggio Emilia approach in Schools*. New York: Teachers College Press.

relaxing and places for active learning; places to be alone and places for interacting with others; and places for creativity and places for familiarity (Klein, 2008).

Four important classroom design qualities have been proposed as essential for meeting the basic needs of children (Rui Olds, 2000; Klein, 2008):

1. The space should foster movement. Children should be able to move around when desired within safe boundaries and where limits are clear. Opportunities should be available for the active child to bounce and spin and wiggle, and there should be places to be still.

2. The space should inspire a sense of comfort where children feel secure and safe and where novelty and familiarity are in balance. Such an environment will support exploration and discovery.

3. The space should empower each child's emerging sense of competence. Organized materials can build organizational skills. A child should readily know where and how to access materials of his choosing and where and how those materials should be returned for ready access in the future.

4. The room should allow a child to feel that he is in control of his space and feel certain of his surroundings. It is often the case that teachers decide what themes, decorations, and artistic creations will adorn the walls of their rooms and hallways. Children will feel more of a sense of belonging if *they* have a say in what gets posted.

TIME

A young child in child care might spend up to 50 hours per week in your program. If you teach at an elementary school, it might be closer to 30 hours, and for part-time preschools, even fewer. Some of this time is determined by circumstance, such as the time when snacks and lunch are ready, or what time the playground or gym is available. Time is a precious resource and every minute needs to be valued. This does not mean that every minute must be filled with activities. To the contrary, the schedule must include down time. The important point is that you are intentional about how each of those precious minutes is allocated to allow children to feel that they are an important part of the community.

One strategy is to schedule large blocks of time so that children have the opportunity to become fully engrossed in activities that are genuinely interesting to them. How those large blocks of time are used will depend on the interests and developmental levels of the children. In a **project-oriented approach**, *children pose the questions, conduct their own investigations, and make decisions about how their time should be used* (Katz, 1994). Your role in a project approach is to closely observe the activities that are naturally interesting to the children in your class and provide opportunities for further exploration into the topics. In an excellent example of the project-oriented approach, Helm and Katz describe a group of toddlers who spent many months learning about fire hydrants and firefighting after their attentive teachers observed their fascination with the subject. The children looked for hydrants on walks, had a visit from a firefighter, created a hydrant with papier-mâché, and ran water through a teacher-constructed hydrant in their classroom, among other related activities (Helm & Katz, 2011). There is no limit to the project-based learning opportunities that can stimulate the learning of groups of children. Such shared learning experiences that last an extended period of time inevitably strengthen the connection among learners.

Extended time for make-believe play is a good way to increase a sense of community. Through play, children explore the complex inner worlds and social connections of the characters they create, as can be seen in the following scenario:

The five-year-olds in Ms. Melanie's class recently visited a local pizza restaurant and, donning hairnets and gloves, were given an exclusive tour of the kitchen before the restaurant opened. Over the next several weeks, the children established and operated a "pizza restaurant" in their classroom. Cal and Cleo designed the oven, prep area, and customer counter with giant boxes they nabbed from the recycling bin. Raquel and Javeon developed the menu. Oona and Mason gathered objects from the room to use as plates, cups, and utensils and solicited help from their classmates to make tablecloths, art for the walls, and centerpieces.

When the restaurant finally opened, the children took turns cooking, taking orders, serving, answering the phone for "take out

LOOKING IN THE MIRROR...

Think about a time that you and a group of classmates, friends, or coworkers worked on a project together over time.

- In what ways did the process of working together create a sense of community among members of the team?
- How were frustrations or disagreements handled?
- Did you enjoy the project-oriented approach?

Regardless of the content or product of the project, you can use the lessons you have learned from group projects in your past to enhance the community-building projects of your young learners.

- What parts of your past collaborative experiences can you apply when using a project-oriented approach with the children in your program?

Suppose the children in your program show an interest in the following content areas. How would you create project-oriented experiences to enrich their understanding?

- Frogs
- A broken arm
- Acorns

and delivery," and being customers. Sometimes the cook spent too much time chatting and burned the pizza. Occasionally, the server had to handle a "dissatisfied" customer. One time, the oven toppled over and customers and employees alike worked together to resolve the crisis with uncooperative duct tape.

The pizza restaurant is closed now but lives on in the memories of the children in that class. Ms. Melanie made herself available for consultation and support but recognized the importance of standing back and letting the children create their world.

Through the pizza play, the children had opportunities to develop character roles and solve problems. Their creation of the kitchen, dining area, menus, and décor enabled all the children to be a part of the action. Dealing with a dissatisfied customer and experiencing the consequence (burned pizza) of a distracted cook prompted empathy and social problem solving. The collapsed oven forced the group to think on their feet and solve a technical problem. The teacher was wise to let the learning happen without interference from scheduled transitions. In fact, at many times when a (real) snack arrived, it was served as part of the pizza restaurant so that the activity did not have to stop.

Expectations and Group Goals

It is important for children to know the behavioral expectations of the group so they may succeed as a member of that group (McMillan & Chavis, 1986). When they participate in the establishment of rules and expectations, children have a greater stake in complying with those rules. In creating a "democratic classroom," McLennan suggests that all the children participate in developing a classroom "bill of rights." The bill of rights delineates the rights and responsibilities for all members and can be discussed often throughout the year (McLennan, 2009).

Open-ended or hypothetical questions can engage children in thinking through the rules that meet needs of the group. For example, you may ask the class, "What should we do when we want to play with a toy that someone else is using?" Sometimes children will offer a rule that would have undesirable consequences, such as, "Just grab the toy." At that time, it is useful to explore potential consequences of the proposed choices. You could say, "OK, let's talk about grabbing the toy. What might happen if we do that?" You can encourage the children to generate several possible outcomes and alternatives to their initial solution. You can then summarize by saying, "OK, we agreed that grabbing might lead to more grabbing or upset feelings. Then we decided that we should use words like, 'May I have it when you're finished?' Should that be one of our rules? What would you like me to write on our list of rules?"

Sense of community and empathy can be enhanced through routines for welcoming a new student to the class. When a new child arrives, let children be the ones to explain the rules, schedules, activities, and other aspects of the class. Giving this authority to the children creates a culture of caring. A new child can also be supported with a buddy or a peer mentor who can show him the ropes. The class can engage in getting-to-know-you activities for new arrivals as well as for all children occasionally throughout the year.

Activities in which children must work together to accomplish group goals can also strengthen the community. Note the following three examples of shared goals:

> Ms. Tiara's pre-K/kindergarten class has a reading train. The cars on the train are about six inches long. Each time a student accomplishes a personal literacy goal (e.g., matches letter sounds to symbols, knows her address, reads a book), the child earns a train piece and attaches it to the train. The literacy activities may occur at school or at home with the family. The class begins the train in September, and by the following June, the train goes around the room two, sometimes three times. Each time the train encircles the room, the class has a pizza or ice cream party to which families are invited. The children encourage each other's accomplishments and enjoy seeing the progress made by the group as a whole.

> A large box sits in the lobby of the preschool. In fall, as the days become colder, the students are led in discussions about

people in their neighborhood who do not have warm winter clothing. Children, staff, and families establish a goal and set out to collect jackets, boots, mittens, hats, and scarves for those less fortunate in the community. In mid-November, the collected items are donated to a local charity.

The three- and four-year-olds have been learning about plants. In a sunny patch along the side of the building, the children don garden gloves, grab shovels, and dig up the earth. High school volunteers dump bags of nutrient-rich soil that the young children spread with child-sized hoes. When the ground is ready, the children plant vegetable seeds. Every day, they water the garden and look for changes. They learn to be careful not to step on the nascent sprouts and discuss the look and feel of the growing crops. Excitement prevails when flowers emerge, and the first appearance of peppers, tomatoes, squash, and cucumbers brings squeals of delight. In September, the children harvest their crops and share the bounty at a feast for the whole child care center.

Everyday Strategies

Although children are born with natural inclinations for empathy and relationships, they also have needs, desires, and impulses that conflict with others and that at times can be hurtful or destructive. These conflicts are common in early childhood settings and should be considered opportunities to teach important interpersonal skills. Biting, hitting, grabbing, and name-calling occur for many reasons and can serve as springboards for direct guidance in empathy and relating. In the following scenario, toddlers who are often quite friendly with each other have an unfriendly moment:

Jaime is quietly playing with a pop-up toy when Kyle toddles over and grabs the toy from her hands. Ms. Nicole was there in an instant but not before Jaime's little teeth put a red dent in Kyle's arm. Ms. Nicole said, "Kyle, are you OK? That looks like it hurts. Jaime, look at Kyle's arm. Your teeth hurt his arm. Let's get some ice so his arm can feel better." While she and Jaime held ice on Kyle's arm, Nicole said, "Kyle, Jaime was playing with that toy and she was not done with it. If you take it from her, she will be upset. She bit you because she was upset. You need to play with something else until Jaime is all done." Nicole said to both children, "We do not take things that other people are playing with. We have to wait until they are all done. And we do not bite each other. Biting hurts people."

Nicole knew that children under age 2 could not fully comprehend all the messages she was trying to give them. She knew she would have to say these same words many more times before the children could really understand and act accordingly. From the very earliest offenses like those of Jaime and Kyle described earlier, we can deliver messages of empathy, caring, and problem solving. Nicole first modeled empathy when she said, "Are you OK?" She pointed out the physical and emotional consequences of Jaime's biting behavior but validated Jaime's right to be upset at Kyle's grabbing behavior. Nicole also acknowledged Kyle's desire to play with the toy but suggested a solution to help him wait: "Play with something else."

By the time children are three, their capacity to link their actions to consequences is emerging. They are increasingly capable of understanding simple cause and effect. They know that if they flip a switch, the light will go on. Their vocabulary has grown by leaps and bounds. If others in their lives have used emotion words such as happy, sad, angry, scared, and hurt, three-year-olds will begin to develop an emotional vocabulary. Increasingly, they can make connections between their actions and the emotions of others. You can support these connections with simple statements, such as, "I feel happy because you made a picture for me!" or "When you pushed Robbie, he felt sad." With a bit more experience, the child will be able to identify the emotion that someone is feeling by looking at his facial expression and body language and listening to his tone of voice. The following conversation occurred with two active three-year-olds:

> Rochelle and Lon were "doctors" at the "hospital" taking care of their patient Clive. Lon put the stethoscope on Clive's chest to hear his heartbeat. Rochelle suddenly grabbed it from Lon's neck so she could listen to Clive's heart. Lon, trying to grab it back, pushed Rochelle and she fell and bumped her head.
>
> Ms. Margie recognized this grabbing/pushing incident as an opportunity to strengthen Rochelle's empathy and impulse control and Lon's ability to express his feelings. She showed the children that it is important to consider the emotions of other people and think about potential unintended consequences. She gave them opportunities to discuss their own feelings and then suggested they practice the behavior they all agreed would have the desired outcome. This approach builds emotional awareness and vocabulary.

Children naturally spend a great deal of time playing roles and developing characters. You can support their empathy and sense of community by inviting children to role-play scenarios that are germane to the issues in the class. For example, Ms. Bev was troubled by a recent epidemic of her four-year-olds excluding each other and saying hurtful things, such as, "You can't play with us."

At story time, Ms. Bev read a story from Betsy Evans's collection, *You're Not My Friend Anymore!* (Evans, 2009). The group talked about the story, including the characters' thoughts and feelings. She asked the children to think about times they had heard or said hurtful things. Then she suggested that the children do a play about different ways friends treat each other, sometimes nice and sometimes not nice. The children enjoyed assigning roles and they played out several scenarios. Some of the children preferred to watch rather than act. After the activity (which the children spontaneously repeated for several days), Ms. Bev invited the children to talk about the characters' thoughts, feelings, problems, and solutions. With younger children, conflict resolution, empathy, sense of community, and other social skills can be supported with puppet or doll play (Center for the Social and Emotional Foundations for Early Learning, 2011).

It is also useful for children to reverse roles in their play. In the earlier scenario with Rochelle and Lon, Ms. Margie could ask the children to reenact what had just happened but this time have Lon grab something from Rochelle. By playing the role of the victim, Rochelle can experience how unpleasant it feels to have something grabbed out of her hand. By playing the role of a child who is pushed down, Lon can feel the discomfort that others feel when he pushes. Young children give us countless real-life conflicts and challenges that we can use as opportunities for role-play, puppet play, and role reversal.

LOOKING IN THE MIRROR...

Several examples of empathetic teacher behavior were presented in this chapter.

- What methods that promote empathy do you use when relating to children?
- Are there times when it is difficult for you to respond to a child's behavior with empathy?

For example, you may feel angry about a child's aggressive behavior and have trouble showing empathy for both the victim and the aggressor. Perhaps you feel annoyed rather than empathetic when a child whines or pouts.

- What makes particular child behaviors so difficult for you?
- What experiences have you had that increased your empathy and sense of community?
- How can you use those experiences to promote empathy and a sense of community in your classroom?
- What aspects of your classroom environment (e.g., space, schedules, and policies) promote a sense of community?
- What community-building activities do you have in place in your class?
- Does your school or center have policies and practices that foster a sense of community?
- What can you do to increase the community spirit in your program right away?
- What steps can you take to make improvements in this area in the long run?
- What books and other resources can you use to promote empathy and sense of community in young children? Research children's literature and generate a list to help you encourage these skills.

Children's literature is full of conflicts and other interpersonal interactions. When you read with children, be sure to reflect on the characters' thoughts, feelings, and desires. The children can explore a character's choices for solving problems and anticipate the likely consequences of the character's solutions. Their experience is enriched when they are the ones to evaluate whether or not the character's choices are effective.

Modeling and Parallel Process

Research consistently confirms that children whose caregivers model empathy and caring will exhibit these behaviors as well (Jennings & Greenberg, 2009; McMullen, et al., 2009). In your day-to-day work, you have many opportunities to model social interactions that are empathetic and build community. For example, at times you will disagree about an issue with a coworker. At these times, you may demonstrate mutually respectful dialogue, compromise, and agreeing to disagree. You may also dramatize conflict resolution by narrating your thinking process. For example, you may say, "I would like for us to go outside right now, but the kindergarten children are already out there and that would be too many children on the playground. They don't look like they are ready to come in right now. What else can we do? I know, let's play a game until we can go outside."

Summary

Each child is born with an intrinsic inclination toward empathy and connection to others. These natural tendencies can be supported by healthy attachment relationships with caregivers or diminished by dysfunctional or absent relationships. Empathy and sense of community can be enhanced in early childhood settings when the space, schedules, policies, and practices are set up to allow children to feel comfortable with themselves and committed to the well-being of the group. Everyday interactions and targeted activities can also be used to promote these important capacities. And, perhaps most important, your awareness of your own level of comfort and competence in this area will help you become intentional about creating situations and seizing existing opportunities that strengthen these competencies in your young learners.

Review and Apply

1. Describe the biological, experiential, and cultural factors that influence the development of empathy and sense of community.
2. You have just inherited a class of six-year-olds from a teacher who is retiring. The children seem to tattle quite a bit, compete for attention, and behave aggressively toward one another.

   a. What steps can you take to build empathy in the children?
   b. Describe the strategies can you use to increase the sense of community in this group of children?

chapter 9

Synchronizing Communication: What Links People to People

"Know how I know Ms. Jen loves me?
She closed her eye like this (tries to wink).
That means we are friends."

—GALE, AGE 3

After reading this chapter, you should be able to

▸ Define communication and describe its components.

▸ Describe the relationship between communication and other social and emotional competencies.

▸ Explain the complex aspects of communication, such as how it differs from language, what is meant by a two-way street, and how context cues can help interpret levels of meaning.

▸ Describe expressive and receptive communication, including verbal and nonverbal aspects.

▸ Create an atmosphere that supports the development of communication skills in all types of communicators.

▸ Describe how you would implement the elements of a communication-rich environment.

▸ Identify and describe multiple strategies that target specific communication skills.

A wink. Thumbs up. A frown. A smile. A question. A story. This is the stuff of communication. At birth, we are endowed with the capacity to express and understand messages, and this capacity becomes more and more fine-tuned throughout our lives. It is the platform on which we regulate ourselves and connect with others. What do we mean by *communication*, and what is the process by which we become so adept at communicating as we grow? How does effective communication contribute to healthy social and emotional development in young children? To understand how communication skills develop, we must first consider the components of communication and the levels and modes by which people communicate.

DEFINING COMMUNICATION AND ITS COMPONENTS

Communication is *a process by which information is exchanged among individuals.* The concept of exchange implies that communication goes back and forth. It has an expressive component and a receptive component, and competence in both is important for effective exchange of information. **Expressive communication** refers to *the process of conveying a message to another person.* Our ability to express ourselves allows us to reveal our desires and needs so that those needs can be met. Proficiency in expressive communication lets people share experiences through stories and images. It enables us to convey our inner states, emotions, thoughts, and ideas. It is critically important for connecting with others. Babies cry, toddlers point and attempt to say "more," and preschoolers often regale us with interesting verbal observations about their world.

Receptive communication is *the process of receiving and understanding information expressed by another.* It requires that the recipient of the message both perceives (sees, hears, or feels) and comprehends the message as it is intended. Receptive communication is necessary for knowing the needs, preferences, and inner states of others. It enables us to learn about their experiences so we may be part of a social dyad or community. We know infants hear us when they look toward our face when we speak to them, and we know preschoolers receive our gentle verbal suggestions when they try to work a puzzle in a different way.

COMMUNICATION AND SOCIAL–EMOTIONAL COMPETENCE INTERACT FOR EFFECTIVE LIVING

Social and emotional competence goes hand in hand with the ability to communicate effectively. When you look at the essential life skills listed in Figure 4.3, you can see that all of the social skills and many of the personal skills require the ability to express feelings, thoughts, needs, or interests and to accurately interpret those expressed by others. For example, to join a group or start a friendship, a child must know how to indicate his desires and common interests.

A child's ability to regulate his emotions and impulses is supported by and also supports communication. Infants are hardwired to read cues for reassurance from their caregivers and it is through those messages that children learn to regulate their own emotional states. When we name those emotions, we give children indispensible emotional expression tools they will use throughout their lives. Similarly, with consistent and clearly expressed expectations and supportive correction, children learn to regulate their impulses. Children who can regulate their emotions and impulses are in a better position to maintain relationships and resolve conflicts through communication. Conflict resolution, including sharing, taking turns, problem solving, negotiating, and compromising all require the ability to assert one's point of view, to listen, and to comprehend the needs and desires expressed by another. Conflict resolution is even more effective when each party can empathize with the other's position, which again illustrates the back-and-forth nature of social, emotional, and communication skills.

THE COMPLEXITY OF COMMUNICATION

Communication is not a simple concept. It consists of many separate but related skills. Communication can be compared to and contrasted with language. It requires synchronous interactions between the individual who expresses messages and the one who interprets the messages. It also requires the ability to recognize and interpret multiple levels of meaning.

Language and Communication

Language is an important aspect of communication and is sometimes used synonymously with communication, but there are differences. **Language** is *a method by which people communicate and often uses symbols such as words, signs, or pictures. It involves coding those symbols to convey a message and decoding the symbols to comprehend the meaning of a message received.*

Language is critically important for complex communication, yet several lines of research suggest that the capacities for language and for communication involve different brain areas and systems (Willems & Varley, 2010). Studies have found that long before most children have mastered verbal language, they are able to express their needs through crying, cooing, gestures, and other means and to interpret messages intended by a speaker (Raikes & Edwards, 2009; Shonkoff & Phillips, 2000). Effective communication requires inference and theory of mind, the ability to understand the intentions and mental states of others. Some evidence notes that even preverbal infants demonstrate this capacity (Willems & Varley, 2010; Liszkowski, Carpenter, & Tomasello, 2008). Research also confirms that many children on the autism spectrum have adequate literal language skills but lack the theory-of-mind component necessary for effective communication (Baron-Cohen, 2001).

In clinical research, patients with severe aphasia (loss of the ability to express or understand speech) have been observed to communicate quite sophisticated messages through nonlinguistic means, such as drawing, facial expressions, and gestures. These observations suggest that the neurological system for coding and decoding symbolic language differs from the system involved in complex communication (Willems & Varley, 2010).

Reggio Emilia founder Loris Malaguzzi refers to the "hundred languages of learning" to describe the various ways children can understand their world and express themselves (Malaguzzi, 1998; Robinson & Aronica, 2009). For our purposes, however, *communication* will refer to *the broad process by which meaningful information is exchanged among individuals*, perhaps what Malaguzzi means by "languages." *Language* will refer to *a more specific method of communication involving symbols such as words, signs, and pictures.* Proficiency in both communication and language are essential for academic success and interpersonal relationships (Jalongo, 2008).

Communication Is a Two-Way Street

The title of this chapter is Synchronizing Communication, which highlights the back-and-forth nature of communication. It is the link that connects people to one another. For communication to be effective, two participants need to be competent in both expressive and receptive communication. Each needs to coordinate his responses to be in synch with the messages conveyed by the other. This is more difficult than it sounds. We enter our interactions with our own agenda, and it can be easy to let our needs and desires distort or even block out the needs and desires a child might be trying to express. We must always remember that our capacity to decipher the meaning of a child's communication as well as to convey messages accurately requires continuous, intentional self-reflection and life-long learning on our part.

Multiple Levels of Meaning

Communication is complex whether it is verbal or nonverbal, written, spoken, or signed. To communicate successfully, a person has to be sensitive to multiple levels of meaning. The words a person selects to express a thought, her tone of voice, her gestures, and her facial expression all convey meaning. Much of the time, these various components of communication are in synch so we don't question or doubt the intended meaning. Sometimes we have less information, such as in an email or a note. Without contextual information, the intended meaning can be unclear, as in the following example:

> The note simply said, "Thanks a lot." Keisha stared at the note left by her new co-teacher, Pam. It was Monday morning and Keisha had only known Pam for a week. Pam had seemed anxious about her new job and it had been a tough week with lots of rain and restless children. Friday afternoon had been particularly hectic, and they did not have a chance to recap at the end of the day. Keisha did not know what to make of the note. Was Pam grateful for something? Was the message sarcastic? What would Pam have to be unhappy about? Did Keisha somehow offend her? Keisha was preoccupied with the mystery of the message for hours. Finally, at noon, Pam came in for her shift, walking tall and smiling. She gave Keisha a hug and said, "Did you get my note? Thank you for making my first week so wonderful!"

Written words on a page or computer screen can easily be misinterpreted. While Pam attempted to communicate her gratitude, the meaning of her note was ambiguous to Keisha, the recipient of that communication. Because communication occurs at multiple levels, words as simple as "Thanks a lot" could be interpreted in many ways. For Keisha to accurately interpret Pam's message, she needed more contextual information. The minute she saw the warm smile on Pam's face, she was able to interpret the note as sincere rather than sarcastic. In this case, Keisha used Pam's facial expression and demeanor as context cues to more fully understand the meaning of her message.

With children, especially those who are not yet proficient in the use of verbal language, we need to constantly tune in to multiple layers of communication. Their gestures, facial expressions, posture, and level of eye contact are all important pieces of information to observe. We need to listen to the tone of their voice and their selection of words to fully understand their intentions. In turn, it is important for us to tune in to those same aspects of communication in ourselves.

TYPES OF EXPRESSIVE AND RECEPTIVE COMMUNICATION

When communicating with others, it is tempting to focus exclusively on the use of words. But people send messages through music, art, drama, clothing, hairstyle, and even fragrance. Children communicate a great deal through play and through behavior, so we need to observe with all our senses and be intentional in our attempts to understand the full meaning of their messages.

Expressive Communication: Verbal

Verbal communication refers to the use of words to express a message and includes speaking, writing, and signing. Verbal language, using words (and signs) as symbols that represent ideas, is essential for conveying and interpreting complex messages (Willems & Varley, 2010). It is a high priority for early childhood educators to promote verbal skills because of the high correlation between verbal skills, literacy, and academic success (Jalongo, 2008, p. 48; Heath & Hogben, 2004; Nation & Snowling, 2004). Children who have preschool experiences where teachers use sophisticated vocabulary and talk analytically with children about books, coupled with early support in the home for literacy, demonstrate significantly higher reading comprehension, word recognition, and vocabulary in fourth grade (Dickinson & Porche, 2011).

Children naturally pick up certain aspects of verbal communication even before they are adept at using the words of their native language. For example, appropriate **intonation**, *the fluctuation of pitch*, and **rhythm**, *the timing of spoken syllables common in a language,* can be heard in a classroom of toddlers who are "talking" before they actually know the words to convey their intended message. These qualities are called **prosodic** features of speech, which also include **stress**, *the emphasis of certain syllables in a word or certain words in a sentence* (Christophe, Millotte, Bernal, & Lidz, 2008).

HELPING CHILDREN USE TONE EFFECTIVELY

We often refer to "tone of voice" when describing intonation. Its relevance to expressive communication is critical. Whining, for example, has a sing-song quality that conveys dissatisfaction or disappointment. It often feels disturbing to the listener and is one of the earliest sound patterns that caregivers attempt to correct. Young children, though, do not yet have the reflective capacity to recognize distinct tonal aspects of their speech. Thus, it is not sufficient to tell a young child to stop whining unless you have first intentionally taught the distinction between the tone he is using and the tone you would prefer he use, as in the following example:

> Three-year-olds Donnie and Andres were engrossed in setting up the train tracks when Gavin sat down and reached for a piece of the bridge.
>
> DONNIE: "Hey! We're using that! Ms. Ma-a-a-rgie! [complaining] Gavin's taking our bri-i-dge." (Imagine the sound of a voice when a syllable is extended over time, with a nasal, sing-song quality, commonly known as "whining.")
>
> GAVIN [DEFENSIVELY]: "I was N-O-T! They won't let me P-L-A-Y."

Ms. Margie [who knows whining when she hears it]:
"Boys, it sounds like you are both troubled. Before we solve the problem of the train bridge, I'd like us to practice something. Listen to my voice and tell me if you can tell the difference between these two things I am saying: 'I W-A-A-NT the BRI-I-I-DGE.' Now this way, 'I want the bridge.' Could you hear the difference?"
Both boys nodded.

Ms. Margie: "Now you try it. Say, 'I want the bridge' using those two different voices. First like this, 'I W-A-A-NT the BRI-I-I-DGE.'"
The boys repeated this (giggling a little).

Ms. Margie: "Now try it the other way. Say, 'I want the bridge.'"
The boys repeated again.

Ms. Margie: "Which one sounds better to you?"
The boys agreed they liked the latter better.

Ms. Margie: "'I W-A-A-NT the BRI-I-I-DGE' is a whining voice. The other way is the way we need to ask for help and talk to each other. People like that better. Sound good?"
The boys nodded, laughing at the exercise.

Ms. Margie: "Now, let's talk about what was bothering you."

Now that the boys are aware, they can catch themselves and change their intonation to communicate more effectively. Like Margie did with whining, when children use a tone of voice that is demanding, mocking, or unassertive, you can draw their attention to the tone they are using and guide them to use a tone that would help accomplish their goal more effectively.

HELPING CHILDREN USE VOLUME EFFECTIVELY

Volume is another feature of speech that sometimes requires direct guidance. Two-year-olds generally begin to know what we mean by inside voice and outside voice. Even before their second birthday, however, some toddlers will modulate their volume in response to an adult who speaks in just over a whisper. In fact, many teachers have observed that when the classroom becomes too loud, simply lowering the volume of their own voice becomes contagious and can inspire a group of young children to quiet down to listen.

HELPING CHILDREN FIND THE WORDS TO SAY

When young children are aggressive, we often tell them, "Use your words," but we don't always explain what that means. As an adult, you have probably had a lifetime of experiences that helped you find effective words to achieve your desired results. Young children may need to be directly taught to assert themselves and guided to find the most effective words to use. For example, we can say, "Tell Bobby you don't like it when he hits you," "Ask Bobby if you can play with the ball when he's finished," or "Tell Bobby to ask you nicely." With direct guidance and modeling, most children will eventually know which words to use to accomplish their goals.

HELPING CHILDREN EXPRESS THEMSELVES USING SIGN LANGUAGE

Sign language requires qualities of both verbal communication (signing words) and nonverbal communication (using gestures) to convey messages. Research suggests that training preverbal babies as young as six months to express their needs, such as "more" and "eat" in sign language, reduces frustration, accelerates the rate at which speech is learned, and results in higher intellectual functioning at age 8 (Acredolo & Goodwyn, 2000; Goodwyn, Acredolo, & Brown, 2000; Vallotton, 2008). Vallotton demonstrated that some preverbal children (age 12 months) were able to use signs for emotions in their spontaneous behavior. Before her study, researchers thought that that emotion concepts did not emerge until the middle of the second year, but the babies in their studies had not been taught the signs for emotions (Vallotton, 2008).

Expressive Communication: Nonverbal

Nonverbal communication is *the process of sending and receiving wordless messages.* Nonverbal communication includes gestures, facial expressions, posture, eye contact, and proximity (how physically close one stands to another). It may also include clothing and hairstyle. People communicate nonverbally through dance, music, art, drama, and other behaviors (e.g., fidgeting). Some types of nonverbal communication are reflexive, such as a startle reaction or gasping. Others may be manifestations of emotions, such as laughing or crying.

PROVIDING ARTS EXPERIENCES

The arts provide modes of expression that do not rely on verbal language. Dance and movement are natural ways for children to express themselves. Whether creating their own music or moving to music created by others, children can communicate emotions and ideas through movement. Similarly, visual arts, such as painting, sculpting with various materials, pounding clay, and drawing, offer enjoyable opportunities for children to express themselves.

PROVIDING MAKE-BELIEVE PLAY OPPORTUNITIES

Perhaps the richest and most common modality through which children express themselves is make-believe play. Early in the second year, toddlers use objects to represent other objects, such as a doll representing a baby or a vacuum cleaner toy representing a real vacuum cleaner. As children venture into the preschool years, their dramatic play becomes more elaborate. The characters in their stories and the themes in their play become increasingly complex as they become more aware of their own and others' inner states. Over the past several decades, mental health practitioners have become more attuned to the emotional content and themes that occur in children's play in the therapy setting. Through play, children act out their fears and fantasies and resolve conflicts and solve problems (Axline, 1947, 1989; Chesley, Gillett, & Wagner, 2008; Frey, 1993). By closely observing children's make-believe play, early childhood professionals can get a glimpse of the complex cognitive and emotional world in which they live. Long-time educator Vivian Gussin Paley presents a fascinating and insightful discussion of children's fantasy play that can help us interpret their underlying messages (Paley, 2004).

OBSERVING, ANALYZING, AND REFLECTING ON BEHAVIOR

Children communicate through their behavior as well, and their actions often tell you more than their words. Whether a child's behavior is prosocial or challenging, the child is telling you something. He might be telling you that he needs support to cope with difficult feelings. He may be telling you that he wants to be a valued member of the group. He might be telling you that the environment is too intense or not stimulating enough. He may be telling you that he lacks the skills to solve his problem in any other way. In any case, his behavior is telling you something, and it is important to observe carefully to be able to accurately read or hear what his behavior is telling you, as illustrated in the following example:

> Four-year-old Chloe looked blankly at the blocks in front of her. When Jackson sat down to build, Chloe grabbed the blocks that were closest to her and said, "These are mine! I was here first!" Jackson was surprised because Chloe didn't appear to be using them and she usually shares pretty well.

Ms. Bev casually sat down at the block table beside Chloe and Jackson so she could get a closer look at what was going on. She had noticed that Chloe was quieter than usual this week. Chloe began to build a house. Her house had no doors and she filled it with countless items from the miniature playhouse nearby. Then she covered her house with a piece of cardboard.

CHLOE: "There."

Ms. BEV: "Chloe, can you tell me about what you are building?"

CHLOE: "It's my house and nobody can come in."

Ms. BEV: "Nobody can come in your house?"

CHLOE: "It's my stuff." She lifted the top slightly. "See? This chair is mine and this brush is mine and this piano is mine and these shoes are mine."

Ms. BEV: "You have a lot of things that are just for you."

CHLOE: "No one can have my stuff. Not David. Not anyone."

Ms. BEV: "This is just yours, but you think David might get it? Who is David?"

CHLOE: "Mommy's friend's boy. He lives at my house with his dad."

Ms. BEV: "He lives at your house now and you don't want him to get your stuff. Do you think he'd try to take it?"

CHLOE: "He can eat the food, but he can't have my stuff."

Through careful observation, Ms. Bev noticed many things about Chloe's behavior that were out of character. Chloe's quiet, pensive mood, her reluctance to share, the inaccessible room she created, and the number of random items that filled the room were nonverbal cues that Chloe had something important on her mind. By listening reflectively, Ms. Bev learned that Chloe was facing a major change at home with the addition of her mother's friend and son. Chloe felt threatened by the intrusion and was compelled to hold her possessions dearly. Ms. Bev received the message Chloe was expressing through her behavior and her play. With this new information, Ms. Bev was able to provide the support Chloe needed.

Receptive Communication

Ms. Bev was astute at picking up Chloe's verbal and nonverbal signals by watching and listening. She created an atmosphere free of judgment that allowed Chloe to feel safe enough to translate her play into verbal language. By being a close observer of the children in her class, she was able to detect and appreciate a change in the emotional quality of this child's play and behavior.

Receptive communication is *the process of receiving and understanding communication.* It involves perceiving, acknowledging, interpreting, and comprehending the messages sent by another. Listening is a critically important skill for effective communication and correlates highly with language development and success in relationships, school, and the workplace (Jalongo, 2006; Nelson, 2007; Smeltzer, 1993; Janusik, Fullenkamp, & Partese, 2007). In her comprehensive book, *Learning to Listen, Listening to Learn,* Mary Renck Jalongo offers the following definition of **listening**: *"the process of taking in information through the sense of hearing and making meaning from what was heard"* (Jalongo, 2008).

Despite the importance of listening for success in school and life, it is a skill that is rarely taught directly (Coakley & Wolvin, 1997). Conaway (1982) administered a listening test to 400 college freshmen at the beginning of their first semester. After their first year of college, about half of those who had scored low on the listening test were on academic probation, while only 4 percent of high-scoring listeners were on academic probation. In contrast, 69 percent of students who scored high on the listening test were considered honors students, while only 4 percent of the poor listeners were honors students (Conaway, 1982). In this study, better listening skills predicted higher academic acheivement.

Jalongo's (2008) thorough review of the literature on the development of listening skills reveals that infants enter the world with preferences for speech and for the primary caregiver's voice. Infants appear to be able to distinguish the sounds of all languages at birth. However, over the first year, this universal capacity becomes native-language specific, and after six months, infants are able to distinguish only the sounds characteristic of their native language (Dietrich, Swingley, & Werker, 2007). Between ages 1 and 3 years, the toddler's receptive vocabulary can be as much as four times his expressive vocabulary, and he becomes progressively skilled at understanding abstract concepts such as *another* and *more* (Nelson, 2007; Jalongo, 2008). Preschool children become more and more able to recognize word parts and use accurate sentence structure. Fascinated by the new worlds that open up to them with their growing language competence, they can often be heard engaging in bedtime monologues during which they experiment with the word combinations that they heard during the day (Nelson, 2007).

Research suggests that people tend to listen through one preferred listening style. A **listening style** is *a set of attitudes, beliefs, and predispositions about the how, where, when, who, and what of the information reception and encoding process* (Watson, Barker, & Weaver, 1995). Your listening style predisposes you to focus on some aspect of a message and not others. The four listening styles are people-oriented, action-oriented, content-oriented, and time-oriented. It is useful to reflect on your own preferred listening style in your

TABLE 9.1 • Listening Styles

Listening Style	Description	Example
People-oriented	Interested in demonstrating concern for other people's emotions and interests, and finding common ground.	Keisha took the time to sit with Charlie so she could hear what his thoughts and feelings were about moving away and going to a new school.
Action-oriented	Interested in direct, concise, error-free communication used for negotiating and accomplishing a goal.	Pauline had difficulty paying attention to Jayla's long-winded explanation of why she didn't want to play with Bryan. She just wanted her to play with him. That's it.
Content-oriented	Interested in intellectual challenge and complex information so they may carefully evaluate all the data before making a decision.	Tony wished he had all day to brainstorm with D'Andre and Colleen as they laid out plans to construct the planter boxes. He was fascinated by their decision-making process.
Time-oriented	Interested in brief, concise communication that gets to the point quickly.	Peggy did not need the details of Leo's home situation, she just wanted his mom to tell him the new address for her records.

Based on Barker, L., & Watson, K. (2000). Listen up. New York: St. Martin's Press.; Jalongo, M. R. (2008). Learning to Listen, Listening to Learn: Building essential skills in young children. Washington, DC: National Association for the Education of Young Children.

efforts to promote listening skills in children (Jalongo, 2008; Barker & Watson, 2000). Please see Table 9.1 to learn more about listening styles.

Because expressive communication occurs in many forms, receptive communication requires the use of multiple senses. Perhaps the most direct form of communication is verbal, but even verbal communication is subject to interpretation, which can be accurate or inaccurate. When a person's words do not match his nonverbal behavior, such as when the speaker has mixed (ambivalent) feelings or is being untruthful, the receiver of the message must listen, look, and empathize to accurately interpret the message. Keeping in mind that receptive communication involves both listening and observing, long-time education leader Judy Jablon and her colleagues suggest that we make a conscious effort to enhance our observational skills through what they call the "Power of Observation Cycle" (Jablon, Dombro, & Dichtelmiller, 2007). In the Power of Observation Cycle, you ask pertinent questions about the child; watch, listen, and literally take notes to gather answers; reflect on your observations; respond to the child by using your reflections; and begin the cycle again. The authors remind us to observe children over time and across situations to note growth, individual preferences, and levels of competence in specific skill areas. They recommend keeping track of observations to notice patterns and obtain a more complete picture of the child (Jablon, et al., 2007). By observing this closely, we can individualize our approach to each child.

Communication can be more challenging to comprehend when messages are sent through art, music, dance, play, or behavior. Such messages are less direct, require more subjective interpretation, and sometimes need translation, as in the previous example of Chloe. When a child is unable to use words, the teacher may look to other sources of information to accurately interpret and understand the child's messages. It is at these times that warm and respectful relationships with families can be especially useful.

Sometimes, even with words, communication breaks down. In the following example, a field trip did not happen because of two simple words:

> To be able to go on the pumpkin patch field trip, the class needed six adult volunteers. Five of the parents showed up at the preschool with time to spare. Jason Wilson's grandfather still had not arrived at 9:00, the planned departure time. Ms. Marsha called Mr. Wilson's home but there was no answer. At 9:15, Mr. Wilson called the school and said he was leaving his shop right then and that he'd be *there* in five minutes. Ms. Marsha said, "Great. Thanks for calling. We look forward to seeing you *here* in five minutes." The class waited and waited at the school. Mr. Wilson arrived at the pumpkin patch and waited and waited for the class to arrive. By 10:00 a.m., it was too late for the class to leave for the field trip, the children were disappointed, and the adults felt angry with Mr. Wilson. Mr. Wilson was upset to have taken time off work for a field trip that the class failed to take.

The ambiguity of the words *there* and *here* resulted in a communication breakdown. The intended meaning of *there* seemed clear to Mr. Wilson. To him, *there* meant the pumpkin patch. The received meaning of *there* seemed clear to Ms. Marsha. To her, *there* meant the school where she and the children were waiting to leave. Both assumed the other had the same meaning, but they did not. In many situations, communication breakdowns can be avoided when we take the time to clarify the intended meanings of words, even if they seem obvious. If Ms. Marsha had said, "So, you will be here at the school in five minutes?" Mr. Wilson would have said, "No, I meant the pumpkin patch."

PRACTICES TO PROMOTE COMMUNICATION SKILLS IN THE EARLY CHILDHOOD SETTING

As we strive to strengthen communication skills in young children, we must be sure to establish an atmosphere that is supportive of all types of communicators and is rich in opportunities for practice.

Creating an Atmosphere That Welcomes All Kinds of Communicators

A communication-rich environment conveys that everyone is valued. In some classrooms, multiple children come from families whose native language differs from the local language. Under these circumstances, it is beneficial for the

LOOKING IN THE MIRROR ...

- What is your listening style?

Think about a time when your listening style did not match the expressive language style of a speaker, or the listening style of the person with whom you were communicating did not match your expressive language style.

- What feelings did those conversations evoke in you?
- What could you do to improve your interactions with people whose listening and expression styles differ from your own?

Think about your own experiences with expressive and receptive communication.

- Have you ever experienced a misunderstanding due to miscommunication?

You thought you were very clear in conveying your message, but it was interpreted inaccurately. Or perhaps you misunderstood the message expressed by someone else.

- Where did things go wrong?
  - Did you or the other person use a term that was ambiguous or unclear?
  - Was the recipient of the message distracted or unable to understand the intended meaning?
- What steps can you take to be certain that the messages you are sending (to colleagues, friends, parents of children in your care, your supervisor or boss, young children) are indeed the messages the recipient is receiving?
- What steps can you take to be sure that you are accurately interpreting the message sent by another person?

professional to learn and to use basic words from each of the languages represented in the classroom to support language development in the children. In addition, teaching those basic words to the other children in the program can build bridges between local communicators and those who speak a different language. This recommendation also applies to children who communicate by signing. When we build signing skills in the rest of the students, all the children will be able to communicate with each another.

Many children jump at the opportunity to tell their stories. Sometimes a child will tell his story in painstaking detail. Sometimes, because of expressive language difficulties, a child will tell his story in a slow and belabored manner. It can be difficult for peers to listen patiently, as in the following example:

Caleb was fascinated with Transformers. He had seen every Transformer movie and owned every imaginable toy that could be transformed. During sharing time, Caleb brought a truck that could be transformed into a heroic character and back again. Caleb elaborated in great detail about the adventures of this character. Despite his enthusiasm, Caleb spoke very slowly and had trouble pronouncing many words. He did not appear to notice that his classmates had lost interest. They were restless and interjected their own ideas.

Ms. Bev reminded the group, "Children, Caleb is sharing a story that is important to him. Let's listen to Caleb and we'll all have a chance to share our stories. Remember the ideas you want to share because they are important, too, and we'll talk about them later."

Ms. Bev was beginning to feel anxious and antsy as well, because Caleb's story seemed to have no end. After several minutes, Ms. Bev said, "Caleb, this is an interesting story and we would like to hear more, but other children have stories to tell, too. How about if during free time, you draw a picture of your story and I'll write down your words?"

Ms. Bev was careful to acknowledge the importance of everybody's ideas. She encouraged the children to demonstrate respect for the needs and ideas of one another. In addition, she modeled respect and patience and offered a strategy for Caleb to express himself that would address his needs and the needs of others.

Note that Caleb was unaware of the needs of his audience. He did not detect their impatience, characterized by squirming and interrupting. In the area of interpreting nonverbal communication and knowing the inner states of others (theory of mind), Caleb resembles some children on the autism spectrum. One cardinal feature of autism spectrum disorders is qualitative impairment in communication. While children with ASD may show adequate speech skills, they often lack skill in the accurate interpretation and effective use of verbal and nonverbal communication (including eye contact and facial expression) (American Psyciatric Association, 2000). Ms. Bev used a sensitive and respectful approach as she guided Caleb to observe the needs of his audience.

Encouraging a Communication-Rich Environment

A communication-rich environment has frequent opportunities for conversation and symbolic play. Such an environment includes many opportunities for children to identify and explore emotions. A communication-rich classroom also contains materials and opportunities for children to express themselves through nonverbal modalities and writing.

SUPPORTING PLENTIFUL AND MEANINGFUL CONVERSATION

Children learn about the values in their community by observing others and engaging in the activities around them. Because communication is one of those values, we must provide children with abundant opportunities to participate in conversations so they may practice their emerging communication skills. A **conversation** is *a verbal or nonverbal exchange of ideas that goes back and forth where each idea expressed by one individual is extended or elaborated by* *the other.* When you engage a child in conversation, you convey to her that you value her thoughts, ideas, feelings, and interests. You build listening, vocabulary, and thinking skills (Dombro, Jablon, & Stetson, 2011). Whether you work with infants, second graders, or any age child in between, the message you send by engaging in mutual and synchronous exchanges has a lasting impact across all domains of development. Not only do these conversations build self-awareness and self-esteem, they also enhance your relationship with the child and strengthen the child's sense of belonging. When you wonder aloud with a child, you prompt him to think in new, creative, and increasingly complex ways. These cognitive gains, in turn, stimulate self-confidence and a desire for more communication.

SUPPORTING OPPORTUNITIES FOR SYMBOLIC PLAY

The use of objects as symbols to represent other objects is a critical step in language and literacy development. Late in a child's second year, he begins to use symbols to express himself. A triangle becomes a piece of pizza. A block becomes a truck. A doll becomes a real baby to feed, change, and cuddle. At the same time, children become more adept at using words as symbols for objects, relationships, activities, and more. As children progress through the early years, their dramatic play becomes more complex. They can describe more and more details in the make-believe world they create independently or with peers. Their stories follow a sequential progression from beginning to middle to end. Their characters have thoughts, feelings, needs, and desires. When we provide opportunities for dramatic play, we foster these critical language, literacy, and social–emotional skills.

USING AND TEACHING EMOTIONAL VOCABULARY

Just as words are symbols for objects, words are also symbols that represent the affective states we all experience. **Emotional vocabulary** refers to *the words we use to describe emotions in others and ourselves.* Emotional vocabulary is a key element of communication that contributes significantly to self-regulation, empathy, conflict resolution, and other emotional and social competencies. When we draw children's attention to the emotions they feel and those that they sense in other people, we help them learn to describe those inner states. We can use puppets, dolls, and characters in stories as well as actual events in the everyday lives of children to highlight emotional aspects. Through this process, children develop the ability to assert themselves and show empathy for others. The following story illustrates the benefits of infusing emotional vocabulary into the environment so that children can communicate effectively in emotionally challenging situations:

> Since the first day of school, Ms. Bev was certain to tie emotion words to many of the daily experiences of her four-year-olds. When reading a story, she would often stop to ask what the

characters might be feeling. Knowing the importance of modeling, she would often describe her own emotional states, for example, "I feel excited that we have a new classmate," or "I am frustrated because the window doesn't open properly." When children would have disagreements, Ms. Bev was sure to ask them to describe what they were feeling as an important consideration in solving the problem. If a child was unable to find the words, she was likely to pick up a couple of puppets and have them "talk to each other" about feelings.

One morning, Ryan was happily playing with the airplane when Chloe called him to look at her block tower. He put the airplane down, intending to return to it. In Ryan's absence, Jackson picked up the airplane and flew it to the other side of the room. When Ryan returned to where he had been playing, he was upset to see that the airplane was gone. He spotted Jackson and Robert with the plane and walked firmly over to them.

RYAN: "I was playing with that airplane."

JACKSON: "We're playing with it now. You put it down. You can have it when we're done."

RYAN: "I know I put it down, but Chloe wanted me to see her tower. I wasn't done with the plane."

JACKSON: "But we have it now."

RYAN: "I know, but I'm disappointed because I wasn't done. May I *please* have it now?"

JACKSON (SHRUGGING HIS SHOULDERS AT ROBERT):   "I guess. Can we have it when you're done?"

RYAN: "Yes. Thank you. I feel better."

It is hard to believe that four-year-olds can carry on such a conversation loaded with emotions and empathy, but it is the product of being in an environment where emotional states are recognized as important and emotional communication is valued.

PROVIDING MATERIALS AND OPPORTUNITIES FOR NONVERBAL COMMUNICATION

As described earlier, some children are more comfortable expressing themselves through music or art than through words. Many young children greatly enjoy experimenting with musical instruments and creating rhythms and melodies. A high-energy five-year-old recently created a rap song for his teacher to describe his feelings related to moving to a new house. He previously had a difficult time sitting down and describing his experience in conversation but was very effective in conveying his message when he put it to percussion and bass. Like many children, the opportunity to move and dance facilitated this child's ability to express himself.

Because some children prefer communicating through the visual arts, it is important to have clay, paper, crayons, markers, paint, and other materials available throughout the day. Children often have a vivid picture in their minds of the objects or events they are creating, even if you, the observer, cannot figure out what the creation represents. When you prompt the child in an open-ended manner, such as, "Can you tell me about your picture?" you convey to him that you are interested in the images and ideas he has in mind.

PROVIDING AUTHENTIC OPPORTUNITIES FOR WRITTEN COMMUNICATION

Even before children have mastered the mechanical capacity to write letters and words, they understand that writing is a way to communicate (Bus, Both-de Vries, de Jong, Sulzby, & de Jong, 2001; Mayer, 2009). Most children begin with pseudo-cursive scribbling (wavy letter-like lines flowing from left to right) and the formation of well-learned elements, such as the child's name and *mom* and *dad*. Another step is nonphonetic strings of real letters or pseudo-letters that are formed intentionally but are not systematically rule based. Once a child acquires the concept that each letter or group of letters corresponds to a specific sound (phonetic understanding), his writing will likely include invented spelling. Bus, et al. (2001) found that when children use their emerging writing skills to communicate their stories, they do not typically use their most advanced level of writing skill. In fact, many children alternate the use of all four of these processes in their productions. When *reading* their written story, they are more likely to relate the story from their mind (memory or imagination) than to attempt to read the *words* they have written.

Remember that our goal is to build communication skills and a child's love for writing. Therefore, in the early years of emergent writing, we should be careful not to inhibit this process by focusing on the mechanical correctness of the writing. Focusing on spelling and penmanship when a child is excited about communicating through writing is likely to stop the flow of the thinking-to-writing process. Instead, we should let the child enjoy the process of creating a written story.

We can greatly enhance children's interest and skill in writing as a form of communication by providing authentic opportunities to practice. Children

should be able to find writing materials in all centers of the classroom that will spur their interest in the usefulness of writing as a way to communicate. For example, paper and pencils in the dramatic play area can be used to create menus for their restaurant, shopping lists for their trip to the store, or prescriptions written by the doctor for a sick patient. Writing materials in the science area enable children to document what they see under the microscope, record changes in the size of their plants, or list the weights of the items they found on the beach. For an excellent summary of the research on emergent writing and ways to promote children's interest in writing to communicate, please see Mayer (2009).

Intentionally Planning Targeted Activities

The early childhood classroom should have ample opportunities for make-believe play. It is through play that children acquire more and more complex ways of thinking and sophisticated ways of communicating (Paley, 2004). In addition, some structured games and activities strengthen the component skills of communication such as listening, observing, and storytelling.

Children enjoy many listening games without even realizing that they are building targeted skills. One listening game is Simon Says. This game requires children to listen for the distinction between a simple command and a command that starts with the words, "Simon says." Of course, the person leading the game can be Simon and use his or her own name, such as, "Julia says...." Another listening game requires players to remember progressively longer lists of objects or activities, as described in the following examples:

JASON: "I'm going on a trip and I'm packing a suitcase. In my suitcase, I will pack a ball."

TOM: "In my suitcase, I will pack a ball and a banana."

PAT: "In my suitcase, I will pack a ball, a banana, and a drum."

Here is a variant of that favorite game, using action words:

JASON: "On my vacation, I'm going swimming."

TOM: "On my vacation, I'm going swimming and diving."

PAT: "On my vacation, I'm going swimming, diving, and dancing."

Such games require children to listen carefully and find ways to remember longer and longer sequences. The possibilities are endless and can include, "In my shopping cart, I will put..." "On our field trip, I saw..." or, "At my house, I have a..."

It is also beneficial to have books available that require listening for or repeating certain words. For example, my favorite children's book is *The Napping House*, by Audrey Wood, with rich and beautiful illustrations by Don Wood (Wood, 1984). *The Napping House* begins with "There is a house, a napping house, where everyone is sleeping....And in that house, there is a bed, a cozy bed, in a napping house, where everyone is sleeping....And on that bed, there is a granny, a snoring granny, on a cozy bed, in a napping house, where everyone is sleeping..." and so on. Children love to anticipate and recite the phrases they have heard over and over. Similar examples that prompt listening skills are *Brown Bear, Brown Bear* and other books by Martin & Carle (1996).

LOOKING IN THE MIRROR ...

It is useful to be aware of our own communication strengths, weaknesses, and preferences. For example, many early educators are very comfortable and confident when communicating with children but not necessarily with parents or groups.

- How do you feel about communicating with parents?
- How do you feel about communicating with supervisors?
- Do you enjoy public speaking?
  - If you do not enjoy speaking to parents, supervisors, or groups, what do you find difficult about it?
  - What steps can you take to improve your skill in these areas?
- What is your preferred mode or style of expression?
  - Do you express yourself best through art, music, or dance?
  - Do you express yourself best through writing, such as in a journal or letters to a friend?
  - Do you prefer to express yourself orally in words?

Think about a child whose communication preferences differ from yours. If you find that your typical ways of communicating are not well understood by a particular child, it may be that the child is unskilled in communicating in your preferred modality. Or the child may communicate in a modality with which you are less familiar. For example, you may be adept at communicating verbally, but the child expresses and comprehends best through art or play and lacks effective verbal skills.

- What steps can you take to improve the effectiveness of the communication between you and the child?

Another enjoyable way to promote communication skills is dialogic reading. **_Dialogic reading_** refers to _a process of reading with individual children or small groups of children during which children participate in the telling of the story._ In _dialogic reading, the adult reads and shares pictures and then pauses to invite input from the children._ The reader assumes the role of active listener, asks questions, adds information, and prompts the children to increase the sophistication of their descriptions of the material in the book (Whitehurst, et al., 1994). The reader begins by asking basic _What_ questions, for example, "What is the puppy eating?" or "What is the boy looking at?" As the children become comfortable with simple questions, the reader asks follow-up questions to help the children elaborate on their observations and ideas. Finally, the reader asks open-ended questions to prompt reflection and stimulate imagination in the children, for example, "I wonder how the tree grew so big," "What do you like to do when you take a walk?" or "Why do you think the boy was crying?"

Dialogic reading has been shown to improve literacy and language skills in children from low- and moderate-income families as well as affluent families. It has been found to be beneficial for children from various cultural groups. In early childhood programs, dialogic reading is most effective when group size is limited to five children, which might require calling on volunteer readers from the community. It has also been found to be most beneficial in early childhood settings when the parents apply dialogic reading practices at home (Whitehurst, et al., 1994).

Summary

Communication refers to the exchange of messages among people and requires numerous component skills. Receptive communication involves the ability to listen to and observe the verbal and nonverbal messages sent by another person. Expressive communication involves the ability to clearly convey one's thoughts, ideas, feelings, and needs in a manner that the recipient of the communication can accurately interpret. Like all people, young children vary in their preferred modes of communication. Some are skilled in expressing and interpreting verbal language and other symbolic forms of communication, like signing or writing. Others express themselves better through art, music, or movement. Most children express themselves and learn a great deal through play and should be provided opportunities for dramatic play throughout the day. Children also communicate through behavior, which requires strong observational skills in the early childhood professional.

Opportunities to build the component skills of communication should be infused into the early childhood classroom environment. Conversations with and around children enrich their emerging communication skills and should abound. Specific activities can also be used to target component skills such as listening, storytelling, and sharing emotions. When children become effective at communicating with peers and adults, they become better at regulating their emotions, have more successful interpersonal relationships, and improve their chances of being more successful academically and in their life pursuits.

Review and Apply

1. Explain what is meant by *synchronizing communication*. Include in your answer concepts related to expressive, receptive, verbal, and nonverbal communication.

2. Describe how you would explain to parents of a group of children (of any age, preschool or primary grades) the importance of communication skills to their development. Write a one-page paper or role-play this scenario with a partner.

3. You have noticed that several four-year-olds in your program have trouble expressing their thoughts or telling stories in much detail. Many of them don't appear to listen or read the nonverbal communication of others very well. You would like to strengthen their capacity to carry on synchronous, back-and-forth conversations.

a. What general strategies can you use in the everyday classroom to build their conversational skills?

b. Describe several targeted activities you could use to address the specific communication needs of the children.

PART 4 SUMMARY

Reflective Support of Social Skills

Each of us is a part of something greater than any one of us alone. We are citizens of the world, and as such, need to know how to relate to each another. The drive to connect with other people is as much a survival instinct as breathing and can be seen in the newborn's first gaze. For children to thrive in this social world, this natural inclination to connect must be nurtured by caregivers who are competent themselves in the social arena. By the time we are adults, we have generally learned to connect and communicate. We learned this through our interactions with others, those who have supported us, and those who have not. And now, we are charged with applying our interpersonal skills to promote the skills of connection and communication in young children.

Every day, children present us with opportunities to bolster their empathy and communication skills. They may have trouble sharing and taking turns. They may exclude their peers, stand too close, talk too loudly, or act aggressively. When they do, we need to identify the underlying social skills that need support and be ready with strategies to guide them.

We can also create a classroom atmosphere that is conducive to building empathy, a sense of community, and communication skills. We can design the space, materials, and schedule in ways that invite cooperation and collaboration. Many activities and games also target specific skills such as listening, sharing, problem solving, and cooperating. The more in tune we are with our own capacities in this area, the more ready and able we will be to enhance these capacities in children.

part 5

· ·

Conclusion

chapter 10

Bringing Reflective Guidance to Your Classroom

"I never realized that everything important is right here in this mirror."

—Mr. Al, Age 26, Teacher of Toddlers

After reading this chapter, you should be able to

▶ Describe the importance of self-reflection in promoting social and emotional development in young children.
▶ Identify several child- and family-related factors to consider when you are individualizing learning experiences for each child.
▶ Recognize the role of goodness-of-fit in children's experiences and interactions.
▶ Create an atmosphere that promotes social competence and emotional well-being.
▶ Use everyday activities and events to promote essential life skills in children.
▶ Use challenging behavior as opportunities to build social and emotional skills.
▶ List activities and experiences that target specific social and emotional skills.

Throughout this book, you have been asked to consider many factors in your interactions with children. Eight themes have emerged as we examined the elements of this reflective approach. Each of the themes is summarized in this chapter as we consider how to bring the reflective approach into your class-room or program. The themes include the following:

1. Engaging in self-reflection
2. Individualizing experiences for each child
3. Enhancing goodness-of-fit between you, the child, and the environment
4. Creating a physical and emotional classroom atmosphere that promotes social competence and emotional well-being
5. Using everyday activities and events to teach essential life skills
6. Viewing challenging behavior as a skill-building opportunity
7. Finding enjoyable activities that target specific skills
8. Building relationships with children and families

A list of reflective questions designed to help you think about your interactions is offered in Figure 10.1.

FIGURE 10.1
Reflective Questions to Guide
Your Approach to Challenging Behavior

You, the Teacher:
- Have I taken the time to get to know this child?
- Have I spent some time in a meaningful interaction with this child today?
- Have my interactions with this child been more positive than negative?
- Do I have an emotional reaction to this behavior that differs from that of my coworkers?
- What is so bothersome to me about this behavior or this child?
- Where in my past or current experiences do those feelings originate?
- How did I learn the behaviors that I would like this child to demonstrate?

The Child:
What do I know about this child that might influence his or her behavior?

- Is there a history of trauma?
- Has he had to adjust to recent changes?
- Has he been in a group setting before? What was the nature of that setting?
- How are his language, cognitive, and social–emotional developmental competencies?
- Has he been physically healthy since birth? If not, do illnesses contribute?
- Does he have difficulty with sensory processing?
- What are some strengths of this child?
- What is important to the child?
- What are the interests of this child?
- What strategies have worked and what strategies have not worked in the past?

(continued)

FIGURE 10.1
(Continued)

The Family:

What do I know about the child's family that might be relevant to the behavior?

- Have there been recent changes?
- Do the adult caregivers get along or is there ongoing conflict at home?
- Are the values, expectations, and practices of the family consistent with ours at school or child care?
- Are those values, expectations, and practices consistent among parental figures?
- What are some strengths of the family?
- Does the family's culture support our expectations at school/child care?
- Do these behaviors occur at home?
- What strategies have worked and what strategies have not worked at home?

The Behavior:

- When do challenging behaviors tend to occur?
  - At a particular time of the day or week?
  - During a particular type of activity?
  - In the presence of a particular person or people?
- What social or emotional skills need support?
- What thoughts or feelings might the child be experiencing?
- What usually precedes the behavior (triggers)?
- What usually follows the behavior (consequences)?

ENGAGING IN SELF-REFLECTION: LOOKING INTO THE MAGICAL MAGNIFYING MIRROR

You bring your own bundle of stuff to any encounter, whether with a child, a parent, or a coworker. That bundle includes your history, your preferences, your biases, strengths, weaknesses, values, and beliefs. Sometimes something in that bundle may catch you off guard. For example, a particular child might sass back at you and you find yourself furious…more furious than your co-teacher and more furious than you might ordinarily be. This is when looking deeply into that magical magnifying mirror is critically important so that you can respond intentionally rather than react impulsively. Which of your beliefs or values did the incident challenge? What memory did that child's behavior trigger in you? When you are willing to look within yourself, you are able to be more present with the child and your responses become more effective.

The importance of self-reflection goes beyond its role in addressing challenging behavior. When you design your classroom, create your schedules, and develop lesson plans, the elements of your temperament, your preferences, and your biases come into play. It is important to acknowledge those aspects of yourself so you can use them to the advantage of the children. For example, you might be someone who likes order and consistency. It can be tempting to offer your students art projects, such as coloring sheets, that will end up looking very much alike despite children's need for creative expression with varied materials. The activities children need to experience can get messy and you may have to work through your discomfort with disorder and unpredictability. Perhaps your listening style is time oriented, but the parent at a conference tends to provide copious details. Knowing that your listening style differs from the communication style of the parent can help you approach the conference differently.

Presumably, we professionals have attained a certain level of social–emotional competence that has enabled us to be where we are today. This is not to say that we cannot improve these skills throughout our lives, but we have had experiences that contributed to our social and emotional development. It is important to reflect on the ways you acquired the specific skills you are trying to promote in a child. Perhaps the adults in your life were supportive and deliberate about helping you develop those skills. Or, perhaps your learning experience was painful and you'd like to find a different approach for the children in your program. Examining those experiences will increase your empathy and can guide your decisions about how to accomplish your goals.

Self-reflection should be a part of every aspect of your work. Each lesson plan, each activity selected, each interaction with a child or parent, and each response to a challenging behavior will be enhanced by your self-reflection.

INDIVIDUALIZING EXPERIENCES FOR EACH CHILD

No two children are alike in their pattern of strengths and weaknesses when it comes to social and emotional competencies. In any group of children, some will be quite articulate while others are not. Some will be able to regulate their emotions and impulses quite well while others will not. Each child will have strengths in some skill areas and weaknesses in others. Thus you must reflect on the developmental needs of each individual child when you plan your activities and respond to children's behavior.

Each child is also unique in his interests, temperament profile, and sensory-processing style. What can be delightful for one child may be quite unpleasant for another. Try to provide a variety of activities that are enjoyable for each child, but also gently challenge children to become more flexible and tolerant.

Children exist in the context of their families. Each family is distinctive in its set of dynamics, circumstances, and

FIGURE 10.2
Gathering and Using Information
to Address Social–Emotional Needs

Exercise 1

Two-year-old Isaiah has been in your classroom for three weeks after having moved from another state. Usually, Isaiah is dropped off in the morning by Aunt Makayla and picked up at the end of the day by his mom, a neighbor, or a teenage cousin. He shows minimal interest in peers but seems to thrive on affection from staff. Isaiah often grabs objects from his classmates and hits peers when they don't give him what he wants. When you or your co-teachers confront Isaiah directly, he pulls away from you and has, at times, kicked or spat at you.

1. What do you wonder about in this situation?
2. What questions should you consider when addressing Isaiah's behavior?
3. What might you suspect are the reasons for Isaiah's behavior?

Exercise 2

Because of your excellent detective work, you learned that Isaiah was in the custody of his grandparents in a neighboring state, and he was removed from his mother at birth because he was born addicted to heroin. Both grandparents work full-time, so they placed Isaiah in the home of a couple who cared for 20–25 children of all ages. The grandparents did not think the babysitters had a program and suspected that peers or the babysitters had treated Isaiah harshly at times.

Isaiah's mother, eighteen months clean and sober, recently moved Isaiah and herself to your community after regaining guardianship and having found a retail job near her cousin's home. Isaiah's biological father's parents live in your community, too, but his dad's whereabouts are unknown to all.

Your initial screening suggests that Isaiah's language development is slightly delayed, but his cognitive skills are average or above. In the social–emotional domain, you have found strengths in autonomy and self-care skills but weaknesses in emotional regulation, impulse control, delay of gratification, and empathy.

1. What is the meaning of or what are the underlying reasons for Isaiah's behavior?
2. What strategies might you use to address his aggressive and impulsive behavior?
3. What else concerns you about Isaiah?

cultures. As a professional, you do not need to sort through all the complicated variables characteristic of the families with whom you interact. Rather, you need to be open to their nature, recognize that they may be very different from you, and respect those differences, as you would want them to respect yours. See Figure 10.2 to apply these concepts in two exercises that focus on gathering and using relevant information.

ENHANCING GOODNESS-OF-FIT BETWEEN YOU, THE CHILD, AND THE ENVIRONMENT

People function at their best when the demands of their environment are compatible with their temperament and preferences. This is true about you just as it is about the children in your program. Teaching a classroom full of children whose sensory needs and preferences differ widely can be quite a balancing act. An environment or activity that is within one child's range of comfort may be at odds with that of another child. The key is to be sensitive to this variable in your planning and flexible about modifying expectations when your selected activities exceed a child's ability to cope with task demands. Our goal is to broaden the range of circumstances with which a given child can function but not so much that the child becomes unregulated and fails.

Goodness-of-fit also relates to your relationship with a child. It is inevitable that you will come across a student whose temperament runs counter to your own. Once your self-reflection has allowed you to recognize the nature of the mismatch, you can work toward increasing the range of experiences and child behaviors you are able to tolerate. The goal is to find ways to synchronize your approach, interactions, and selected activities so they align with the needs of the child or children.

CREATING A PHYSICAL AND EMOTIONAL ATMOSPHERE THAT PROMOTES SOCIAL COMPETENCE AND EMOTIONAL WELL-BEING

Never underestimate the importance of the physical indoor and outdoor classroom environment in promoting social and emotional competence in children. In creating an atmosphere conducive to development in this domain, we must consider our use of space, time, and materials. Look around your classroom. Are there spaces for quiet time, detail work, small group interactions, dramatic play, and full-body activities? Designating spaces for these purposes can enhance several social–emotional skills, such as self-regulation, autonomy, empathy, and communication. Is the space well organized or is it cluttered? Is it friendly and inviting? Be sure to lay out your classroom with these important objectives in mind.

The daily schedule must balance predictability and flexibility. Young children benefit from routines and knowing what to expect. On the other hand, the schedule has to allow for spontaneous learning opportunities, or teachable moments, as they occur. The schedule should also balance quiet, calming activities with opportunities to be boisterous and physically active. Keep in mind the critical importance of having periods of time for rich conversation. Children benefit greatly from sharing and listening to personal stories and engaging in back-and-forth exchanges about subjects of interest to them. It is important to be intentional about the use of time to optimize children's learning experiences.

The materials you choose should support both general and targeted opportunities for social–emotional skill building. Posters on the walls and characters in books should resemble the children and families in your program so that the children can identify with them. The set of accessible materials should balance familiarity and novelty. Developmentally appropriate materials are those that are interesting, enjoyable, and challenging for the specific children in your group.

Beyond the use of time, space, and materials, healthy development in all domains relies heavily on the program's emotional environment. The warmth of our gestures, comfort in our tone of voice, and our genuine interest in the children's experiences all blend to create an atmosphere that builds trust and a sense of belonging. From trust grow self-regulation and autonomy. Empathy and commitment to the goals of the group grow when a child has a sense of belonging. We can enhance all the important elements of social and emotional development by being intentional about what we are communicating verbally and nonverbally and how we are listening and observing. In a nutshell, we create a nourishing environment when we synchronize communication.

USING EVERYDAY ACTIVITIES AND EVENTS TO TEACH ESSENTIAL LIFE SKILLS

Everyday activities and events are natural resources for promoting social skills and emotional competence. All day long, children interact with you, with their peers, and with materials in their environment. These interactions present opportunities for skill building that we can enhance through conversation, modeling, and even staging potential challenges that we can help children navigate.

Play is perhaps the greatest vehicle for essential skill building, whether it is structured in games, unstructured on the playground, or child-organized in the dramatic play area. Structured games require children to agree on and follow rules, wait their turns, solve problems, and cope with disappointments. It is inevitable that children will struggle with these or other task demands. Don't think of their struggle as a problem, but rather consider it your opportunity to support the development of coping skills.

Unstructured playtime allows children to exercise choice and develop autonomy while providing you with natural opportunities to observe their interests, preferences, and talents. Unstructured play can be rife with incidents of spontaneous prosocial behavior and mini-crises for children to resolve. When we play close attention, we can be there to reinforce children's positive choices and support their efforts to settle conflicts.

In their make-believe play, children experiment with various roles that emerge from their experiences and imaginations. Make-believe play builds competence in many areas, including autonomy, empathy, theory of mind, creativity, and communication as well as literacy and other cognitive skills. The characters children create offer us glimpses through a window to their inner thoughts and understandings. The information we glean from our observations can help us fine-tune our approach to guidance.

VIEWING CHALLENGING BEHAVIOR AS A SKILL-BUILDING OPPORTUNITY

For many reasons, children behave in ways that are contrary to rules and expectations. Rather than reacting with frustration, put on your detective hat, grab your magnifying glass, and look for clues to the possible factors underlying the challenging behavior. What is the meaning of this behavior at this time to this child? Should you focus your intervention on a social or emotional skill that you have noticed is weak or lacking? What is the child trying to accomplish with this behavior? These basic questions should be asked, explored, and answered before you respond to the child's behavior. This process of inquiry requires that you be open to changing habitual ways of responding, and instead address the skill-building needs of the child in an intentional manner.

Sometimes, in the heat of the moment, it is hard to stand back and look so objectively at a child's behavior. The early childhood classroom is a busy, flurried place with multiple demands competing for your attention at any given time. For this and other reasons, try to establish relationships with colleagues in your building, a supervisor, or a mental health consultant who can be available to lend an extra set of eyes to problematic and complex situations.

FINDING ENJOYABLE ACTIVITIES THAT TARGET SPECIFIC SKILLS

Once we notice that particular social or emotional skills are weak in a child or a group of children, we can introduce activities that target those skills. Suppose you discover that a child has difficulty regulating his emotions, especially anger. Recognizing that anger management entails a specific set of subskills, such as self-awareness, identification of triggers, calming strategies, and selecting from among various responses, you can tailor the child's activities to address those subskills. For example, you can read stories with characters who work through angry situations. You can have the children make collages with pictures of emotion-laden faces. In circle time, you may pass a beanbag, and the child holding it can share the memory of an anger-arousing event, their level of anger, how they handled it, and what consequences followed. All the children benefit from hearing the experiences of their peers. It would also be useful for you to share your own stories, including mistakes you have made and how you could have handled a situation more effectively. The list of potential targeted activities is limitless for anger management as well as other essential skills.

The process just outlined can be used with any social or emotional skill for which a child needs assistance. By using games, dialogic reading, circle-time activities, rich conversations, role-plays, puppet plays, art, and movement, you can enhance children's competence without their even knowing they are working on something difficult.

Your lesson plans should include a variety of activities that target the emotional and social developmental needs of each child. For example, the three-year-olds in Ms. Jennifer's class sing a whisper song and take a deep breath before eating lunch. This activity is designed to target impulse control and delay-of-gratification skills in several children. Ms. Ramona engages her two-year-olds in yoga-like calisthenics to improve body awareness, especially for those who have highly unregulated activity levels. The kids love it.

Brainstorm with colleagues about fun ways to promote children's skills that are underdeveloped and need bolstering. For example, when we challenge children with tasks that are just a little above their ability level (perhaps a difficult puzzle or fine-motor task), they can learn to cope with uncertainty and frustration while building confidence and persistence. Dress-up areas promote role-playing skills so vital to the development of empathy and sense of community. Structured games build skills in impulse and emotional regulation as well as social skills like sharing and communication. Always keep in mind which social skills and emotional competency you hope to strengthen when you select materials and activities. Please see Figure 10.3 for an exercise in applying everyday and targeted activities to promote essential skills in children.

FIGURE 10.3
Using Everyday and Targeted Activities to Promote Social and Emotional Skills

Exercise 3

1. Six-year-old Ming is a master of the sneak attack. She is has been known to say hurtful things to her friends and then tell on them for retaliating. She often sits and leans in such a way as to block the view of her classmates during story time. She hides their crayons and glue sticks during art.
   a. What specific skills does Ming need assistance to develop?
   b. What are some activities in which the whole class can participate that will help Ming and similar students build these skills?
   c. What are some targeted activities you could use to strengthen these skills in Ming and others who need more support?

2. Three-year-old Calvin stares blankly at the art materials in front of him with no idea how to begin. On the playground, he clings to you and follows you everywhere you go. His most frequent phrases are "I can't" and "I don't know."
   a. What specific skills does Calvin need assistance to develop?
   b. What are some activities in which the whole class can participate that will help Calvin and his classmates build these skills?
   c. What are some targeted activities you could use to strengthen these skills in Calvin and others who need more support?

3. Two-year-old Casimir frequently pushes his way to the front of the line and grabs toys right out of the hands of his classmates.
   a. What specific skills does Casimir need assistance to develop?
   b. What are some activities in which the whole class can participate that will help Casimir and his classmates build these skills?
   c. What are some targeted activities you could use to strengthen these skills in Casimir and others who need more support?

4. Four-year-old Jaden reacts with physical aggression to almost any provocation. Chloe bumped Jaden near the cubby, and Jaden pushed her down. James reached for the purple paint dish, and Jaden slapped his hand. Impatient waiting for her turn on the swing, Jaden threw sand in Jack's face, forcing him to stop and get off.
   a. What specific skills does Jaden need assistance to develop?
   b. What are some activities in which the whole class can participate to help Jaden and her classmates build these skills?
   c. What are some targeted activities you could use to strengthen these skills in Jaden and others who need more support?

BUILDING RELATIONSHIPS WITH CHILDREN AND FAMILIES

More important than any technique or strategy is the quality of your relationship with the child. Like most individuals, children want to cooperate with people who have taken the time to get to know them and genuinely like them. Healthy attachment relationships form the foundation for all social and emotional development. A child's sense of safety and security in relationships paves the way for his emerging capacities for self-regulation, autonomy, empathy, and communication. Your strong, mutually respectful relationships with each child will facilitate your individualized planning that is so important for their early education. Getting to know each child as an individual is the first step in promoting competence in the social–emotional domain.

Your relationships with family members are equally important. Parents first and foremost want to know that you genuinely like their children. Parents also want to know that you view them as partners and value their opinions, respect their cultural background, and appreciate their efforts and practices. A warm, positive relationship with a parent will increase your comfort level when discussing concerns and facilitate the process of finding solutions to challenging behavior. You and the parents are a team.

Always remember the platinum rule: "Do unto others as you would have *others* do unto others" (Pawl, 1998). When you treat children with compassion and respect, when you model empathy and use the language of community, children will internalize those behaviors and practice them with others.

Sit in front of a mirror with a child on your lap and look closely at yourself and the child. There is much to see. Each of you is complex and full of unique characteristics that influence how you feel and think and interact with others. The better you know those characteristics, the more effective you will be in everything you do. A reflective approach is your most valuable resource in your efforts to promote the essential social and emotional skills that each and every child needs to succeed in school and life.

GLOSSARY

Adaptability a temperament characteristic referring to how quickly and readily a child adjusts to a new or changed situation.

Angels in the nursery a term coined by the field of infant mental health to describe the influence of positive early relationships on ongoing present caregiving relationships.

Antecedents events or triggers that preceded or stimulated the behavior.

Anterior cingulate sometimes considered the chief operating officer of the brain because it helps to allocate attention and coordinate what we do with our thoughts and bodies.

Antisocial behaviors behaviors that show disregard for and violation of the rights of others and may include theft, bullying, deceitfulness, irresponsibility, fighting, lack of remorse, and reckless disregard for the safety of others.

Attachment an emotional bond that forms between an infant and his primary caregiver; an important aspect of caregiving that supports a child's sense of security and safety from a particular adult—the attachment figure—especially in situations that arouse anxiety or distress.

Attention the ability to focus selectively on a desired stimulus or task; alertness, selection, and allocation of energy to the area of focus.

Attention regulation the ability to focus selectively on the task at hand, to sustain that focus for the length of time necessary to complete the task, and to resist distractions.

Attunement a state of interaction between a caregiving adult and a child in which the adult aligns her own internal state with that of the child, accomplished by attending to the nonverbal, often subtle communication of the child.

Autism spectrum disorders (ASD) a group of developmental disabilities that can cause significant social, communication, and behavioral challenges.

Autonomy the sense that one is able to do things for oneself, think for oneself, and govern one's own decisions and direction.

Brainstem the part of the brain that develops first and regulates the sleep-arousal cycle and fight-or-flight response.

Caregiving providing physical and emotional care and support.

Challenging behavior actions on the part of a child that are disruptive, offensive, dangerous, or hurtful; conduct that interferes with a child's functioning, learning, or relationships.

Classical conditioning in the context of empathy development, a mode of empathic arousal in which the child observes signs of distress in another person such as a caregiver, and the child pairs her own distress with that of the caregiver.

Collectivist culture a culture in which the individual is seen first and foremost as a member of the group, and individuality and autonomy are deemphasized. The goal is interdependence, where a person's uniqueness is primarily for the benefit of the group, not the person himself.

Co-regulation sharing of emotional regulation between child and caregiver through which the child becomes able to regulate his own internal states.

Communication the broad process by which meaningful information is exchanged among individuals.

Confidence the belief in oneself and one's abilities or power.

Context the circumstances that surround behavioral expectations.

Conversation a verbal or nonverbal exchange of ideas that goes back and forth where each idea expressed by one is extended or elaborated by the other.

Creativity the ability to generate new ideas or combinations of ideas to solve problems or develop new forms.

Cultural competence knowing, respecting, appreciating, and honoring the diversity of cultures in our work with others.

Cultural scripts the combination of elements that forms the ways in which a person views the world, thinks, and behaves.

Culture a shared system of meaning, which includes values, beliefs, and assumptions expressed in daily interactions of individuals within a group through a definite pattern of language, behavior, customs, attitudes, and practices; the array of values and teachings stemming from the child's family and community.

Delay of gratification or deferred gratification the ability to postpone immediate satisfaction for the sake of future consequences.

Developmental screening a procedure used to determine if a behavior pattern is aberrant enough to warrant further evaluation and intervention; a system for measuring developmental skills in all domains, including the social–emotional domain.

Dialogic reading a process of reading with children during which children participate in the telling of the story; the adult reads and shares pictures and then pauses to invite input from the children.

Direct association in the context of empathy development, a mode of empathic arousal in which one sees a person in a difficult situation that reminds him of a similar situation from his own life and feels distress for that person.

Early childhood mental health the child's ability to experience, regulate, and express emotions; form close and secure interpersonal relationships; explore the environment; and learn in the context of family and community.

Emotional regulation the ability to inhibit, enhance, maintain, and modulate emotional arousal to accomplish one's goals.

Emotional vocabulary the words we use to describe emotions in ourselves and others.

Empathy a person's emotional response that stems from apprehension of another's emotional state and is similar to what another person is feeling; an affective response that is more appropriate for another person's situation than one's own; an emotional connection to the inner experiences of others that leads a person to feel connected to them.

Environmental history the child's past and current experiences that may support or disrupt his development.

Ethnicity a person's or family's country of origin.

Evaluation a detailed procedure conducted by a specially trained professional to determine a child's unique profile of strengths, weaknesses, and intervention needs and to develop a comprehensive individualized plan for remediation.

Executive functions the higher-order cognitive activities necessary for adaptive and goal-oriented behavior that exert control over basic sensory, attention, emotional, and behavioral processes.

Expressive communication the process involved in the transmission of oral, nonverbal, or symbolic communication to another person; the process of conveying a message to another person.

Extended discourse reciprocal interactions with opportunities to hear and produce explanations and personal narratives.

Extrinsic motivation the willingness to apply oneself to a task only with the promise or expectation of an external reward.

Family dynamics the quality and nature of relationships within the family—that is, how people relate to one another.

Filter to inhibit the expression of words or gestures that will offend other people, have negative consequences, or interfere with accomplishing one's goals.

Fulfillment of needs a component of a person's sense of community; the understanding that associating with the group will meet the needs of its members.

Functional analysis (FA) a specific procedure where a child is observed directly in a variety of situations on multiple occasions using clearly defined behavior indicators that reflects a running account of antecedents, behaviors, and consequences (ABCs).

Functional behavior assessment (FBA) an organized effort to understand the function that a child's difficult behavior is serving in order to decide the best way to address it using direct and indirect information.

Ghosts in the nursery a term borrowed from the field of infant mental health that suggests that the ways in which our primary caregivers (our parents and guardians) related to us, for better or for worse, profoundly influence our present relationships with children in our care.

Goodness-of-fit the degree to which an individual's temperament is compatible with the demands and expectations of his environment.

Habituation/dishabituation a preference technique used to research infant learning that assumes that infants prefer to look at novel stimuli. When an object becomes familiar, the infant looks away and heart rate and other physiological activity decrease. When a different stimulus is introduced and the infant looks again, dishabituation is said to have occurred.

Helpless an orientation in which a person believes that his innate intelligence determines success or failure on a task and that he has a certain immutable level of intelligence and there is nothing he can do to change it.

Impulse control the ability to resist the inclination to act immediately without consideration of other behavior choices or possible consequences; involves inhibition of the impulse to do one thing and to stop and think about what is most appropriate or needed.

Individualistic culture a culture that encourages individuals to think for themselves, empowers them to solve their own problems, promotes independence in personal care, and welcomes their expression of thoughts and feelings; high value is placed on autonomy and independence.

Inductive approach a guidance strategy in which adults make explicit the likely consequence of the child's action on the other person.

Influence a component of sense of community that reflects the belief that one has an impact on the activities or the success of the group, and the group has an impact on the behavior or the well-being of the individual.

Instinct an inherent inclination toward a certain behavior that occurs below a conscious level.

Internal working models cognitive-emotional expectations for relationships that influence how a child experiences and reacts to a caregiver and, over time, to other people.

*Inter*personal **intelligence** a person's capacity to understand the intentions, motivations, and desires of other people and, consequently, work effectively with others.

Intonation the fluctuation of pitch in speech.

*Intra*personal **intelligence** the capacity to understand oneself, to have an effective working model of oneself, including desires, fears, and capacities, and to use such information effectively in regulating one's own life.

Intrinsic motivation an orientation in which a person is purely motivated by the sheer pleasure of learning or doing.

Joint attention the manner in which two or more individuals simultaneously attend to a common or goal object.

Knowledge need when a child does not know, and might not be expected to know, how to behave appropriately in a given situation and must be taught.

Language a specific method by which people communicate that uses symbols such as words, signs, or pictures. It involves coding those symbols to convey a message and decoding the symbols to comprehend the meaning of a message received.

Limbic system brain structures and processes that mediate emotion and motivation.

Listening style a set of attitudes, beliefs, and predispositions about the how, where, when, who, and what of the information reception and encoding process.

Listening the process of taking in information through the sense of hearing and making meaning from what was heard.

Mastery-oriented an orientation to tasks in which a person believes that his success is within his control and that with effort his skills will improve.

Mediated association a mode of empathic arousal that is invoked when a more experienced person points out and names the emotion experienced by another.

Membership a sense that one belongs within the boundaries of a group.

Mental health consultant a specially trained mental health professional who works collaboratively with the adults in a child's life (e.g., early childhood educators, parents, and early intervention providers) to increase their skills and expertise so that they may, in turn, promote social and emotional competence in children.

Mental states (or inner states) thoughts, feelings, preferences, biases, and intentions.

Meta-cognition the process of thinking about thinking.

Mirror neurons neural firings (signals between nerve cells) in the brain of an observer that occur in the same brain areas as in a person who is experiencing the emotion herself.

Motivation or mastery motivation a psychological force that stimulates an individual to attempt independently, in a focused and persistent manner, to solve a problem or master a skill or task that is at least moderately challenging for him or her.

Motor mimicry the process whereby one spontaneously imitates the facial, vocal, or postural expression of distress in another and the resulting change in one's own expression is experienced as a feeling of distress.

Need for skill building the circumstances in which a child clearly knows what is expected but lacks the skill to behave in the appropriate manner consistently across situations.

Neurons nerve cells.

Nonverbal communication the process of sending and receiving wordless messages; includes gestures, body language, facial expressions, posture, eye contact, proximity, clothing, and hairstyle. People communicate nonverbally through dance, music, art, drama, and other behaviors.

Object permanence knowledge that an object continues to exist even when it is out of sight.

Orbitofrontal cortex a brain area that connects virtually all the essential brain processes involved in self-regulation, including the brainstem (arousal), the limbic system (emotions), and the frontal cortex (reasoning and logic).

Parallel process a term borrowed from the literature on reflective supervision in the field of infant mental health and refers to the process by which the nature of one relationship is replicated in another relationship.

Parasympathetic nervous system (PNS) part of the autonomic nervous system that enables us to calm down, relax, and rest; sometimes referred to as the relaxation response.

Persistence a temperament dimension that facilitates autonomy and refers to the capacity to sustain attention to the task at hand for a sufficient amount of time to attain a goal.

Personality the stable set of traits, or patterns of affect, behavior, and cognition that define a person, as well as his characteristic adaptations to situation and self-defining life narratives.

Platinum rule created by Jeree Pawl, "Do unto others as you would have **others** do unto **others**."

Prefrontal cortex an area of the brain involved in response inhibition, problem solving, reasoning, and other executive functions; an essential brain area for self-regulation and the last to fully mature.

Problem of will an active choice on the part of the child to defy expectations or authority.

Project-oriented approach an approach to teaching in which children pose the questions, conduct their own investigations, and make decisions about how their time should be used.

Proprioception the system of communication between the muscles and the nervous system initiated by receptors in the muscles, tendons, and joints that provide information about movement or position of the body in space, including internal organs.

Prosocial babies infants who show communications and behaviors that help create a positive emotional climate in the group and that involve reaching out—positive, discernable, outward social expressions on the part of one baby toward one or more other individuals, whether infant or adult.

Prosocial behaviors voluntary behaviors intended to benefit others that include helping, taking turns, sharing, and comforting others.

Prosodic features of speech that include intonation, rhythm, and stress.

Reaction an emotion or behavior that immediately follows a triggering event with no time taken for consideration of outcomes or other factors.

Reactivity one's level of response to sensory input.

Receptive communication the process of receiving and understanding communication; involves perceiving, acknowledging, interpreting, and comprehending the messages sent by another.

Reciprocal determinism a term Bandura used to describe the process of personality development where the forces of the person component (cognitive and emotional factors), environmental reinforcers, and behaviors interact to create one's personality.

Reflection the ability to look within ourselves and to look in depth at others so that we may use our enhanced understanding to determine the most effective ways to interact; the ability to see ourselves as others see us; a thinking process that allows us to consider the many variables that result in the behavior of self and others.

Reflective functioning the essential human capacity to understand behavior in light of underlying mental states and intentions.

Reflective listening a listening approach in which the listener serves as a mirror to the speaker such that rather than answering the client's question, challenging his idea, asking questions or offering advice, the reflective listener confirms the idea expressed by the speaker.

Reflective practice an approach to teaching or practicing that involves stopping to consider various strategies and the reasons for them, thinking critically about alternative perspectives, and changing practices based on new understandings.

Relationship-based guidance an approach to teaching and guidance that emphasizes the emotional connection between two individuals, the adult and the child.

Relaxation response the process of calming down, relaxing, and resting; activation of the parasympathetic nervous system.

Response an emotion or behavior that follows a triggering event and is the result of thoughtful examination of personal and contextual variables, determination of desired outcomes, exploration of all possible actions, and an intentional selection of the most effective course of action.

Responsiveness the quality in a relationship in which one person responds intentionally and very specifically to the emotional states and needs of another.

Rhythm the timing of spoken syllables that are common in a language.

Role- or perspective-taking a mode of empathic arousal characterized by the ability to create an image in one's mind of the thoughts, feelings, and needs of another.

Screening (See Developmental Screening) a preliminary way to see if a behavior pattern is aberrant enough to warrant further exploration by a professional.

Self-efficacy the sense that one's actions matter and that one can have an effect on the world.

Self-regulation the ability to monitor and manage one's thinking, attention, feelings, and behavior to accomplish goals.

Self-theory one's beliefs about himself.

Sense of community a feeling of belonging, a belief that members matter to one another and the group, and a shared faith that members' needs will be met through their commitment to being together.

Sensitivity the capacity to take in and process sensory input.

Sensory integration the process of organizing sensations from the body and the environment for adaptive use.

Sensory processing the ability to organize sensations from the body and the environment and put them to adaptive use.

Sensory regulation the ability to take in, modulate, and organize sensations to engage in the task at hand.

Sensory threshold the point of detection of sensory input in a given person at a given time.

Shared emotional connection a necessary element for promoting a sense of community that relates to the intensity, frequency, importance, and desirability of the interactions with the group.

Skills aptitudes, competencies, abilities.

Social referencing the act on the part of an infant or toddler of looking back at the attachment figure for reassurance and approval.

Stress a condition in which circumstances in one's life increase their level of arousal; in speech, the emphasis of certain syllables in a word or certain words in a sentence.

Sympathetic nervous system (SNS) a component of the autonomic nervous system that enables a person to mobilize the body's resources under stress. The sympathetic nervous system governs the fight-or-flight response, characterized by increased heart rate and force of contraction, dilation of the pupils, reduced digestion, and other physical changes.

Synapse the space between neurons where electrochemical reactions connect neurons to each other as a result of experience.

Temperament individual differences in emotional reactivity and regulation that appear early in life, are relatively stable, and are at least partly biologically based.

Theory of mind a set of beliefs a person develops to describe, explain, and make predictions about other people's knowledge, beliefs, and behavior based on inferences about their mental states; awareness of the mental states of others.

Trigger an object or event that stimulates emotional arousal.

Vestibular processing one's sense of balance and perception of his or her body in space, with its locus of processing in the inner ear.

Will determination, desire, or motivation to behave in a certain manner.

Wonder a feeling of surprise and awe caused by something unexpected, unfamiliar, or inexplicable; like curiosity with a dash of amazement, an important ingredient in autonomy.

REFERENCES

Accardo, P., Tomazic, T., Fete, T., Heaney, M., Lindsay, R., & Whitman, B. (1997). Maternally reported fetal activity levels and developmental diagnoses. *Clinical Pediatrics, 36,* 279–283.

Acredolo, L., & Goodwyn, S. (2000, July 18). *The long-term impact of symbolic gesturing during infancy on IQ at age 8.* Retrieved September 25, 2011, from Baby Signs, Inc.: https://www.babysigns.com/index.cfm?id=113

Adamson, L., & Frick, J. (2003). The Still Face: A History of a Shared Experimental Paradigm. *Infancy, 4* (4), 451–473

AGBeat News. (2011, August 15). *Agent Genius.* Retrieved September 2, 2011, from Surprising statistics about social media use in America—infographic: agentgenius.com/real-estate-technology-new-media/surpising-statistics-about-social-media-in-america

Alter, P. J., Conroy, M. A., Mancil, G. R., & Haydon, T. (2008). A Comparison of Functional Behavior Assessment Methodologies with Young Children: Descriptive Methods and Functional Analysis. *Journal of Behavior Education, 17,* 200–219.

American Pregnancy Association. (2008, October 1). *Using illegal drugs during pregnancy.* Retrieved April 24, 2011, from www.americanpregnancyassociation.org: www.americanpregnancyassociation.org/pregnancyhealth/illegaldrugs.html

American Psychiatric Association. (2000). *Diagnostic and Statistical Manual of Mental Disorders: Fourth Edition Text Revision.* Washington, DC: American Psychiatric Association.

Arnold, D., Ortiz, C., Curry, J., Stowe, R., Goldstein, N., & Fisher, P. (1999). Promoting academic success and preventing disruptive behavior disorders through community partnerships. *Journal of Community Psychology, 27* (5), 589–598.

Arthur, L., Beecher, B., Death, E., Dockett, S., & Farmer, S. (2005). *Programming and planning in early childhood settings* (3rd ed.). Sydney: Thomson Publications.

Axline, V. (1947, 1989). *Play Therapy.* New York: Ballentine Books.

Ayres, A. J. (1979). *Sensory integration and the child.* Los Angeles, CA: Western Psychological Services.

Bandura, A. (1989). Social cognitive theory. *Annals of Child Development, 6,* 1–60.

Bandura, A., Ross, D., & Ross, S. (1961). Transmission of aggression through imitation of aggressive models. *Journal of Abnormal & Social Psychology, 63,* 575–582.

Barker, L., & Watson, K. (2000). *Listen up.* New York: St. Martin's Press.

Baron-Cohen, S. (2001). Theory of Mind and Autism: A Review. *International of Research in Mental Retardation, 23,* 169–184.

Belsky, J., Bakermans-Kranenburg, M., & van IJzendoorn, M. (2007). For better and for worse: Differential susceptibility to environmental influences. *Current Directions in Psychological Science, 16,* 300–304.

Benson, H., & Klipper, M. Z. (2000). *The Relaxation Response.* New York: Harper Paperbacks.

Bijou, S. W., Peterson, R., & Ault, M. (1968). A method to integrate descriptive and experimental field studies at the level of data and empirical concepts. *Journal of Applied Behavior Analysis, 1,* 175–191.

Bodrova, E., & Leong, D. (2007). *Tools of the Mind.* Upper Saddle River, NJ: Pearson Education.

Boris, N., Aoki, Y., & Zeanah, C. (1999). The development of infant-parent attachment: Consideration for assessment. *Infants and Young Children, 11,* 1–10.

Bos, K., Zeanah, C., Fox, N., Drury, S., McLaughlin, K., & Nelson, C. (2011). Psychiatric outcomes in young children with a history of institutionalization. *Harvard Review of Psychiatry, 19* (1), 15–24.

Boyd, D. R., & Bee, H. (2010). *The Growing Child.* Boston: Allyn & Bacon.

Boyd, J., Barnett, S., Bodrova, E., Leong, D., & Gomby, D. (2005, March 1). *Promoting children's social and emotional development through preschool education.* Retrieved November 18, 2011, from National Institute for Early Education Research: http://nieer.org/resources/policyreports/report7.pdf

Bredekamp, S., & Copple, C. (1997). *Developmentally Appropriate Practice in Early Childhood Programs*. Washington, DC: National Association for the Education of Young Children.

Bronfenbrenner, U. (1979). *The Ecology of Human Development: Experiments by Nature and Design*. Cambridge, MA: Harvard University Press.

Bronson, P., & Merryman, A. (2009). *Nurture Shock: New thinking about children*. New York: Twelve Hatchett Book Group.

Bus, A., Both-de Vries, A., de Jong, M., Sulzby, E., & de Jong, E. (2001, November 5). *Center for the Improvement of Early Reading Achievement*. Retrieved October 16, 2011, from ciera.org: www.ciera.org/library/reports/inquiry-2/2-015/2-015.pdf

Buss, A., & Plomin, R. (1984). *Temperament: Early developing personality traits*. Hilldale, NJ: Erlbaum.

Calkins, S. D. (2011). Caregiving as Coregulation: Psychobiological Processes and Child Functioning. In A. Booth, S. M. McHale, & N. S. Landale, *Biosocial Foundations of Family Processes* (pp. 49–59). New York: Springer Science and Business Media, LLC.

Carlson, S. M., Moses, L. J., & Claxton, L. J. (2004). Individual differences in executive functioning and theory of mind: An investigation of inhibitory control and planning ability. *Journal of Experimental Child Psychology, 87,* 299–319.

Caspi, A., Moffitt, T., Newman, D., & Silva, P. (1996). Behavioral observations at age three years predict adult psychiatric disorders: Longitudinal evidence from a birth cohort. *Archives of General Psychiatry, 53,* 1033–1039.

Cassidy, J., & Shaver, P. (1999). *Handbook of attachment*. New York: The Guilford Press.

Center on the Social and Emotional Foundations for Early Learning. (2011, January). *CSEFEL: Center on the Social and Emotional Foundations for Early Learning*. Retrieved November 19, 2011, from Vanderbilt University: http://csefel.vanderbilt.edu/

Centers for Disease Control and Prevention. (2011, March 25). *Autism Spectrum Disorders (ASDs)*. Retrieved November 19, 2011, from Centers for Disease Control and Prevention: www.cdc.gov/ncbddd/autism/index.html

Chau, M., Thampi, K., & Wight, V. R. (2010, October 1). *Basic Facts about Low-income Children, 2009: Children Under Age 6*. Retrieved November 19, 2011, from National Center for Children in Poverty: www nccp.org/publications/pub_972.html

Chau, M., Thampi, K., & Wight, V. R. (2010, October 30). *Basic Facts About Low-income Children, 2009*. Retrieved January 14, 2011, from National Center for Children in Poverty: http://nccp.org/publications/pub_971.html

Chesley, G., Gillett, D., & Wagner, W. (2008). Verbal and Nonverbal Metaphor With Children in Counseling. *Journal of Counseling & Development, 86,* 399–411.

Christiansen, M., Emde, R., & Fleming, C. (2004). Cultural perspectives for assessing infants and young children. In R. Delcarment-Wiggins, & A. Carter, *Handbook of infant, toddler and preschool mental health assessment* (pp. 7–23). New York: Oxford University Press.

Christophe, A., Millotte, S., Bernal, S., & Lidz, J. (2008). Bootstrapping lexical and syntactic acquisition. *Language & Speech, 51,* 61–75.

Coakley, C., & Wolvin, A. (1997). Listening in the educational environment. In M. Purdy, & D. Borisoff, *Listening in everyday life: A personal and professional approach* (2nd ed.) (pp. 172–212). Lanham, MD: University Press of America.

Cohen, E., & Kaufmann, R. (2005). *Early childhood mental health consultation*. Substance Abuse and Mental Health Servies Administration, Center for Mental Health Services. Rockville, MD: Department of Health and Human Services.

Colle, L., & Del Giudice, M. (2011). Patterns of Attachment and Emtional Competence in Middle Childhood. *Social Development, 20* (1).

Conaway, M. (1982). Listening: Learning tool and retention agent. In A. Algier, & K. E. Algier, *Improving reading and study skills* (pp. 51–63). San Francisco: Jossey-Bass.

Conn-Powers, M. (2010, April). *Essential Skills for Successful School Readiness*. Retrieved November 20, 2011, from Early Childhood Center, IIDC, Indiana University: www.iidc.indiana.edu/styles/iidc/defiles/ECC/EssentialSkills.pdf

Conn-Powers, M., Cross, A. F., & Dixon, S. (2011, June). *The First Days of Kindergarten and What They Mean for Preschool Teachers*. Retrieved November 20, 2011, from Indiana Institute on Disability and Community Early Childhood Center: www.iidc.indiana.edu/styles/iidc/defiles/ECC/ECCKindergartenResearchPaper2011.pdf

Cumming, T., & Lesniak, G. (2000). *Improving Employability Skills through Cooperative Education and Tech Prep*. Retrieved November 20, 2011, from Education Resources Information Center (ERIC): www.eric.ed.gov/PDFS/ED442978.pdf

DeYoung, C. G., & Gray, J. (2009). Personality Neuroscience: Explaining Individual Differences in Affect, Behavior and Cognition. In P. Corr, & G. E. Matthews, *The Cambridge handbook of personality psychology* (pp. 323–346). New York: Cambridge University Press.

Dickinson, D. K., & Porche, M. (2011). Relation Between Language Experiences in Preschool Classrooms and Children's Kindergarten and Fourth-Grade Language and Reading Abilities. *Child Development, 82* (3), 870–866.

Dickinson, D. K. (2003). Why We Must Improve Teacher-Child Conversations in Preschools and the Promise of Professional Development. In L. Girolometto, & E. Weitzman (Eds.), *Enhancing caregiver language facilitation in childcare settings*. (pp. 4-1–4-8). Toronto, Canada: The Hanen Institute.

Dietrich, C., Swingley, D., & Werker, J. (2007, October 2). *Native language governs interpretation of salient speech sound differences at 18 months*. Retrieved September 29, 2011, from PNAS Online: www.pnas.org/content/104/41/16027.full

Dombro, A.L., Jablon, J., & Stetson, C. (2011). *Powerful Interactions: How to connect with children to extend their learning*. Washington, DC: NAEYC.

Donne, J. (1839). *The Works of John Donne* (Vol. 3). (H. Alford, Ed.) London: John W. Parker.

Dougherty, L., Bufferd, S., Carlson, G., Dyson, M., Olino, T., Durbin, C. E., et al. (2011). Preschoolers' Observed Temperament and Psychiatric Disorders Assessed with a Parent Diagnostic Interview. *Journal of Clinical Child & Adolescent Psychology, 40* (2), 295–306.

Drotar, D. S. (2008). *Pediatric Developmental Screening: Understanding and selecting screening instruments*. New York: The Commonwealth Fund.

Dweck, C. S. (1999, Spring). Caution - Praise can be dangerous. *American Educator*, 1–5.

Dweck, C. S. (2000). *Self-theories: Their Role in Motivation, Personality and Development*. Philadelphia: The Psychology Press.

Dweck, C. S. (2006) *Mindset: The New Psychology of Success*. New York: Random House.

Edwards, C., Gandini, L., & Forman, G. (1998). *The Hundred Languages of Children: The Reggio Emilia Approach—Advanced Reflections*. Greenwich, CT: Ablex.

Eisenberg, N., & Fabes, R. A. (1990). Empathy: conceptualization, measurement and relation to prosocial behavior. *Motivation and Emotion, 14*, 131–149.

Eisenberg, N., Fabes, R. A., Shepard, S. A., Murphy, B. C., Guthrie, I. K., Jones, S., et al. (1997). Contemporaneous and Longitudinal Prediction of Children's Social Functioning from Regulation and Emotionality. *Child Development, 68* (4), 642–664.

Elicker, J. & Fortner-Wood, C. (1995). Research in review: Adult-child relationships in early childhood settings. *Young Children 51* (1), 69–78.

Eisenhauer, M. J., & Katz, J. E. (2011). R.E.A.L.K.I.D.S.: A Framework for Intentional Social–Emotional Guidance. *Early Years, 32* (3), 22–25.

Emde, R. N. (2006). Culture, diagnostic assessment and identity: Defining concepts. *Infant Mental Health Journal, 27*, 606–611.

Epstein, A. S. (2009). *Me, you, us: social–emotional learning in preschool*. Ypsilanti, MI: HighScope Press.

Ericsson, K. A. (2007, June 7). The Making of an Expert. *Harvard Business Reveiw*, 1–6.

Ericsson, K. A., Prietula, M. J., & Cokely, E. T. (2007, July 30). The Making of an Expert. *Harvard Business Review*. Retrieved May 9, 2011, from Harvard Business Online: http://hbr.org/2007/07/the-making-of-an-expert/ar/1

Erikson, E. (1993). *Childhood and Society* (2nd ed.). New York: W. W. Norton, Inc.

Espinosa, L. (2010). *Getting it Right for Young Children from Diverse Backgrounds: Applying Research to Improve Practice*. New Jersey: Pearson Education, Inc.

Evans, B. (2009). *You're not my friend anymore!* Ypsilanti: High/Scope.

Facebook (2011). *Statistics/Facebook*. Retrieved March 29, 2012, from Facebook website: http://newsroom.fb.com/content/default.aspx?NewsAreaId=22

Fisher, B. (1995). *Thinking and learning together: Curriculum and community in a primary classroom*. Portsmouth, NH: Heinemann.

Fox, N., Almas, A., Degnan, K., Nelson, C., & Zeanah, C. (2011). The effects of severe psychosocial deprivation and foster care intervention on cognitive development at 8 years of age: findings from the Bucharest Early Intervention Project. *The Journal of Child Psychology and Psychiatry, 52* (9), 919–928.

Fraiberg, S., Adelson, E., & Shapiro, V. (1975). Ghosts in the nursery: A psychoanalytic approach to the problems of impaired infant-mother relationships. *Journal of the American Academy of Child Psychiatry, 14*, 338–421.

Frey, D. (1993). Learning by metaphor. In C. Schaefer, *The therapeutic powers of play* (pp. 223–239). Northvale, NJ: Aronson.

Galinsky, E. (2010). *Mind in the Making*. New York: Harper Collins Publishers.

Gardner, H. (1999). *Intelligence Reframed: Mulitiple Intelligences for the 21st Century*. New York: Basic Books.

Gillespie, L. G., & Seibel, N. L. (2006, July 15). *Self-Regulation: A Cornerstone of Early Childhood Development*. Retrieved February 22, 2011, from Beyond the Journal-Young Children on the Web: www.naeyc.org/yc/files/200607/Gillespie709BTJ.pdf

Gilliam, W. (2005). *Prekindergarteners left behind: Expulsion rates in state prekindergarten programs*. New York: Foundation for Child Development.

Gladwell, M. (2005). *Blink: The Power of Thinking Without Thinking*. New York: Little, Brown and Company.

Goldsmith, H. H., Lemery, K., Aksan, N., & Buss, K. A. (2000). Temperament substrates of personality development. In V. J. Molfese, & D. L. Molfese, *Temperament and personality development across the life span* (pp. 1–32). New Jersey: Erlbaum.

Goleman, D. (1995). *Emotional Intelligence: Why it can matter more than IQ*. New York: Bantam.

Gonzalez-Mena, J. (2008). *Diversity in Early Care and Education: Honoring Differences*. New York, NY: McGraw-Hill.

Goodwyn, S., Acredolo, L., & Brown, C. (2000). Impact of symbolic gesturing on early language development. *Journal of Nonverbal Behavior, 24*, 81–103.

Grossberg, S., & Vladusich, T. (2010). How do children learn to follow gaze, share joint attention, imitate their teachers, and use tools during social interactions? *Neural Networks, 23*, 940–965.

Hansen, R., & Hansen, K. (2011, January). *What Do Employers Really Want: Top Skills and Values Employers Seek from Job-Seekers*. Retrieved November 20, 2011, from Quintessential Careers: www.quintcareers.com/job_skills_values.html

Harvard (2012). *Toxic Stress: The Facts*. Retrieved May 13, 2012, from Center on the Developing Child at Harvard University: http://developingchild.harvard.edu/topics/science_of_early_childhood/toxic_stress_response

Hauser-Cram, P., & Mitchell, D. (2009). I Think I Can, I Knew I Could: Understanding and Encouraging Mastery Motivation in Young Children. In M. M. Burnham, & E. L. Essa, *Informing Our Practice: Useful Research on Young Children's Development* (pp. 136–140). Washington, DC: National Association for the Education of Young Children.

Heath, S., & Hogben, J. (2004). Cost-effective prediction of reading difficulties. *Journal of Speech, Language and Hearing Research, 47*, 751–765.

Heffron, M. C., Ivins, B., & Weston, D. R. (2005). Finding an Authentic Voice, Use of Self: Essential Learning Processes for Relationship-based Work. *Infants & Young Children, 18* (4), 323–336.

Helm, J. H., & Katz, L. (2011). The Fire Hydrant Project: Adapting the Approach for Toddlers. In J. H. Helm, & L. Katz, *Young Investigators: The Project Approach in the Early Years* (pp. 89–97). New York: Teachers College Press.

Hoffman, M. L. (2000). *Empathy and Moral Development: Implications for Caring and Justice*. Cambridge, UK: Cambridge University Press.

Hoffman, M. L. (2007). The Origins of Empathic Morality in Toddlerhood. In C. Brownwell, & C. Kopp, *Socioemotional development in the toddler years: transitions and transformations* (pp. 132–149). New York: The Guilford Press.

Hofstede, G. (1991). Empirical models of cultural differences. In N. Bleichrodt, & P. J. Drenth, *Contemporary issues in cross-cultural psychology* (pp. 4–20). Lisse, The Netherlands: Swets & Zeitlinger.

Hyson, M. (2008). *Enthusiastic and Engaged Learners: Approaches to Learning in the Early Childhood Classroom*. Washington, DC: National Association for the Education of Young Children.

Hyson, M., & Taylor, J. (2011, July). Caring about Caring: What Adults Can Do to Promote Young Children's Prosocial Skills. *Young Children*, 74–83.

Jablon, J., Dombro, A., & Dichtelmiller, M. (2007). *The Power of Observation for Birth through Eight* (2nd ed.). Washington, DC: Teaching Strategies, Inc.

Jalongo, M. (2006). *Early childhood language arts* (4th ed.). Boston: Allyn & Bacon.

Jalongo, M. R. (2008). *Learning to Listen, Listening to Learn: Building essential skills in young children*. Washington, DC: National Association for the Education of Young Children.

Janusik, L., Fullenkamp, L., & Partese, L. (2007, January 1). *Listening Facts*. Retrieved September 29, 2011, from Listen.org: http://d1025403.site.myhosting.com/files.listen.org/Facts.htm

Jennings, P., & Greenberg, M. (2009). The Prosocial Classroom: Teacher Social and Emotional Competence in Relation to Student and Classroom Outcomes. *Review of Educational Research*, 79 (1), 491–525.

Johnson, S. (1998). *Who Moved My Cheese?* New York: Putnam Adult.

Kagan, J. (2005, September 28). *Temperament. 1–4*. Montreal, Quebec, Canada: Centre of Excellence for Early Childhood Development. Retrieved June 30, 2011, from Encyclopedia on Early Childood Development: www.child-encyclopedia.com/documents/KaganANGxp.pdf

Kagan, J., & Snidman, N. (2004). *The long shadow of temperament*. Cambridge, MA: Harvard University Press.

Kaplan, P. S., & Werner, J. S. (1986). Habituation, response to novelty, and dishabituation in human infants: Tests of a dual process theory of visual attention. *Journal of Experimental Child Psychology*, 42 (2), 199–217.

Katz, L. (1994). *The project approach*. Champaign, IL: ERIC Clearninghouse on Elemenentary and Early Childhood Education.

Kennedy, R. F. (1966, June 6). *Day of Affirmation Address* (news release text version). Retrieved December 15, 2011, from John F. Kennedy Presidential Library and Museum: www.jfklibrary.org/Research/Ready-Reference/RFK-Speeches/Day-of-Affirmation-Address-news-release-text-version.aspx

Keyser, J. (2006). *From Parents to Partners: Building a Family-Centered Early Childhood Program*. St. Paul, MN: Redleaf Press.

Kim, J., & Deater-Deckard, K. (2011). Dynamic changes in anger, externalizing and internalizing problems: attention and regulation. *Journal of Child Psychology and Psychiatry*, 52 (2), 156–166.

Klein, A. S. (2008, December 1). *Creating Peaceful Environmental Designs for the Classroom*. Retrieved September 10, 2011, from Early Childhood News: www.earlychildhoodnews.com/earlychildhood/article_view.aspx?ArticleID=390

Kochanska, G., Forman, D., Aksan, N., & Dunbar, S. (2005). Pathways to conscience: early mother-child mutually responsive orientation and children's moral emotion, conduct, and cognition. *Journal of Child Psychology and Psychiatry*, 46 (1), 19–34.

Ladd, G., Kochenderfer, B., & Coleman, C. (1997). Classroom peer acceptance, friendship and victimization: Distinct relational systems that contribute uniquely to children's school adjustment. *Child Development*, 68 (6), 1181–1197.

Lansford, J. E., Malone, P. S., Stevens, K. I., Dodge, K. A., Bates, J. E., & Pettit, G. S. (2006). Developmental trajectories of externalizing and internalizing behaviors: Factors underlying resilience in physically abused children. *Development and Psychopathology*, 18(1), 35–55.

Lapsley, D. (2011). Landmarks of Moral Formation in Early Childhood. *Indiana Association for Infant and Toddler Mental Health Annual Conference* (pp. 1–52). Indianapolis: IAITMH.

Lieberman, A. F., & Van Horn, P. (2005). *"Don't Hit My Mommy!"* Washington, DC: ZERO TO THREE Press.

Lieberman, A., Padron, E., Van Horn, P., & Harris, W. (2005). Angels in the Nursery: The intergenerational transmission of benevolent parental influences. *Infant Mental Health Journal*, 26 (6), 504–520.

Liszkowski, U., Carpenter, M., & Tomasello, M. (2008). Twelve-month-olds communicate helpfully and appropriately for knowledgeable and ignorant partners. *Cognition, 108*, 732–739.

Loh, A. (2006, December 1). *Reggio Emilia Approach.* Retrieved September 10, 2011, from Brainy-child.com: www.brainy-child.com/article/reggioemilia.shtml

Malaguzzi, L. (1998). History, ideas and basic philosophy: An interview with Lella Gandini. In C. Edwards, *The Hundred languages of children: The Reggio Emilia approach* (pp. 49–98). Greenwich, CT: Ablex.

Mangione, P. (1995) *"Acknowledge, Ask, and Adapt,"* *A Guide to Culturally Sensitive Care,* developed by WestEd and California Department of Education, Sacramento.

Mann, T., Steward, M., Eggbeer, L., & Norton, D. (2007, May). ZERO TO THREE's Task Force on Culture and Development: Learning to Walk the Talk. *Zero to Three*, 7–15.

Marshall, P., Fox, N. A., & Group, T. B. (2004). A comparison of the electroencephalogram between institutionalized and community children in Romania. *Cognitive Neuroscience, 16* (8), 1327–1338.

Martin, J. B., & Carle, E. (1996). *Brown Bear, Brown Bear, What Do You See?* New York: Henry Holt and Co.

Maschinot, B. (2008). *The Changing Face of the United States: The Influence of Culture on Early Child Development.* Washington, DC: ZERO TO THREE.

Massey, S. L. (2004). Teacher-Child Conversations in the Preschool Classroom. *Early Childhood Education Journal, 31* (4), 227–231.

Mayer, K. (2009). Emergent Knowledge About Emergent Writing. In E. L. Essa, M. M. Burnham, & Eds., *Informing Our Practice: Useful Research on Young Children's Development* (pp. 111–118). Washington, DC: National Association for the Education of Young Children.

McCabe, A., & Peterson, C. (1991). Getting the story: A longitudinal study of parental styles of eliciting narratives and developing narrative skill. In A. McCabe, C. Peterson, & Eds., *Developing narrative structure* (pp. 217–253). Hillsdale, NJ: Lawrence Erlbaum Associates.

McCann, C., & Yarbrough, K. (2006, July 1). *Snapshots: Incorporating Comprehensive Developmental Screenings into Programs for Young Children.* Ounce of Prevention Fund, Retrieved September 4, 2012, from www.ounceofprevention.org/news/pdfs/Snapshots.pdf

McClelland, M., Morrison, F., & Holmes, D. (2000). Chlidren at risk for early academic problems: The role of learning-related social skills. *Early Childhood Research Quarterly, 15* (3), 307–329.

McFarland, L., Saunders, R., & Allen, S. (2009). Reflective Practice and Self-Evaluation in Learning Positive Guidance: Experiences of Early Childhood Practicum Students. *Early Childhood Education Journal, 36*, 505–511.

McKenzie, J. (1998). From Now On. *The Educational Journal, 7* (6), 33.

McLennon, D. M. (2009, July). Ten Ways to Create a More Democratic Classroom. *Young Children*, 100–101.

McMillan, D. W., & Chavis, D. M. (1986). Sense of community: A definition and theory. *Journal of Community Psychology, 14* (1), 6–23.

McMullen, M., Addleman, J., Fulford, A., Moore, S., Mooney, S., & Sisk, S. (2009, July). Learning to Be ME While Coming to Understand WE: Encouraging Prosocial Babies in Group Settings. *Young Children*, 20–28.

Mesman, J., van IJzendoorn, M. H., & Bakermans-Kranenburg, M. J. (2009). The many faces of the Still-Face Paradigm: A review and meta-analysis. *Developmental Review, 29* (2), 120–162.

Michel, W., Shoda, Y., & Peake, P. (1988). The nature of adolescent competencies predicted by preschool delay of gratification. *Journal of Personality and Social Psychology, 54*, 687–696.

Mischel, W. (1996). From good intentions to willpower. In P. Gollwitzer, J. Bargh, & Eds., *The psychology of action: Linking cognition and motivation to behavior* (pp. 197–218). New York: The Guilford Press.

Mischel, W., Ebbesen, E., & Zeiss, A. (1972). Cognitive and attentional mechanisms in delay of gratification. *Journal of Personality and Social Psychology, 21*, 204–218.

Mistry, J. (1995). Culuture and Learning in Infancy: Implications for Caregiving. In J. Cortez &

C. L. Young-Holt, *Infant/Toddler Caregiving: A Guide to Culturally Sensitive Care* (p. 2). Sacramento, CA: California Department of Education.

Moffitt, T., Caspi, A., Harrington, H., & Milne, T. (2002). Males on the life-course-persistent and adolescent-limited antisocial pathways: Follow-up at age 26 years. *Development and Psychopathology, 14,* 179–207.

Morgan, G., Harmon, R., & Maslin-Cole, C. (1990). Mastery motivation: Definition and measurement. *Early Education and Development, 1,* 318–339.

Nation, K., & Snowling, M. (2004). Beyond phonological skills: Broader language skills contribute to the development of reading. *Journal of Research in Reading,* 342–356.

National Association for the Education of Young Children (NAEYC). (2011, May). *NAEYC Position Statement Code of Ethical Conduct.* Retrieved April 17, 2012, from www.naeyc.org/files/naeyc/file/positions/Ethics%20Position%20Statement2011.pdf

National Association for the Education of Young Children (NAEYC). (2009, January 1). *Developmentally Appropriate Practice in Early Childood Programs Serving Children from Birth through Age 8.* Retrieved April 29, 2011, from National Association for the Education of Young Children: www.naeyc.org/files/naeyc/file/positions/positions%20statements%20Web.pdf

National Research Council and Institute of Medicine. (2000). *From Neurons to Neighborhoods: The Science of Early Childhood Development.* (J. Shonkoff, & D. A. Phillips, Eds.) Washington, D.C.: National Academy Press.

Nelson, C. A., Furtado, E., Fox, N., & Zeanah, J. C. (2009). The Deprived Human Brain: Developmental deficits among institutionalized Romanan children—and later improvements—strengthens the case for individualized care. *American Scientist,* 222–229.

Nelson, K. (2007). *Young minds in social worlds: Experience, meaning and memory.* Cambridge, MA: Harvard University Press.

Oberman, L., Hubbard, E., McCleery, J., Altschuler, E., Ramachandran, V., & Pineda, J. (2005). EEG evidence for mirror neuron dysfunction in autism spectrum disorders. *Cognitive Brain Research, 24* (2), 190–198.

O'Connor, A., & Diggins, C. (2002). *On reflection: Reflective practice for early childood educators.* New Zealand: Open Mind Publishing.

Osofsky, J. D. (1995). The effects of exposure to violence on young children. *American Psychologist, 50,* 782–788.

Paley, V. G. (2004). *A child's work: The importance of fantasy play.* Chicago: The University of Chicago Press.

Parlakian, R. (2001). *Look, listen and learn: Reflective supervision and relationship-based work.* Washington, DC: ZERO TO THREE.

Pawl, J. S., & St. John, M. (1998). *How you are is as important as what you do. In Making a positive difference for infants, toddlers and their families.* Washington, DC: ZERO TO THREE: National Center for Infants, Toddlers and Families.

Pena, E. D., & Mendez-Perez, A. (2006, September). Individualistic and Collectivistic Approaches to Language Learning. *Zero to Three,* 34–41.

Perry, B. D., Pollard, R. A., Blakely, T. L., Baker, W. L. & Vigilante, D. (1995). *Childhood Trauma, the Neurobiology of Adaptation & Use-dependent Development of the Brain: How States Become Traits.* Infant Mental health Journal, Vol. 16, No. 4, Winter 1995.

Perry, B. D. (2001, March 1). *Curiosity: The Fuel of Development.* Retrieved June 27, 2011, from Scholastic: www.teacher.scholastic.com/professional/bruceperry/curiosity.htm

Perry, B. D. (1997). Incubated in Terror: Neurodevelopmental Factors in the "Cycle of Violence." In Joy D. Osofsky (Ed.), *Children in a violent society* (pp. 124–149). New York: The Guilford Press.

Perry, D., & Kaufmann, R. (2009, November 1). *Issue Brief: Integrating Early Childhood Mental Health Consultation with the Pyramid Model.* Retrieved December 4, 2011, from Technical Assistance Center on Social Emotional Intervention for Young Children: http://www.challenging.behavior.org/do/resources/documents/brief_integrating.pdf

Piaget, J. (1972). *The Psychology of the Child.* New York: Basic Books.

Pianta, R. C. (1997) Adult-Child Relationship Processes and Early Schooling. *Early Education and Development, Volume 8, Number 1,* (pp. 11–16).

Pink, D. H. (2009). *Drive: The Surprising Truth about What Motivates Us*. New York: Riverhead Books.

Powell, B., Cooper, G., Hoffman, K., & Marvin, R. (2009). The Circle of Security. In C. H. Zeanah (Ed.), *Handbook of Infant Mental Health* (3rd ed.) (pp. 450–467). New York: The Guilford Press.

Raaijmakers, M., Smidts, D., Sergeant, J., Maassen, G., Posthumus, J., van England, H., et al. (2008). Executive Functions in Preschool Children with Aggressive Behavior: Impairments in Inhibitory Control. *Journal of Abnormal Child Psychology, 36*, 1097–1107.

Raikes, H., & Edwards, C. P. (2009). *Extending the Dance in Infant and Toddler Caregiving*. Baltimore, MD: Paul H. Brookes Publishing Co.

Rankin, B. (1997). Education as collaboration: Learning from and building on Dewey, Vygotsky and Piaget. In J. Hendrick, *First steps toward teaching the Reggio way* (pp. 70–83). Upper Saddle Creek, NJ: Prentice Hall.

Reyes, I., & Moll, L. C. (2006). Bilingualism and Latinos. In I. Stavans, *Encyclopedia Latina: History, culture, and society in the United States* (pp. 181–185). New York: Grolier.

Robinson, S. K., & Aronica, L. (2009). *The Element: How finding your passion changes everything*. New York: Penguin Group, Inc.

Rogers, C. (1951). *Client-centered Therapy: Its Current Practice, Implications and Theory*. London: Constable.

Rossman, B., Hughes, H. M., & Rosenberg, M. S. (2000). *Children and interparental violence: The impact of exposure*. Philadelphia: Brunner/Mazel.

Rothbart, M. K., & Bates, J. E. (2006). Temperament in children's development. In W. Damon, R. Lerner, N. Eisenberg, & Eds., *Handbook of child psychology, sixth edition: Social, emotional and personality development* (Vol. 3, pp. 99–166). New York: Wiley.

Rui Olds, A. (2000). *Child care design guide*. New York: McGraw-Hill.

Saarni, C. (1999). *The development of emotional competence*. New York: The Guilford Press.

Sameroff, A., & MacKenzie, M. (2003). A quarter-century of the transactional model: How have things changed? *Zero to Three*, 14–22.

Schiller, P. (2009). *Seven Skills for School Success*. Silver Spring, MD: Gryphon House.

Schore, A. N. (1994). *Affect Regulation and the Origin of Self*. Hillsdale, NJ: Lawrence Erlbaum Associates.

Schuder, M. & Lyons-Ruth, K. (2004). "Hidden Trauma" in Infancy: Attachment, Fearful Arousal and Early Dysfunction of the Stress Response System. In J. Orsofsky (Ed.), *Young Children and Trauma: Intervention and Treatment* (pp. 75–82). New York, NY: The Guilford Press.

Shoda, Y., Mischel, W., & Peake, P. K. (1990). Predicting Adolescent Cognitive and Self-Regulatory Competencies from Preschool Delay of Gratification: Identifying Diagnostic Conditions. *Developmental Psychology, 26* (6), 978–986.

Shonkoff, J., & Phillips, D. A. (2000). *From Neurons to Neighborhoods: The Science of Early Childhood Development*. Washington, DC: National Academy Press.

Siegel, D. J. (2001). Toward an Interpersonal Neurobiology of the Developing Mind. *Infant Mental Health Journal, 22* (1–2), 67–94.

Siegel, D. J. (2011). *Mindsight: The new science of personal transformation*. New York: Bantam Books.

Siegel, D. J., & Hartzell, M. (2003). *Parenting from the Inside Out: How a deeper self-understanding can help you raise children who thrive*. New York: Tarcher/Penguin Group.

Silverthorn, D. U., Garrison, C. W., Silverthorn, A. C., & Johnson, B. R. (2009). *Human Physiology: An Integrated Approach* (4th ed.). New York: Pearson/Benjamin Cummings.

Slade, A. (2005). Parental reflective functioning: An introduction. Attachment & Human Development, 7 (3), 269–281.

Slater, A. (2004). Born to love pretty faces. *New Scientist, 183* (2464), 14.

Smeltzer, L. (1993). Emerging questions and research paradigms in business communication research. *Journal of Business Communication, 30* (2), 181–198.

Squires, J., & Bricker, D. (2007). *An Activity-Based Approach to Developing Young Children's Social Emotional Competence*. Baltimore, MD: Paul H. Brookes Publishing Co.

Sroufe, L. A., Coffino, B., & Carlson, E. A. (2010). Conceptualizing the role of early experience: Lessons from the Minnesota Longitudinal Study. *Developmental Review, 30* (1), 36–51.

Sroufe, L. A., Egeland, B., Carlson, E., & Collins, W. (2005). Placing early attachment experiences in developmental context. In K. E. Grossman, K. Grossman, & E. Waters, *Attachment from infancy to adulthood: The major longitudinal studies* (pp. 48–70). New York: The Guilford Press.

Stoiber, K. C., Gettinger, M., & Fitts, M. (2007). Functional Assessment and Positive Support Strategies: Case Illustration of Process and Outcomes. *Early Childhod Services, 1* (3), 165–179.

Stone, Sandra J. (1995, September). Wanted: Advocates for Play in the Primary Grades. *Young Children*.

Swenson, K. J. (2010). *The Effects of Non-Directive Play Therapy on Children with Anxiety*. Winona: Winona State University College of Education.

Tarullo, A., Obradovic, J., & Gunnar, M. (2009). Self-Control and the Developing Brain. *Zero To Three, 29* (3), 31–37.

Thomas, A., & Chess, S. (1977). *Temperament and development*. New York: Brunner/Mazel.

Thompson, R. A. (2009). Doing What Doesn't Come Naturally: The Development of Self-Regulation. *Zero to Three, 30* (2), 33–39.

Tierney, A. L., & Nelson, I. C. (2009, November). Brain Development and the Role of Experience in the Early Years. *Zero to Three*, 9–13.

Tomlin, A., Sturm, L., & Koch, S. M. (2009). Observe, Listen, Wonder and Respond: A Prelimary Exploration of Reflective Function Skills in Early Care Providers. *Infant Mental Health Journal, 30* (6), 634–647.

Toth, K., Munson, J., Meltzoff, A. N., & Dawson, G. (2006). Early Predictors of Communication Development in Young Children with Autism Spectrum Disorder: Joint Attention, Imitation and Toy Play. *Journal of Autism Developmental Disorders, 36*, 993–1005.

Tronick, E., Adamson, L. B., Als, H., & Brazelton, T. B. (1975, April). Infant emotions in normal and pertubated interactions. Paper presented at the biennial meeting of the Society for Research in Child Development, Denver, CO.

Twombly, E., & Fink, G. (2004). *Ages & Stages Learning Activities*. Baltimore: Paul H. Brookes Publishing Co.

U.S. Census Bureau. (2011, July 1). *Table 11. Resident Populations Projections by Race, Hispanic-Origin, Status, and Age: 2010 and 2015*. Retrieved August 1, 2011, from Statistical Abstract of the United States: 2011: www.census.gov/compendia/statab/2011/tables/11s0011.pdf

Vallotton, C. (2008). Signs of Emotion: What can preverbal children "say" about internal states? *Infant Mental Health Journal, 29* (3), 234–258.

Van Hecke, A. V., Meyer, J., Neal, A. R., & Pomares, Y. B. (2007). Infant Joint Attention, Temperament, and Social Competence in Preschool Children. *Child Development, 78* (1), 53–69.

van IJzendoorn, M., & Kroonenberg, P. (1988). Cross-cultural patterns of attachment: A meta-analysis of the Strange Situation. *Child Development, 59*, 147–156.

Viorst, J. (1972). *Alexander and the Terrible, Horrible, No Good, Very Bad Day*. New York: Anthem.

Vohs, K. D., & Baumeister, R. F. (2004). *Handbook of self-regulation: Research, theory and applications*. New York: The Guilford Press.

Vygotsky, L.S. (1987). *Thinking and speech* (Vol. 1). New York: Plenum Press.

Walden, T. (1991). Infant social referencing. In U. Garber, & K. Dodge, *The development of emotion regulation and dysregulation* (pp. 69–88). Cambridge, England: Cambridge University Press.

Walton, G., Armstrong, E. S., & Bower, T. (1998). Newborns learn to identify a face in eight/tenths of a second? *Developmental Science, 1* (1), 79–84.

Waterhouse, L. (2006). "Inadequate Evidence for Multiple Intelligences, Mozart Effect, and Emotional Intelligence Theories." *Educational Psychologist, 41*(4), 247–255.

Watson, K., Barker, L., & Weaver, I. J. (1995). The listening styles profile (LSP-16): Development and validation of an instrument to assess four listening styles. *International Journal of Listening, 9*, 1–13.

Weigand, R. F. (2007). Reflective supervision in child care: The discoveries of an accidental tourist. *Zero to Three, 28* (1), 17–22.

Wein, C. A. (2008). *Emergent curriculum in the primary classroom: Interpreting the Reggio Emilia approach in Schools*. New York: Teachers College Press.

Wentzel, K., & Asher, S. (1995). The academic lives of neglected, rejected, popular and controversial children. *Child Development, 66* (3), 756–763.

Whitehurst, G. J., Arnold, D., Epstein, J., Angell, A., Smith, M., & Fischel, J. (1994). A Picture Book Reading Intervention in Day Care and Home for Children from Low-Income Families. *Developmental Psychology, 30* (5), 679–689.

Wiggins, C., Fenichel, E., & Mann, T. (2007) *Literature Review: Developmental Problems of Maltreated Children and Early Intervention Options for Maltreated Children.* ZERO TO THREE Maltreatment and development report. Task 6: Child Protective Services Project Integrated Literature Review. Washington, DC: ZERO TO THREE. Retrieved September 4, 2012, from http://aspe.hhs.gov/hsp/07/Children-CPS/litrev/report.pdf

Willems, R., & Varley, R. (2010, October 25). *Frontiers in Human Neuroscience.* Retrieved September 20, 2011, from www.frontiersin.org: www.frontiersin.org/human_neuroscience/10.3389/fnhum.2010.00203/full

Williamson, G., & Anzalone, M. (2001). *Sensory Integration and Self-Regulation in Infants and Toddlers: Helping very young children interact with their environment.* Washington, DC: ZERO TO THREE.

Wood, A. (1984). *The Napping House.* San Diego: Harcourt Brace Jovanovich, Publishers.

Zeanah, C. H., & Zeanah, P. D. (2009). Three Decades of Growth in Infant Mental Health. *Zero to Three, 30* (2), 22–27.

Zeanah, C. (2009). Institutional Rearing and Psychiatric Disorders in Romanian Preschool Children. *The American Journal of Psychiatry, 166* (7), 777–785.

Zeanah, C., Nelson, C., Fox, N., Smyke, A., Parker, S., & Koga, S. (2003). Designing research to study the effects of institutionalization on brain development: The Bucharest Early Intervention Project. *Development and Psychopathology, 15,* 885–907.

Zentner, M., & Bates, J. E. (2008). Child Temperament: An Integrative Review of Concepts, Research Programs, and Measures. *European Journal of Developmental Science (EJDS), 2* (1/2), 7–37.

ZERO TO THREE. (2001). *Definition of infant mental health.* Washington, DC: ZERO TO THREE Infant Mental Health Steering Committee.

ZERO TO THREE Infant Mental Health Task Force. (2002). Infant Mental Health. In R. Parlakian, & N. Seibel, *Building strong foundations: Practical guidance for promoting the social–emotional development of infants and toddlers.* Washington, DC: ZERO TO THREE.

ZERO TO THREE. (2005). *Diagnostic classification of mental health and developmental disorders of infancy and early childood: Revised edition (DC 0-3R).* Washington, DC: ZERO TO THREE Press.

INDEX